MW01240656

Interracial Lovers in Revolutionary China

Interracial Lovers in Revolutionary China

D. E. Mungello

ROWMAN & LITTLEFIELD
Lanham • Boulder • New York • London

Published by Rowman & Littlefield
An imprint of The Rowman & Littlefield Publishing Group, Inc.
4501 Forbes Boulevard, Suite 200, Lanham, Maryland 20706
www.rowman.com

86-90 Paul Street, London EC2A 4NE, United Kingdom

Copyright © 2023 by The Rowman & Littlefield Publishing Group, Inc.

All rights reserved. No part of this book may be reproduced in any form or by any elec-
tronic or mechanical means, including information storage and retrieval systems, without
written permission from the publisher, except by a reviewer who may quote passages
in a review.

British Library Cataloguing in Publication Information Available

Library of Congress Cataloging-in-Publication Data

Names: Mungello, D. E. (David Emil), 1943- author.
Title: Interracial lovers in revolutionary China / D.E. Mungello.
Description: Lanham : Rowman & Littlefield, [2023] | Includes bibliographical
    references and index.
Identifiers: LCCN 2023009741 (print) | LCCN 2023009742 (ebook) | ISBN
    9781538176252 (cloth) | ISBN 9781538176269 (paperback) | ISBN
    9781538176276 (epub)
Subjects: LCSH: Interracial couples—China—History—20th century.
Classification: LCC HQ801.8 .M864 2023 (print) | LCC HQ801.8 (ebook) | DDC
    306.7308900951—dc23/eng/20230330
LC record available at https://lccn.loc.gov/2023009741
LC ebook record available at https://lccn.loc.gov/2023009742

∞™ The paper used in this publication meets the minimum requirements of American
National Standard for Information Sciences—Permanence of Paper for Printed Library
Materials, ANSI/NISO Z39.48-1992.

Contents

Illustrations

Acknowledgments

In 2012, Professor Bert Stern of Wabash College, after reading my *Western Queers in China*, sent an email telling me about the biography he was writing on Robert Winter. Winter was a largely unknown American expatriate who had gone to China in 1923 where, apart from brief departures, he remained until his death in 1987. Stern met him in 1984/1985 when he taught English at Beida (Beijing University) and returned to attend his ceremonial one hundredth birthday party in 1987. In 2014 Stern published his detailed and carefully documented *Winter in China: An American Life*. His book has become rare and difficult to find, although a Chinese translation, published in Hong Kong in 2016, is available. I am indebted to him and to his study for information on this remarkable expatriate.

I am, as on so many previous occasions, indebted to Professor Jonathan Chaves for assisting me in questions involving the Chinese language and literature. I am indebted to my friend Jules Nadeau for his assistance on several points. I am indebted to John Mofett, the librarian of the Needham Research Institute, Cambridge, England, for his assistance in obtaining a high-resolution image of Joseph Needham, Lu Gwei-djen, and Dorothy Needham. I am indebted to Dr. Robin Hesketh, the unofficial historian of the Biochemistry Department at Cambridge University, for his graciousness in granting permission to use this image.

I am indebted to the Baylor University Library for the use of its facilities and to the Library of Congress Prints and Photographs Division for the use of its images.

A special note of gratitude to my daughter Dr. Elise Anne Howard. Long ago in 1971, at the beginning of my Sinological career, I remember her squeezing her tiny girl's body into a plastic bucket of cool water for relief from the hot, humid Taipei weather. Now in her maturity she has provided crucial technical assistance in producing this book. I dedicate this book to her with a father's love.

Map 1. China in the twentieth century with marked sites referred to in the book.

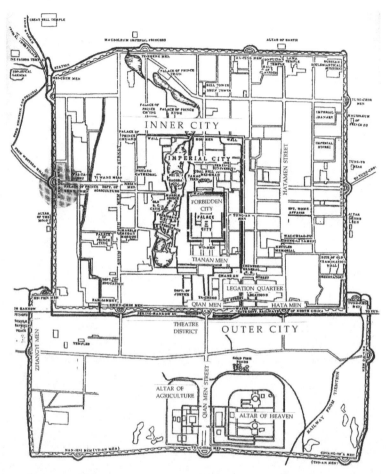

Map 2. Beijing, ca. 1922. Beijing was built in the traditional style of Chinese capitals on a north-south axis in order to harmonize political and cosmological forces. Qianmen Street lay at the core of this axis, linking the imperial palace at the center of the city (and the universe) with the Temples of Heaven and Agriculture to the south. Qianmen (Front Gate) (see cover) was the most central and important of the city gates. It straddled the main north-south thoroughfare of Qianmen Street and divided the Inner City from the Outer City to the south. The Summer Palace was located only a short distance northwest of the Beijing city wall. Edmund Backhouse initially lived in the western part of the city apart from Europeans. In 1939 after the Japanese occupation, he moved into the British Embassy Compound in the Legation Quarter and, at the end of his life, into the French Saint Michael's Hospital. (Adapted from "Cook's Skeleton Map of Peking," 1922.)

Map 3. Shanghai in 1936. Unlike Beijing, which was founded on traditional Chinese cosmological principles, Shanghai was a product of colonialist forces that divided the city into the old Chinese city, French Concession, and British-dominated International Settlement. The Bund (central business district) was linked by the Garden Bridge (Waibaiduqiao 外白度橋) over Suzhou Creek into the part of the International Settlement that lay north of the Whangpoo (Huangpu) River. This bridge led into an industrial area of Hongkew (Hongkou) where many Portuguese and Eurasians lived. An adjoining American Settlement lay to the east. Prior to the Japanese invasion of 1937, Shao Xunmei's home was located in the northeastern section of the International Settlement called Yangtszepoo. The Jesuit orphanage of T'ou-se-we (Tushanwan 土山灣) was part of the Catholic educational and scholarly center of Zi-ka-wei (Xujiahui 徐家匯). (From American Jesuits of Gonzaga College, *Portraits of China* [Shanghai: Tou-sè-wè Orphanage Printing Press, 1936], 42–43.)

Chronology of Love Affairs

Introduction

This book is about the interracial love affairs of twenty-two people who lived during a period of twentieth-century revolutionary turmoil in China— eight Chinese, six Britons, three Americans, one Manchu, one Belgian, one Eurasian, one Australian, and one Indian. Apart from four of them who were characters in a novel, they were all historical. Race for them was a complex mixture of physical features (such as skin color), family relationships, and culture. This period was a time of political and social upheaval in China. The traditional dynastic structure of emperors was giving way to a malformed republic in 1912 which collapsed under revolutionary pressure and was replaced by a Communist state in 1949. It was a time of economic transformation from an agrarian society with oppressive landlords to richly rewarding and exploitive forms of capitalism. It was a time when China opened its gates to foreign influence by sending students to Europe and North America and by welcoming foreign residents, particularly to places like Beijing and Shanghai. It was a time of Japanese invasion and destruction. It was a time of revolutionary fervor, of xenophobic outbursts, of the restoration of national pride, of constructive as well as devastating Communist programs, and of frightful oppression by the youthful Red Guards. In the midst of these revolutionary changes very different people began to mingle in new relationships that not only produced emotional bonds but crossed color lines to fall in love.

The first of these accounts of interracial lovers (1904–1908) blends sexual fantasy and historical reality in a relationship between the Manchu Dowager Empress Cixi (1835–1908) and the British Sinologist Sir Edmund Backhouse (1873–1944). Backhouse had fantasist tendencies, and yet he is such a knowledgeable source of information that his account cannot be dismissed as pure fabrication. At the very least, it is filled with the rich symbolism of a Manchu dynasty that had exhausted its ability to generate virile male heirs to the throne who could reproduce. Cixi and Backhouse are riotously implausible as lovers because Backhouse was a reclusive expatriate and homosexual while Cixi was thirty-eight years older and the actual ruler of China. Nevertheless, the possibility of a complex blending of fantasy and reality compels us to examine their relationship as interracial lovers, particularly since it anticipated by only a half century an equally striking and largely substantiated parallel interracial love affair that developed between the emerging leader of neighboring India Jawaharlal Nehru (1889–1964) and the wife of the last British Viceroy to India, Lady Mountbatten (1901–1960).

The second love affair to be considered comes from literary fiction and was an account of the dual love affairs of a Chinese father and son in London based on the residence there of the famous author Lao She in the late 1920s. Just as Backhouse's tendencies toward literary exhibitionism and pornography influenced the account of his love affair with the Dowager Empress Cixi, so too did Lao She's early tendencies toward Chinese nationalism and satire affect his account of the abortive love affairs of the father Ma Zeren and the son Ma Wei with their British landlady Mrs. Wendell and her daughter Mary.

More historically grounded lovers in these affairs of the heart are found in the third set of relationships that began with the troubled marriage of the Chinese Zhou Wei 周煒 (b. 1886) and the Belgian Marguerite Denis (1885–1966) and their prolific Eurasian daughter Han Suyin 韓素音 (the penname for Rosalie Matilda Chou, a.k.a. Zhou Guanghu 周光瑚) (1916–2012). Also included are Han Suyin's love affairs with the Nationalist general Tang Baohuang 唐保璜 during 1935–1947, the Australian journalist Ian Morrison during 1949–1950, and the Indian colonel Vincent Ratnaswamy during 1960–2003. Their love affairs revolved around China and Han Suyin's identity as a Eurasian with all the painful implications which that identity involved.

The fourth set of love affairs involved the American novelist Pearl Sydenstricker Buck (Sai Zhenzhu 賽珍珠) (1892–1973) and her love for East Asians that encompassed not only the Chinese poet Xu Zhimo 徐志摩 (1896–1931), but also abandoned Amerasian children.

The fifth love affair involved the American writer Emily Hahn (Ding Meili 頂美麗) (1905–1997) and the Chinese author Zao Simay (Shao Xunmei 邵洵美) (1906–1968). Their affair (and Chinese marriage in concubinage) was set in and inseparable from the history of Shanghai in the 1930s.

The sixth set of love affairs involved the American expatriate Robert Winter (Wen Te 溫特) (1890–1988) and his Chinese male lovers whose secretive affairs were necessitated by American homophobia, fostered by Winter's Sinophilia (admiration for China), and finally violently suppressed by Maoist revolutionary fervor.

The seventh love affair involved a concubinage relationship between the eminent British scientist and Sinologist Joseph Needham (1900–1995) and his wife the scientist Dorothy Needham (1896–1987) and his Chinese mistress and scientist collaborator Lu Gwei-djen (1904–1991).

The eighth love affair involved a classic long-term relationship of the famous husband-and-wife translation team of Yang Xianyi 楊憲益 (1915–2009) and the Briton Gladys (née Taylor) Yang (Dai Naidie 戴乃迭) (1919–1999) whose relationship survived the surrounding revolutionary turmoil because of their mutual devotion. Some of these love affairs were short-lived and others endured for over a half-century. Some were impressionistic and others were deeply emotional. Ironically, several of the lovers treated in this book were acquainted with one another although their acquaintances were more a reflection of the overlapping expatriate circles in which they lived rather than close personal affinities.

II.

The children of interracial love affairs in the setting of this book were called Eurasians (European Asians) and Amerasians (American Asians). These are terms that belong more to history than to the present because they reflect the early interracial procreation in these parts of the world. These were to me exotic and abstract categories until I arrived at Lingnan College 嶺南書院 in Hong Kong in 1973 to begin my college teaching career. In Hong Kong, I entered into my first colonialist setting and acquired my first Eurasian student. This Eurasian girl stood out from the others simply because her classmates had Han 漢 (Chinese) physical features while she blended Chinese and European features. She was intriguing to me because she was the child of an interracial love affair. Hong Kong at that time was still a crown colony of the British, a vestige of imperialism, and so this girl was apparently the child of historical forces that brought together a Chinese and a European (probably a Chinese woman and a British or Scottish man). I wondered how she felt living in a sea of Chinese faces. In one sense, this was merely a personal story of one girl, but over the years it evolved into a much larger story involving the numerous interracial relationships in this study.

Most Americans view colonialism as an alien concept and, apart from the uncomfortable experiences with the Philippines and the Panama Canal, the United States has prided itself on being a former colony rather than having colonies of its own. But the reality was that from 1619 to 1862 the United States did have African slaves. The vestiges of slavery lingered for years in the miscegenation laws that prohibited Blacks and whites from fornicating and marrying. Maryland passed the first miscegenous or anti-amalgamation law in 1664 and by 1914 forty-one other states had enacted laws prohibiting interracial marriage between whites and "colored" people. In 1935, the law in Maryland was extended to forbid marriage between Malaysians and whites. Even in my hometown movie theatre in southwestern Pennsylvania, I remember the segregated seating section for Blacks that persisted well into the 1950s. In 1967 the bans on interracial marriage were nullified by the US Supreme Court, although negative racial stereotypes lingered.

The situation in the United States with regard to Chinese people was more complicated and based on both class and race. In 1882 the Chinese Exclusion Act was passed, barring all Chinese laborers from entering the United States for ten years and prohibiting Chinese immigrants from becoming naturalized citizens.[1] Chinese merchants, teachers, students, diplomats, and travelers were exempt from this exclusion. Because of the fear that Chinese immigrants were contaminated with contagious illnesses and parasites, all new and some returning Chinese immigrants were sent to Angel Island in the San Francisco Bay where they were subjected to intense physical examinations and other interrogations. Growing American nativism was reflected in the 1924 Immigration Act which dealt not only with Asian exclusion, but also restricted immigration from southern and eastern Europe.[2] Finally, in 1943 the exclusion laws were repealed.

The deepening of interracial relations between people from the Western world (Europe and North America) and the Chinese began with the encounter that could be dated from July 20, 1579, when the first Catholic missionary, Fr. Michele Ruggieri, arrived in Macau.[3] The Jesuits were the primary early intermediaries in this encounter because, unlike early European traders, they were notable for their deeper interest in the Chinese culture and people.[4] The Jesuits learned the Chinese language, studied Chinese culture, made friendships with Chinese people, served at the imperial court, became the earliest interpreters of China to Europe, cultivated a sense of respect among Europeans for Chinese culture, and sought an interaction with the Chinese on several cultural and spiritual levels.[5] Largely because of Jesuit works which admired the Chinese, sixteenth- and seventeenth-century European writings tended to refer to the Chinese as "white," but in the eighteenth century, there was an increase in references to the Chinese as "yellow" which paralleled the declining European respect for China.[6] Jesuit contacts and publications with European savants like Gottfried Leibniz (1646–1716) created some of the earliest intellectual exchanges between China and Europe.[7] Although Catholic priests were required to be celibate, there were some inevitable lapses and sexual scandals in these relationships between priests and Chinese parishioners.[8] There were the first Chinese seminarians who studied in Europe in the eighteenth century.[9] There were Western homosexuals who fled to China and were attracted to Chinese men in the nineteenth and twentieth centuries.[10]

This book explores these Sino-Western contacts by dealing with interactions between Chinese (*Zhongguoren* 中國人) and foreigners (*waiguoren* 外國人) and Eurasians (*Ouyaren* 歐亞人) on a personal plane, namely, the *affaires de coeur* (affairs of the heart) or love affairs (*fengliu yunshi* 風流韻事). The nature of these relationships varied, ranging from casual affairs to lasting devotion. By examining several interracial lovers who lived in this century of Chinese revolution, we confront touching and troubled stories of our past and ourselves. And we also confront our emotional and cultural evolution.

NOTES

1. Erika Lee, *At America's Gates: Chinese Immigration during the Exclusion Era, 1882–1943* (Chapel Hill: University of North Carolina Press, 2002), 2–4.

2. Lee, *At America's Gates*, 11–13.

3. For a thoughtful attempt to articulate the intellectual confluence of Europe and China since the seventeenth century, see Stefan Gaarsmand Jacobsen, "Chinese Influences or Images? Fluctuating Histories of How Enlightenment Europe Read China," *Journal of World History* 24 (2013): 623–60.

4. D. E. Mungello, *Curious Land: Jesuit Accommodation and the Origins of Sinology* (Stuttgart: Franz Steiner Verlag, 1985).

5. D. E. Mungello, *The Great Encounter of China and the West*, fourth revised edition (Lanham, MD: Rowman & Littlefield, 2013).

6. Walter Demel, "Wie die Chinesen gelb wurden: Ein Beitrag zur Frühgeschichte der Rassentheorien," *Historische Zeitschrift* 255 (1992): 625–66.

7. David E. Mungello, *Leibniz and Confucianism: The Search for Accord* (Honolulu: University of Hawaii Press, 1977).

8. D. E. Mungello, *The Spirit and the Flesh in Shandong, 1650–1785* (Lanham, MD: Rowman & Littlefield, 2001).

9. D. E. Mungello, *This Suffering Is My Joy: The Underground Church in Eighteenth-Century China* (Lanham, MD: Rowman & Littlefield, 2021).

10. D. E. Mungello, *Western Queers in China: Flight to the Land of Oz* (Lanham, MD: Rowman & Littlefield, 2012)

Chapter 1

Fantasy and Reality

The Dowager Empress
and Sir Backhouse

I.

The Dowager Empress Cixi 慈禧 (1835–1908), commonly known as the Old Buddha, was the last powerful ruler of imperial China (see figure 1.1). She came from an obscure Manchu family and entered the palace in 1851 as a low-ranking concubine to the Xianfeng emperor (r. 1851–1861). Her status was elevated by producing the only male heir to the throne.[1] Unlike during the early Qing dynasty when male fertility was very fecund and Manchu emperors produced many heirs—the Kangxi emperor (r. 1661–1716) had begotten thirty-six sons—the lack of male heirs in the late Qing dynasty was symbolic of the dynasty's decline.[2] Cixi's ascent to power began when the Xianfeng 咸豐 emperor died in 1861 and her son was declared the Tongzhi 同志 emperor (r. 1862–1874). He later died without a male heir. The official announcement claimed he died of smallpox, but other unverified accounts claim that he died due to diseases that he had contracted in brothels.[3] After his death, several officials and eunuchs were removed and blamed for having been his companions. Sir Edmund Trelawny Backhouse gives detailed descriptions of his own visits to male brothels of that period in Beijing.[4]

Over the years, Cixi's power increased through the manipulation of her son and then her nephew the Guangxu 光緒 emperor (r. 1875–1908). However, she lost face when she supported the rebellion of the reactionary anti-foreign martial arts group called the Society of Righteous Fists (Boxers) (*Yihequan* 義和拳) in 1899 and 1900. After the destruction of the Boxers by foreign forces, political realities forced her to become more accommodating to foreigners in China. She posed in a famous 1903 photograph with the wives of foreign diplomats at a palace reception for a carefully staged photo op.[5] Because of

1

The Empress Dowager of China was one of the most famous rulers in the history of the Orient. This photograph was taken by an American woman artist who painted her portrait.

Figure 1.1. The Dowager Empress Cixi (1835–1908). She rose from obscure origins through marriage and manipulation of filial piety to become the last powerful monarch to reign in China. (Carpenter Collection. 1890–1908. Library of Congress Prints and Photographs Division, Washington, DC.)

the power and fame and secrecy that she embodied, Cixi became a chameleon figure who authors tended to interpret in terms of their own preoccupations. A negative view of Cixi was expressed by many Han Chinese who were loyal to the previous dynasty—the Ming—and opposed Manchu rule. By 1900, this anti-Qing (*fan Qing* 反清) feeling was growing into a revolutionary force. The Overseas Chinese scholar Lim Boon Keng 林文慶 (1869–1957), writing in Singapore in 1901, expressed anti-Qing sentiments in viewing Cixi as the symbol of a reactionary Manchu court that was impeding the advance of progressive Chinese reformers like Kang Yuwei. She had been "trained in the polluted and licentious seraglio of the dissolute Emperor Hsien Feng."[6] She was "crafty as a fox" and "vixenish."[7] Lim claimed that many of the eunuchs under Cixi were chosen for their "fine physique and comely features" and suffered sudden deaths after entering the imperial palace.[8] Lim implied that Cixi's chief eunuch Li Lianying 李蓮英 (d. 1911), her partner in accumulating power and wealth, had not undergone castration.[9] However, other biographers, such as Pearl Buck or, more recently, Jung Chang, portrayed Cixi as a proto-feminist.[10] Unlike Lim, Buck rarely alluded to Cixi's promiscuous affairs, but rather focused on her frustrated and secret love for a Manchu kinsman named Jung Lu (Ronglu 榮祿) (1836–1903). More controversial is the claim that her efforts at accommodation involved taking European lovers.

Sir Edmund Trelawny Backhouse (1873–1944) stood out for his eccentricity among the collection of foreign merchants, missionaries, adventurers, and aesthetes who flocked to Beijing in the late nineteenth century during the last, fading years of the Qing dynasty. At Oxford he had been part of a group of homosexuals; in 1895 Oscar Wilde was jailed for homosexual acts, and Backhouse helped to raise money for Wilde's defense.[11] It is clear that he was a timid man who fled from danger, and the timing of his journey from England to China would indicate that he fled from the double threat of being caught-up in the Wilde-related purge of homosexuals and in escaping from unpaid debts.[12] Having fled England owing the considerable sum of twenty-three thousand pounds sterling, he was declared bankrupt and his family settled his debts, providing him a small allowance.[13]

Backhouse said that he arrived in Beijing in 1898 on "the day of Guangxu's reforms."[14] He was referring to the "Hundred Days' Reforms," a comprehensive set of educational reforms sanctioned by the Guangxu emperor. The forces of reaction led the Dowager Empress to cancel the reforms and secretly confine the emperor to house arrest.

Backhouse was a recluse who avoided Westerners and lived in the western area of Beijing, apart from most other Europeans who resided in the Legation Quarter (see map 2).[15] Except for brief trips back to Europe and North America, he remained in China for the rest of his life. In 1913, he contributed twenty-nine crates of valuable Chinese works to the Bodelian Library at Oxford as part of an unsuccessful attempt to become the Professor of Chinese at Oxford.[16] In 1939, after the outbreak of the Pacific War, he moved into a single room in a modestly furnished house on the British Embassy compound.[17] Because of medical problems, he entered the French St. Michael's Hospital on April 6, 1943, and remained there until his death in January 1944. Since he had become a Catholic in 1942, he was given a funeral service in St. Joseph's Church (the Dongtang 東堂) and buried in the Catholic cemetery of Zhalan 柵, which was the burial site of several prominent Jesuits.[18]

Backhouse had a gift for languages and became known for his colloquial fluency in Chinese, serving at times as a translator for imperial court proceedings with foreigners. According to Reinhard Hoeppli, the Swiss physician who had almost daily contact with Backhouse during the last years of his life, Backhouse was a complex character who wore long Chinese gowns of dark colors and had a charming manner. He combined an extraordinary gift for languages with an overactive imagination, a life of shady activities that probably included work for the British Intelligence Service, tendencies toward dishonesty, and a strong sexuality that Hoeppli compared to an "old satyr."[19] The most remarkable rumor related by Hoeppli came from his Manchu rickshawman who after the outbreak of the Pacific War claimed that Backhouse had been a lover of the Dowager Empress.[20]

Backhouse collaborated with *The Times* of London correspondent J.O.P. Bland in producing two works, the most famous of which was *China under the Empress Dowager* (1910).[21] However, Backhouse's knowledge of Chinese and of Beijing was superior to that of Bland. The central text in this work was said to be the diary of the Beijing court official Jing Shan 景善 (1823–1900) who was killed by his son shortly after the foreign expeditionary force entered Beijing to disperse the Boxers.[22] Backhouse claimed he had recovered this diary during the looting following the Boxer Rebellion. He wrote: "The Diary was found by the translator in the private study of Ching Shan's house on August 18th and saved, in the nick of time, from being burnt by a party of Sikhs."[23] Several scholars have convincingly argued that the diary of Jing Shan was forged by Backhouse.[24] But even if the diary was a forgery, it reflected a superior knowledge of the language and details of life at that time in China—a knowledge that makes Backhouse more complicated than a mere serial liar.

In 1973, long after Backhouse's death, Trevor-Roper received a query from Hoeppli asking if he would be willing to receive and transmit to the Bodelian Library at Oxford a substantial work by Backhouse.[25] Trevor-Roper agreed and received the parcel by hand at the Basel airport.[26] The package contained two manuscripts written by Backhouse at the end of his life—one entitled "The Dead Past" which dealt with his early years in England and the other "Décadence Mandchoue" (Manchu Decadence) which dealt with the final years of the Qing dynasty. These works were obscene and incendiary and included Backhouse's detailed descriptions of sexual relations with Chinese figures as well as Europeans like Oscar Wilde, Aubrey Beardsley, Paul Verlaine, and the British Prime Minister Lord Robert Cecil Salisbury.[27] Consequently, Trevor-Roper decided that because these works were too offensive and unreliable as a source from which to quote excerpts, he would instead construct a book on their contents drawing from external sources.[28]

The Bodelian copy of the manuscript of *Décadence Mandchoue* consists of 1,393 pages, divided between 327 pages written in Backhouse's hand and the remaining pages in typewritten transcription by Dr. Reinhard Hoeppli.[29] Hoeppli encouraged him to write his life story and supported Backhouse financially in his impoverished old age. Hoeppli was less skeptical of Backhouse's veracity than Trevor-Roper, although he conceded that Backhouse sometimes confused his imagination with actual events. *Décadence Mandchoue* was finally edited and published by Derek Sanders in 2011.

II.

Backhouse claimed that he had a sexually intimate six-and-one-half year relationship with the Dowager Empress dating from 1902 until her death in 1908.[30] The relationship was said to have begun in May 1902 when Backhouse returned twenty-five thousand volumes and six hundred pieces of art objects (bronzes, jades, porcelain, ivories, paintings, calligraphy, cloisonné, lacquer, tapestries, and carpets) which had been recovered from the looting that followed the Boxer Rebellion.[31] Backhouse claimed that he had recovered these objects with the assistance of trustworthy Manchus, but there is evidence that Backhouse himself had profited from the looting. At this hand-over meeting, the Empress recalled having seen him a few days before at the ceremony of burning incense at the God of War's shrine.[32]

In the fourth chapter of *Décadence Mandchoue*, Backhouse gives a detailed account of his first purported sexual encounter with the Dowager Empress.[33] His writing style blends Victorian pornography with sophisticated literary allusions drawn from classical Greek and Roman as well as Chinese literature. Its perspective is as much homoerotic as heteroerotic. The chapter title "Summer Palace Nocturne: The Pastimes of Messalina" was an allusion to Cixi as Messalina, the promiscuous wife of the Roman emperor Claudius. The use of classical literary allusions was commonplace in Victorian literary culture, but it also reflected Backhouse's exhibitionism in using obscure terminology as well as redundant French terminology. This chapter begins on August 8, 1904, with the arrival of a note from the Dowager Empress' favored eunuch Li Lianying 李蓮英 (d. 1911), commanding Backhouse (Bakesi 巴恪思) to come to the Summer Palace that evening.[34]

The Summer Palace (*Yiheyuan* 頤和園) (Garden of Peace and Harmony) was located only a short distance to the northwest of Beijing. It had originally been part of a much grander Garden of Perfect Clarity (*Yuanmingyuan* 圓明園) built in the seventeenth and eighteenth centuries but was destroyed by Anglo-French armies in 1860. In 1886 the Dowager Empress diverted Navy funds to rebuild a small part of the Old Summer Palace into the garden known as the Summer Palace. Although the Summer Palace was occupied by the foreign expeditionary forces that destroyed the Boxers in 1900, the damage was later repaired. The Dowager Empress was passionately fond of the Summer Palace and, as she aged, she spent more and more time there.[35] She wandered the grounds with her entourage—picnicking and boating and enjoying the vegetation (figures 1.2 and 1.3).

Backhouse arrived at the Summer Palace in a sedan chair and was greeted by Li Lianying who would be his guide. He introduced him to the "Old Ancestress" who welcomed him and invited him to eat a special meal she ordered for him.[36] After she had "a whiff or two of opium," she would take him on an excursion on the lake (figure 1.4). Over the meal, the eunuch prepared Backhouse for his encounter by describing the Dowager Empress' desires and her abnormally large clitoris (*yindi* 陰蒂).[37] The eunuch had a sandalwood scent applied to his genital area and Backhouse was exhilarated to note the great interest the Manchu elite took in the anal area of the body.

After the boat outing and casual conversation with Cixi, which included a curious and friendly discussion of his homosexuality, Backhouse was given a powerful aphrodisiac to enhance his erection. Several electric fans as well as large blocks of ice cooled the room to control the European's perspiration which Cixi "held in abhorrence."[38] Cixi told Backhouse that he must forget that she was an empress (she was sixty-nine and he was thirty-three) and that he should see her as Yang Guifei. Yang Guifei was the famous eighth-century concubine and femme fatale of the Tang dynasty with whom

Figure 1.2.   Marblebridge, Summer Palace, Beijing. (Photoglob Company, ca. 1890–1910. Yiheyuan 頤和園 [Garden of Peace and Harmony]. Library of Congress Prints and Photographs Division, Washington, DC.)

Figure 1.3. The 17-Arches Bridge and lake at the Summer Palace, Beijing, 1901. (Yiheyuan 頤和園 [Garden of Peace and Harmony]. Library of Congress Prints and Photographs Division, Washington, DC.)

Emperor Xuanzong became so infatuated that he allowed his kingdom to fall into rebellion. Backhouse, ever at pains to exhibit his knowledge, responded with a corresponding metaphor from Chinese culture by saying that he would regard her as Avaloitesvara (Guanyin), the Buddhist Goddess of Mercy.

There followed fellatio, cunnilingus, and penile as well as clitoral penetration in three sessions with intervening pauses for aphrodisiacs, opium, and food. The empress had Backhouse ejaculate into her mouth, and she observed that his semen had a "sourish taste" (*suan bu jide* 酸不積的).[39] It is impossible to know if these things actually happened or whether they were generated by Backhouse's imagination. Some events that Backhouse related sound plausible, such as the interruption for the Empress' morning opium pipe (*qing shui yin* 清水癮), but other things sound dubious, such as Backhouse walking alone along the lake and encountering the Guangxu emperor (r. 1875–1907).[40] The increasingly reactionary Cixi had placed this emperor under house arrest in 1898 because of his backing of reformers and had since confined his activity. Backhouse states that his meeting with the Dowager Empress was at the Summer Palace (*Yiheyuan* 頤和園) which lay a short distance northwest of Beijing.[41] However, the Guangxu emperor was imprisoned in the center of Beijing on the Yingtai island in the South Lake (*Nanhai* 南海), one of the chain of lakes located on the west side of the Forbidden City.[42] But otherwise

Figure 1.4. In a first-class opium joint, "hitting the pipe," Beijing, 1901. Opium was introduced into China from India and Afghanistan by English merchants ca. 1770. The opium trade transformed China's profitable trade surplus from the export of tea and silk trade into a destructive trade deficit caused by the import of opium. The Western trading powers circumvented China's efforts to ban opium, leading to the Opium War (First Anglo-Chinese War) of 1839–1842. Opium was an inexpensive drug that caused widespread addiction in China. Attempts to eradicate opium addiction failed until the Communists took control in 1949. (Library of Congress Prints and Photographs Division, Washington, DC.)

throughout his account, Backhouse included descriptions that demonstrated his knowledge of the court and of obscure Chinese terminology. He concluded by describing the state of physical exhaustion in which he left the palace.

III.

Backhouse's description of his sexual contact with the Dowager Empress is more salacious than romantic. And yet his account is too literary to represent mere sexual titillation of the reader. It is more likely to have been a mixture of truth and literary exhibitionism. The two participants were said to demonstrate friendly warmth that stopped short of love. Their encounter was more exploratory than romantic. To modern tastes, the combination of literary allusions with the details of sexual arousal are jarring. Or perhaps the strange quality reflects a homosexual's way of describing a heterosexual experience. In any case, it is more descriptive of a performance rather than an act of sexual passion. In fact, Backhouse devotes far more attention and enthusiasm in *Décadence Mandchoue* to describing the activity in the male bordellos that he visited in Beijing than he does in this sexual interlude with Cixi, which is presented as an exotic heterosexual aside.

Backhouse claimed that he was not the only foreigner who had a sexual encounter with Cixi because he learned that there were two other Europeans who shared her bed. One evening in 1905 during a visit to the Xinjing 新淨 (Turkish bath), a male bordello for the Manchu aristrocracy, Backhouse again encountered Cixi's favorite eunuch Li Lianying.[43] At that encounter Backhouse claimed Li told him that a member of the French Legation named Wa Lun 瓦倫 (Wallon) had also had sexual relations with Cixi.[44] This Frenchman had been working at the Zhonghai 中海 (Central Lake) palace, just west of the Forbidden City, where Cixi preferred to live in the winter months.[45] It coincided with the time (1886–1887) when the old North Church (Beitang 北堂) in the Canchikou 蠶池口 section of Beijing was decommissioned before being reconstructed at a nearby location in Xishiku 西十庫.[46] The eunuch told how Cixi on one of her lakeside walks was attracted to the well-built twenty-three-year-old Wallon who was casting amorous glances at her. It was arranged for Wallon to meet with the Dowager Empress the following evening in the Palace of Eternal Spring (*Changqunpo* 長春波) in the Forbidden City. According to Backhouse, she forced Wallon to have coitus five times in one evening, after which she had an "invigorating" drug prepared for him and arranged for him to make a second visit. Wallon died a few hours afterward. The Legation physician gave "heat apoplexy" as the cause of death. Backhouse claimed that the numbers of Cixi's lovers must have amounted to "many scores." The number of deaths of those of low birth (*xiajian* 下賤) who had been lovers of the Dowager Empress grew so large that it evoked a perfunctory apology from Cixi.[47] Backhouse expressed no sympathetic or moral regret over their deaths.

The third instance of a European having had a sexual liaison with Cixi is referred to by Backhouse as the La Ba 喇叭 affair. He explained La Ba as meaning "apparently *Rab* or *Raab*, but it may not be his surname, *Rab* being Russian for slave, while *Raab* is, I believe, a German patronymic."[48] According to Backhouse, Cixi claimed that Rab had intercourse with her five or six times and that he was "very full of lust" (*sefeixiao* 色非小). She knew that this Russian or German died a few hours after leaving the palace. The tea-house gossip was that Cixi caused his death by arsenic poisoning in order to silence rumors. Cixi assured Backhouse that he was not in a similar danger for having had sex with her and offered to eat shark fins from the same dish to prove it. As a further assurance, Backhouse claims she then had him rise from his knees and drew him toward her and kissed him on the mouth several times in front of an important court official, saying "you are one of us" (*ni bu shi wairen* 你不是外人).[49]

Laying aside the complexities of Backhouse's relationship with the Dowager Empress, it is doubtful that her purported sexual encounters with Wallon and Raab could be characterized as affairs of the heart. For Cixi, these encounters—assuming that they were not entirely products of Backhouse's imagination—appear to have been motivated, at least in part, by a sexual curiosity about Europeans. (Conversely, one must concede that these sexual encounters might represent the projections of overly imaginative European minds in an age of imperialism.) What gives these incidents a possible plausibility and an important significance is the decline in male virility among the members of the Manchu imperial house. These Manchu males, who had conquered the Chinese in 1644, had maintained their separate language and customs, but had lost their martial prowess along with their ability to procreate. For Backhouse, who was supposedly obeying an imperial summons rather than initiating a seduction, the purported interlude with Cixi seems to have involved a badge of pride in having sex with the most powerful woman in China as well as the fascination of a Sinophile in crossing a cultural and racial sexual barrier.

This fascination with crossing a cultural and racial sexual barrier was shared by other Europeans of that time, notably by the Frenchman Victor Segalen (1878–1919) who also had deeply homoerotic inclinations.[50] Although Segalen was trained as a naval physician, he developed a romantic infatuation with China and began studying Chinese with the Parisian Sinologist Edouard Chavannes in 1908. Shortly thereafter he went to Beijing where in 1910 he met and became infatuated with a young heterosexual Frenchman named Maurice Roy. Segalen sublimated his infatuation with Roy by chronicling the incredible tales of Roy's sexual relations with members of the Manchu imperial family in a novel entitled *René Leys*, which was published in Beijing in 1912.[51]

Leys is portrayed in Segalen's novel as having an affair with the Dowager Empress Long Yu (Longyu Huangtaihou 龍裕皇太后). She had previously been a wife of the Guangxu emperor and was called Empress Xiaoding 孝定 景皇后. She was a cousin, three years older than the Guangxu emperor, and had been chosen by Cixi to control the emperor.[52] However, the emperor "had no affection for her" because he appears to have been sexually impotent with women. By contrast, the novel *René Leys* claims that the seventeen-year-old Leys is said to have conceived a child with this thirty-eight- to forty-year-old Dowager Empress who gave birth to a boy. The assumption has long been that this illegitimate boy was the product of Segalen's literary imagination. Segalen describes Leys as an *amouroux triumphant* (triumphant lover) who has taken revenge for the Boxer assault on the Legations in 1900.[53] He calls their relationship a *miracle d'amour* (miracle of love).

The Guangxu emperor produced no heirs.[54] Just before Cixi died, the preponderant evidence is that she had him murdered (either by poisoning or strangulation) and named his nephew (and her grand-nephew) Puyi 溥儀 (1906–1967) as the heir. Puyi, the last Manchu emperor of China, was impotent with women and had homosexual tendencies.[55]

Segalen's story of René Leys is a mixture of fantasy and reality that has striking parallels to Backhouse's account. However, there are other possible explanations besides imitation. One possibility is that the story, along with Backhouse's palace encounter, may suggest that the Manchu ruling house, faced with a radical decline in male fertility and growing homosexuality, was experimenting with European men as a source of fertility. Conversely, an equally plausible possibility is that the claims of these sexual encounters (whether by Backhouse or Leys) were a projection of European imaginations and an expression of European imperialism. Curiosity might have justified Cixi's interest in having a sexual encounter in 1902 with Backhouse who was a familiar personality and fluent in Chinese, but by 1908, Cixi was dead. In chronological comparison, the entries in Leys' journal indicated that his friendship with Maurice Roy began at the beginning of June in 1910 and continued until October 30, 1911.[56]

In terms of belonging to the category of love affairs (*fengliu yunshi* 風流 韻事), the interracial relationship between Backhouse and Cixi had a lack of emotional intensity and scarcely qualifies. And yet it helps to establish the outer parameters in the wide range of human emotions and commitment that characterized the interracial love affairs under discussion in this book and which range from causal affairs to lasting devotion. Accounts of other very different bonds of affection follow.

NOTES

1. Fang Chao-ying, "Hsiao-ch'in Hsien Huang-hou," in *Eminent Chinese of the Ch'ing Period (1644–1912)*, edited by Arthur W. Hummel (Washington, DC: Government Printing Office, 1943), 295.

2. The sons of the Kangxi emperor are listed in Jonathan D. Spence, *Emperor of China: Self-portrait of K'ang-hsi* (New York: Vintage, 1975), 119–22.

3. Fang Chao-ying, "Tsai-ch'un," in *Eminent Chinese of the Ch'ing Period*, 731.

4. See chapter V "Eunuch Diversions" and chapter VI "The Hammam and the Intrusion," in Edmund Trelawny Backhouse, *Décadence Mandchoue: The China Memoirs of Sir Edmund Trelawny Backhouse* (Hong Kong: Earnshaw Books, 2011), 75–94, 95–111.

5. This photograph is reproduced in John K. Fairbank's *East Asia: Tradition and Transformation* (Boston: Houghton Mifflin Co, 1973), 639. References to Cixi's diplomatic receptions for foreign women are made in Backhouse, *Décadence Mandchoue*, 20, 26.

6. Lim Boon Keng (Wen Ching), *The Chinese Crisis from Within* (London: Grant Richards, 1901), 88.

7. Lim, *The Chinese Crisis from Within*, 85, 120.

8. Lim, *The Chinese Crisis from Within*, 89–90.

9. Lim, *The Chinese Crisis from Within*, 148.

10. Pearl S. Buck, *Imperial Woman, A Novel by Pearl S. Buck* (New York: John Day Company, 1956); Jung Chang, *Empress Dowager Cixi: the Concubine Who Launched Modern China* (New York: Alfred A. Knopf, 2013).

11. Hugh Trevor-Roper, *Hermit of Peking: The Hidden Life of Sir Edmund Backhouse* (Harmondsworth, Middlesex, England: Penguin Books, 1976), 33.

12. Trevor-Roper, *Hermit of Peking*, 34, 96–97.

13. Edmund Trelawny Backhouse, *The Dead Past*, third edition, edited by Reinhard Hoeppli and Peter Jordaan (Coppell, TX: Alchemie Books, 2021), 6.

14. Backhouse, *The Dead Past*, 280.

15. Reinhard Hoeppli, "Postscript," in Backhouse, *The Dead Past*, 300.

16. Trevor-Roper, *Hermit of Peking*, 125–29.

17. Hoeppli, "Postscript," in Backhouse, *The Dead Past*, 310–11.

18. Hoeppli, "Postscript," in Backhouse, *The Dead Past*, 307, 311–12. On Zhalan, see Edward J. Malatesta and Gao Zhiyu, eds., *Zhalan: Departed, Yet Present, the Oldest Christian Cemetery in Beijing* (Macau: Instituto Cultural de Macau & Ricci Institute, University of San Francisco, 1995).

19. Hoeppli, "Postscript," in Backhouse, *The Dead Past*, 302.

20. Hoeppli, "Postscript," in Backhouse, *The Dead Past*, 301.

21. J. O. P. Bland and Edmund Backhouse, *China under the Empress Dowager: the History of the Life and Times of Tzu Hsi* (1910; Hong Kong: Earnshaw Books, 2009). The second work on which they collaborated was E. Backhouse and J. O. P. Bland, *Annals & Memoirs of the Court of Peking (from the 16th to the 20th Century)* (Boston: Houghton Mifflin Company, 1914).

22. Fang, "Jung-lu," in *Eminent Chinese of the Ch'ing Period*, 409.

23. Bland and Backhouse, *China under the Empress Dowager*, 254.

24. See Derek Sandhaus, "Foreword," in *China under the Empress Dowager* (2009), vii. The Sinologist J. J. L. Duyvendak questioned the diary's authenticity in "Ching-Shan's Diary a Mystification," *T'oung-Pao*, second series, volume 33, book 3/4 (1937), 268–94. Forty years later Hugh Trevor-Roper questioned the diary's authenticity in *Hermit of Peking*, 348–50. More recently Lo Hui-min has pointed out historical discrepancies in "The Ching-shan Diary: A Clue to Its Forgery," *East Asian History*, 1 (June 1991): 98–124.

25. Trevor-Roper, *Hermit of Peking*, 14–15.

26. Trevor-Roper, *Hermit of Peking*, 15.

27. Sandhaus, "Introduction," in *Décadence Mandchoue: The China Memoirs of Sir Edmund Trelawny Backhouse*, edited by Derek Sandhaus (Hong Kong: Earnshaw Books, 2011), xi.

28. Trevor-Roper, *Hermit of Peking*, 16–17.

29. Sandhaus, "Introduction," in *Décadence Mandchoue*, xii–xiv.

30. Backhouse, *The Dead Past*, 241.

31. Backhouse, *The Dead Past*, 20.

32. Backhouse, *The Dead Past*, 24.

33. Backhouse, *The Dead Past*, 59–74.

34. Fang, "Hsiao-ch'in," in *Eminent Chinese of the Ch'ing Period*, 298.

35. L. C. Arlington and William Lewisohn, *In Search of Old Peking* (Beijing: Henri Vetch, 1935), 285.

36. Backhouse, *The Dead Past*, 61.

37. Backhouse, *The Dead Past*, 61, 71.

38. Backhouse, *The Dead Past*, 70.

39. Backhouse, *The Dead Past*, 72

40. Backhouse, *The Dead Past*, 74.

41. Backhouse, *The Dead Past*, 59.

42. Arlington and Lewisohn, *In Search of Old Peking*, 96.

43. Backhouse, *The Dead Past*, 95.

44. Backhouse, *The Dead Past*, 98.

45. Arlington and Lewisohn, *In Search of Old Peking*, 52.

46. Anthony E. Clark, *China Gothic: The Bishop of Beijing and His Cathedral* (Seattle: University of Washington Press, 2019), 103–07.

47. Backhouse, *The Dead Past*, 98–99.

48. Backhouse, *The Dead Past*, 236.

49. Backhouse, *The Dead Past*, 237.

50. Mungello, *Western Queers in China*, 109–14.

51. Victor Segalen, *René Leys.* Édition présentée et annotée par Marie Dollé et Christian Doumet. (Paris: Librairie Génerale Française, 1999); Victor Segalen, *René Leys*, translated by J. A. Underwood (New York: New York Review of Books, 2003).

52. Fang, "Tsai-t'ien," in *Eminent Chinese of the Ch'ing Period*, 732.

53. Segelan, *René Leys*, edited by Dolle et Doumet, 184.

54. Fang, "Tsai-t'ien," in *Eminent Chinese of the Ch'ing Period*, 733.

55. Jerome Ch'en, "The Last Emperor of China," *Bulletin of the School of Oriental and African Studies* 28 (1965): 340–41 [336–55].

56. Marie Dollé and Christian Doumet, preface, in Segalan, *René Leys*, 12–13.

Chapter 2

Literary Fiction versus History

Lao She's Two Ma's (Er Ma 二馬)

I.

One of the earliest Chinese novels to treat love affairs between Chinese men and Western women was written in 1929 by Lao She 老舍 (the pen-name for Shu Qingchun 舒慶春) (1899–1966). This was one of Lao She's earliest novels in a prolific career as one of the leading novelists of early twentieth-century China. However, just as Backhouse's account of his love affair with the Dowager Empress Cixi was influenced by his tendencies toward literary exhibitionism and pornography, so too was Lao She's account of these interracial love affairs between a Chinese father and son with a British mother and daughter shaped by his use of parody and feelings of Chinese patriotism. The result is that while the accounts of Backhouse and Lao She are based on history, both diverge from history in distinctive ways. Lao She's primary concern was to satirize the racist attitudes of the British and the lack of national pride of many Chinese. But an equally important theme involved the humiliations that Chinese experienced living abroad, especially in Western settings. Unlike today, China in the 1920s was a weak and disrespected nation. Lao She was very sensitive to the fact that people from strong nations were called human beings while those from weak nations, such as China, were called "dogs."[1]

As a member of the ruling ethnic minority born as the Qing (Manchu) dynasty was ending, Lao She lived in a transitional age when Manchus faced intense hostility from the majority Han Chinese. His father, like most Manchu males, had been a soldier in a Banner unit. In 1900, a xenophobic martial arts force called the Righteous Fists (*Yihequan* 義和拳) or Boxers attacked foreigners in Beijing. When a foreign expeditionary force marched on Beijing to destroy the Boxers, Lao She's father was killed during the hostilities, leaving the family impoverished. When the Manchu Bannermen were demobilized

15

after the 1911 Revolution, most of them became either policemen or rick-shaw pullers.[2] Shu Qingchun instead pursued the traditional Chinese path of academic achievement, studying hard at Yanjing (Yenching) 燕京 University and teaching English at a middle school.

In his free time, Lao She taught English to poor Manchu children at the West City New Church in the Old Tartar City near the West Gate in Beijing. This church had been established by the London Missionary Society (LMS) in the 1860s, but it was transformed by the radical pastor Bao Guanglin who saw the need for Christianity in China to become indigenized and completely independent from the British mission.[3] After teaching briefly at the Nankai Middle School in Tianjin, Lao She returned to Beijing to enroll in English classes at Yanjing University with the assistance of an LMS Arts college grant. In the summer of 1924, he was awarded a five-year teaching appoint-ment in London. He bought a second-class boat ticket with a loan from the LMS and departed from Shanghai for England. In London, he taught Chinese at the School of Oriental Studies and lived in relative comfort.

Lao She's five-year stay in England was crucial to his development as a novelist. He read widely in English novels to improve his English. He began writing novels that were deeply influenced by the works of Charles Dickens and Joseph Conrad. In his novels, he was preoccupied with the theme of injustice, which he treated satirically. After writing his first three novels in England, he returned to China in 1930/1931. His greatest nov-els, such as *Camel Xiangzi* (*Luoto Xiangzi* 駱駝祥子) (1937) and *Four Generations Under One Roof* (*Sishi tongtang* 四世同堂), were written after he returned to China.

Lao She's novels are individualistic and humorous.[4] His protagonists are usually flawed men struggling against overwhelming social forces, and they practically never deal with romance. Female characters are usually limited to being foils to the main male characters. However, in the last novel Lao She wrote during his stay in London, *The Two Ma's*, he applied his perspective to the topic of interracial love. This novel attained a certain popular status when it was later transformed into a twenty-episode television series in 1999.[5]

The Two Ma's is about the generational and cultural conflicts between a Chinese father and son who traveled to London for the purpose of assuming ownership of a curio shop that the father had inherited from his deceased brother and to enable the son to study English and earn a degree.[6] The father, Ma Zeren 馬則仁, almost fifty years old, saw himself as someone in the old scholarly tradition of China. However, Lao She described him in satirical fashion as someone who was too lazy to study and had "never really devel-oped the habit" of reading![7] Moreover, he was filled with disdain for shop-keepers and too proud to work in the curio shop.[8] Missing his late wife, he fell in love with his widowed landlady, Mrs. Wendell (*Wendou Taitai* 溫都太太).

The son, Ma Wei 馬威, twenty-two or twenty-three years old, represented the generational divide then prominent in Republican China. He was the antithesis of his father. He was patriotic, tragic, and sentimental. White race colonialism had generated two myths that for a time were very pervasive in popular novels and films. One was that non-white men secretly lusted after white women.[9] The other myth was that a non-white man was too intimidated to fight a white man in self-defense. Unlike his father who fit the then-current Chinese stereotype of timidity and lack of courage, Ma Wei fought back when a young Englishman provoked him by aggressively grabbing Ma Wei's collar and saying: "Don't you get any uppity ideas that you can run around with our women!"[10] A bloody fistfight ensued in which Ma Wei triumphed.

Ma Wei fell in love with his landlady's daughter, Mary (*Mali* 瑪力) Wendell. Mrs. Wendell and Mary were poorly educated, lower-middle-class Londoners. Mrs. Wendell's basic decency was flawed by her absorption of the widespread prejudice in British society that viewed Chinese as criminals and murderers. Unlike her mother who was practical-minded, Mary was a flighty, superficial character who refused to help with the cooking and was preoccupied with wearing fashionable clothes and hats and finding a husband.[11] Although she was younger and more sexually attractive than her mother, her heart was more prejudiced against the Chinese. When Ma Wei fell in love with her, a minor tragedy ensued.

II.

The Chinese in London in the 1920s could be divided into two groups: workers and students.[12] Most of the workers lived in poverty in the eastern part of London in Chinatown and were regarded by most of the British as members of the Yellow Peril who smoked opium, gambled, and molested very young white girls.[13] The student group was more middle class and consisted almost entirely of males. Consequently, since few suitable Chinese women were available in London for the Ma's, they sought romance with British women.

Old Ma was passive about most things, except with women where he took the initiative. He saw Mrs. Wendell as beautiful, although Lao She voiced Ma's affection in the form of parody: "Mrs. Wendell had just finished eating lunch; she blinked her tired eyes. The powder had worn off her nose, revealing its red pointed form, but to Mr. Ma that red pointy nose was indescribably beautiful."[14] Being in London and far away from China, Ma thought foreign women were more attractive than Chinese girls in the sense that "even the ones who don't have a pretty face—at least they have nice figures."[15] Mrs. Wendell's bias against the Chinese was largely based on widespread social prejudice in England and her concern about what others would think. She claimed that she could not marry Mr. Ma because it would ruin her daughter's chances of finding a husband.[16] Her daughter Mary's bias was more personal. After planning to go to the circus with her mother, she backed out when she learned that the elder Ma was going too. Ma Wei was angry when Mary refused to go to the circus because of his father, but that did not stop him from becoming infatuated with Mary.

Lao She treated the love affairs of father and son with a mixture of pathos and humor. At one point in the novel Mr. Ma wandered into Mrs. Wendell's room and as he smelled the scent of her powder, "an aching pang ran through his heart."[17] Then he came upon Ma Wei kneeling in front of the bed in Mary's room with his head on the bed, crying. Old Ma was conflicted. While, on one hand, he was in love with Mrs. Wendell and "sometimes had felt great affection for Mrs. Wendell's cute red nose," on the other hand he felt that "marrying a foreigner would be a disgrace."[18] And yet while it would be a "disgrace" to give Ma Wei a foreign mother and prevent him from ever taking her home to China, he found foreign ladies so "pretty."[19]

Ma Wei was also conflicted about his love for Mary. His hardworking and stable youthful counterpart Li Zirong 李子榮 had kept the curio shop running through his hard labor, but Li had a very different attitude toward love and willingly accepted the bride his mother had arranged for him. Ma Wei told him he would be a fool if he didn't see the importance of love. The practical Li Zirong replied that he would "be a fool—*if* he loved a girl who didn't love [him]."[20] Ma Wei realized he could never forget Mary, so he tried to take refuge in the idealistic belief that to die for China would be a much more meaningful sacrifice than to die for a beautiful woman.[21] Consequently, he undertook a bodybuilding routine of morning runs in the park and rowing on the river, trying to convince himself that "there's no way beauty can balance on the scales with glory!" Meanwhile, Mary's world fell apart when her fiancé, Washington (*Huashengtun* 華盛頓), abandoned her for another woman. It was anticipated that Mary would sue Washington for breach of promise and ask for five hundred to six hundred pounds sterling in compensation.[22]

The attitude of other characters in the novel toward the Chinese was even more caustic than that of the Wendells. The Wendells' relative Aunt Dory declined their invitation to Christmas dinner because she did not feel safe around Chinese people.[23] Rev. Evans' son Paul (*Paoluo* 保羅), who had been raised as a missionary child in China, was particularly hostile. He was ungracious in refusing to reciprocate after receiving a box of Christmas cigars from Mr. Ma because of his disdain for the Chinese.[24] He was the one who challenged Ma Wei to a fight. And yet his sister Catherine (*Kaisalin* 凱薩林)

was one of the kindest hearted characters in the novel even though she ran off with Mary's fiancé Alexander!

III.

Lao She's satirizing of Rev. Evans (*Yimushi* 伊牧師) shows how he later distanced himself from British missionary endeavors.[25] Some of Lao She's sharpest satire is directed at the LMS missionary Reverend Evans who spent over twenty years in China. Evans' portrait is thought to have been based on the actual LMS Rev. Evans who helped Lao She get to London and who met him on his arrival in London on September 14, 1924.[26] Lao She mocked his knowledge of China by saying that Evans "knew everything about China" when, in fact, he was unable to translate Chinese texts.[27] His description of Mrs. Evans is even more scathing, particularly in regard to her large size and hirsute face which contrasts with the smaller bodies and notably smooth and hairless faces of Chinese women. He described her as having a hefty body and being a head taller than her husband. But in his most cutting remark, Lao She wrote "Mrs. Evans had a small mustache that was soft, dark and long; and this extra endowment was [soft] certainly the reason for her husband's compete absence of facial hair; he didn't dare grow one himself, for if he did it would be seen as a blatant attempt to compete with her."[28] During their years in China, Mrs. Evans had not allowed her son and daughter to learn Chinese or to play with Chinese children. This is a literary account, and it probably had some basis in truth for many missionaries in China. However, it was not true of all missionaries, and it was contradicted by the actual missionary childhood of Pearl Sydenstricker Buck in China in 1892–1911. Buck played with Chinese children and learned Chinese while her father Absalom Sydenstricker dedicated himself to making a new Chinese translation of the New Testament (see chapter 4).

After returning to China, Lao She became a famous novelist and was honored by its Communist leaders. However, the novel *The Two Ma's* contributed to his death. Thirty-seven years after its composition, Mao Zedong stirred up the political frenzy known as the Great Proletarian Cultural Revolution by radicalizing the youth of China to attack his opponents in the educational and party bureaucracies of China. Millions of these Red Guards were given free passage on the national railroad to come to Beijing where they attacked a wide range of objects and hunted down enemies. They smashed art objects, beat up "former capitalists," changed "reactionary" street signs, kidnapped officials, and burned the British legation to the ground.[29] Lao She was included as a target in this broad sweep of attack. His five-year residence in

London and the Western influence of Charles Dickens' novels on his writings made him vulnerable by tainting him in the minds of the young and xenophobic Red Guards.

In August 1966, when Lao She was sixty-seven and recuperating from bronchial bleeding and other health problems, he was ordered to attend several "study sessions" with members of the revolutionary committee in Beijing. On August 23, he was summoned to a "struggle session" with a group of middle-school Red Guards who forced him to stand for hours of verbal and physical abuse. In their eyes, his residence abroad in London had contributed to his development as a reactionary. He was beaten and made to kneel while a placard "Unrepentant Counter-revolutionary" was hung around his neck.[30] He resisted and, although bleeding, flung the placard to the ground. During the struggle session, Lao She's house was ransacked and many of his possessions and books were destroyed. He was allowed to go home for the night, but the next day he was called to another meeting and suffered more beatings. Later, his body was found in the Taiping Lake. It is unknown whether he had been murdered or had completed suicide.

IV.

The gap in Lao She's *Two Ma's* between literary fiction and historical reality is apparent in comparing the fictional love affairs of Ma Zeren and Ma Wei in London in 1929 with the actual love affairs treated in this book. In 1905–1908 in Brussels, Han Suyin's father Zhou Wei 周煒 (Chou Yentung) and the Flemish girl Marguerite Denis began their love affair (see chapter 3). In 1937 at Oxford Yang Xianyi and the British student Gladys Taylor began their love affair (see chapter 10). Unlike in Lao She's *Two Ma's*, these love affairs had long-term consequences. Also unlike in Lao She's *Two Ma's* where the love affairs were literary constructs created for the sake of parody and to foster Chinese patriotism, history shows that love was a powerful force that drew interracial lovers together and created complicated consequences for their Eurasian children.

NOTES

1. Lao She 老舍者, *Mr. Ma & Son a Sojourn in London* 二馬, translated by Julie Jimmerson 吉姆遜. (Beijing: Foreign Language Press, 2001), 25–27.

2. Anne Witchard, *Lao She in London* (Hong Kong: Hong Kong University Press, 2012), 5.

3. Witchard, *Lao She in London*, 28–30.

4. C. T. Hsia, *A History of Modern Chinese Fiction 1917–1957* (New Haven: Yale University Press, 1961), 165.

5. Li Mingguang, "Chen Daoming shuo 'Er Ma,'" ("Chen Daoming on the *Two Mas*"), *Renmin ribao* (*People's Daily*), February 23, 1999.

6. Hsia, *A History of Modern Chinese Fiction*, 172.

7. Lao She, *Mr. Ma & Son a Sojourn in London* 二馬。, translated by Julie Jimmerson (Beijing: Foreign Language Press, 2001), 347.

8. Lao She, *Mr. Ma & Son*, 179. Also see Louis Kam, "Constructing Chinese Masculinity for the Modern World: With Particular Reference to Lao She's *The Two Mas*," *The China Quarterly* 164 (December 2000): 1067.

9. Hsia, *A History of Modern Chinese Fiction*, 176.

10. Lao She, *Mr. Ma & Son*, 465–67.

11. Lao She, *Mr. Ma & Son*, 175.

12. Lao She, *Mr. Ma & Son*, 25.

13. Kam, "Constructing Chinese Masculinity for the Modern World," 1063.

14. Lao She, *Mr. Ma & Son*, 143.

15. Lao She, *Mr. Ma & Son*, 407.

16. Lao She, *Mr. Ma & Son*, 521–23.

17. Lao She, *Mr. Ma & Son*, 347–49.

18. Lao She, *Mr. Ma & Son*, 351.

19. Lao She, *Mr. Ma & Son*, 407

20. Lao She, *Mr. Ma & Son*, 421

21. Lao She, *Mr. Ma & Son*, 376–77.

22. Lao She, *Mr. Ma & Son*, 547.

23. Lao She, *Mr. Ma & Son*, 401.

24. Lao She, *Mr. Ma & Son*, 389–91.

25. Witchard, *Lao She in London*, 32.

26. Witchard, *Lao She in London*, 34.

27. Lao She, *Mr. Ma & Son*, 21, 487.

28. Lao She, *Mr. Ma & Son*, 189.

29. Jonathan D. Spence, *The Gate of Heavenly Peace: The Chinese and Their Revolution, 1895–1980* (New York: Viking Press, 1981), 345–49.

30. Britt Towery, *Lao She China's Master Storyteller* (Waco, TX: Tao Foundation, 1999), 189–92.

Chapter 3

A Many-Splendored Fabricator

Han Suyin

I.

A Many-Splendoured Thing, the most famous novel (and later film and television series) of an interracial love affair in the 1950s, was based on the actual experience of the Eurasian Han Suyin 韓素音. Her real name was Rosalie Matilda Kuanghu Chou (Zhou Guanghu 周光瑚) (1916–2012), and the key to her fame as an author lay in her blending of personal experiences with the larger events of Chinese history. Her literary imagination recast and transformed her life both in terms of the men she loved and the Communist China that she romanticized (but only infrequently visited). She presented herself as the great interpreter and defender of a revolutionary China to the rest of the world, but her interpretations of history were shaped by her personal struggles.

Han Suyin was a fabulist who created fables about love and China filled with literary passion. When Mao Zedong forcibly collectivized the peasants into people's communes during the Great Leap Forward, causing an estimated forty-five million deaths, she wrote: "Especially in that winter of 1960. Fiercely, wholeheartedly, I was defending China, even lying through my teeth (with a smile) to the diplomats and the newsmen who probed. . . . I had not chosen this. It has chosen me. All the more so when the wind howled like a wolf and winter fastened its iron will upon the land, and the whole world seemed to rise with glee to threaten China. Then above all, I was Chinese."[1]

Han Suyin's father was a Chinese named Zhou Wei 周煒 (Chou Yentung) (b. 1886). Zhou came from a formerly prosperous family in Sichuan province descended from Hakkas (*kejia* 客家, or Chinese Guest People) who had migrated from north China in the twelfth century. In 1903, he departed from Sichuan to board a ship in Shanghai that carried him to study in Europe. When the ship stopped in Singapore, he took the bold step of having his queue cut off.[2] The queue (*bianzi* 辮子) or "pigtail" had been imposed on all Chinese males during the Qing dynasty as a mark of their submission to the Manchus. As the Qing dynasty came to an end, revolutionary-minded young Chinese began cutting off their queues, although there were punishments in China for doing so. Arriving in Marseilles in 1904, Zhou and his fellow Chinese were met by the Chinese vice-consul and guided by train to Belgium where he began his study at the University of Brussels.

In May 1905, Zhou met the Flemish girl Marguerite Denis (1885–1966) at a cheese market in Ixelles and is said by Han Suyin to have fallen instantly in love with her.[3] Han Suyin romanticized her parents as contrasting personalities. She said her mother was attractive, high-spirited and—unlike her father—"wayward and headstrong."[4] Han Suyin inherited the rebellious nature of her mother. Much later, when she returned to China while it was undergoing a Communist re-education campaign, she told her father "I did not want to be re-educated, my skin crawled at the thought."[5] However, her father, remembering her mother's rebelliousness, told her that she must not "show temper."

Marguerite viewed Zhou as an "Asiatic prince" and said she wanted to go to his country. Their relationship developed over three years from 1905 to 1908, becoming an interracial scandal. The Denis family tried to end the relationship by locking Marguerite in her room, but she kicked a hole in the door and escaped.[6] Marguerite became pregnant. Zhou received permission from his family in China to marry her. The bishop in Belgium allowed the marriage to go forward despite Zhou's refusal to become a Catholic. In October 1908, four months after their marriage, their child Son of Spring was born. Zhou completed his engineering degree at the University of Brussels in October 1910 and returned to China with Marguerite and their son in 1913.[7]

Zhou's impoverished family looked to him for financial support. The entire country of China was financially exhausted by having most of its revenues diverted to foreign powers to repay war indemnities.[8] During the years 1880 to 1894, the leading official Li Hongzhang had led the industrialization effort in updating China's transportation system by building its first railroad, but Europeans funded and drained the profits in colonialist style from most of the consequent railroad building.[9] Zhou Wei's engineering training in Belgium made him ideally suited to contribute to this construction effort.

After arriving back in China, the fairy-tale romance of Zhou and Marguerite began to disintegrate. When Zhou attempted to buy first-class tickets on an English boat en route to Sichuan, he was told that no "coloured person" was allowed in the first-class section of the boat and, in any case, the first-class section was already full.[10] However, when they collected their second-class tickets, the European ticket agent told Marguerite that she could travel by first class, but not Zhou because it was not allowed. Of course, she refused.

Son of Spring was returned to Belgium in 1914 where, caught up in the First World War, he remained until 1925 when he once again came to China, but eventually returned to live in Europe.[11] Marguerite gave birth to Sea Orchid, Second Son, while Zhou was working on the Lunghai Railway on the northern plains of Henan province. According to Han Suyin, Marguerite thought he was "the most beautiful child in the world."[12] She called him Gabriel, after the archangel who announced the birth of Jesus to Mary (Luke 1:19–36). When Sea Orchid suddenly died, Marguerite began drinking brandy. At that time her isolation was duplicated by numerous European women who suffered nervous breakdowns in China, although most of the European women, unlike Marguerite, were married to other Europeans. The conditions along the railroads were plagued by warlords, bandits, and famine (see figure 3.1).

While Marguerite was still grieving for Sea Orchid, First Daughter Rosalie (later Han Suyin) was born in 1916 in Sinyang, Henan province. She was later told that she was "a long thin child" and that Marguerite refused to look at her for a whole week, saying: "Take the halfcaste brat away. It is not my

Figure 3.1. A hysterical boy crying to his mother "please don't sell me" as his elder sister had already been sold. Red Cross famine relief. January 1920. (Library of Congress Prints and Photographs Division, Washington, DC.)

child."[13] Marguerite refused to nurse Rosalie until Zhou slapped her.[14] Han Suyin claims that although her mother tried to love her, Marguerite could not overcome her resentment over the loss of Sea Orchid. They would be forever estranged. The birth of Rosalie was followed by the births of Tiza, then a little brother, a little sister, and another little brother, the last three of whom died because the European doctors were negligent in their treatment of "half-castes."[15] Finally the last child, Marianne, was born and survived, at the expense of mental illness.[16] Han Suyin summarized her mother's ambitions for her daughters by saying that Marguerite felt resentment toward Rosalie, thought that Tiza was lovely, and viewed Marianne as beautiful.[17] At first, Marguerite tried to cope with conditions in revolutionary China, but after losing four children, she departed China in 1956 with one daughter (Tiza) and a granddaughter. She never returned. Later, Han Suyin tried to arrange a reunion of her parents in Singapore, but the obstacles to obtaining a visa for her father to leave China were insuperable.[18]

Han Suyin said that skin color bias existed in India, Singapore, and Malaya, as well as among overseas Chinese and Eurasians.[19] It also existed among the Chinese in China. The amah Lao Jie criticized Han Suyin for going out without a parasol, saying: "You'll get so black." Han Suyin married a Chinese, then an Englishman, and finally an Indian, to whose dark skin she was sexually attracted. She described his skin as being "the most gorgeous, sensuous, satin chocolate colour in the world for me. Then and there I fell out of frigidity into the most blazing need to put my hands on him."[20]

Han Suyin grew up in Beijing.[21] However, since her knowledge of Chinese was deficient, she studied for two years at Yanjing University which had an enrollment of eight hundred students.[22] When she began studying at Yanjing University in 1933, she felt the bias against her as a Eurasian. Then she shed the name of Rosalie like an old skin that she was leaving behind and traveled to Brussels via the Trans-Siberian railway in 1935[23] (figure 3.2). In London she met Tang Baohuang 唐保璜, where he was studying as a cadet at the Sandhurst Royal Military Academy.[24] Tang was a graduate of the Whampoa Military Academy founded in south China near Guangzhou (Canton) by the Nationalist leader Sun Yatsen in 1924 with Chiang Kai-shek as the commandant. The Academy had been founded in order to develop a disciplined officer corps that could overcome the northern warlords and reunify China. Tang Baohuang was an idealistic patriot and Han Suyin became infatuated with him, following him back to China in 1938. While many Chinese viewed Han Suyin as Eurasian rather than Chinese, Tang assured her that her blood was Chinese saying "blood comes from the father, the mother is only the receptacle."[25] Later, when Han Suyin became disillusioned with the Nationalists, she mocked Tang's view as "pre-scientific," although her own view of China's history and her role in it was more far romantic than "scientific." But in 1938,

Figure 3.2. A Trans-Siberian train at Mukden, Manchuria, on the longest railroad in the world. In the 1920s and 1930s, the Trans-Siberian railway was the fastest and most direct route between China and Europe. Published 1904. (Library of Congress Prints and Photographs Division, Washington, DC.)

she felt that marriage to Tang would allow her to be recognized as Chinese. When she followed him back to China, she wrote: "it was for China, not for a man, that I had left Europe. This was my grand illusion."[26] The rich ambiguity of that statement is a hallmark of Han Suyin's writing.

In 1938, Han Suyin followed Tang back to China to the battlefield in Wuhan where the Nationalists were attempting to repel the Japanese invasion and she married him. Later she accompanied him in returning to London where he was a military attaché and where she completed her medical training. Tang became a general and returned to China to lead Nationalist troops on the battlefield against the Communist forces, but the Nationalist cause was becoming hopeless. Late in 1947, his troops "either abandoned him or killed him."[27] However, Han Suyin had lost sympathy for her first husband. She came to condemn Tang Baohuang's politics and transformed it into the cause of her sexual frigidity. Nor did she love her second husband, Leonard Comber, the British Assistant Superintendent in the Special Branch in

Malaya, on leave in Hong Kong (married 1952–1958), who she married only to provide stability for her daughter Yungmei.[28] She wrote: "How does one explain a total inability to function sexually? Of course I knew the cause. It was Bao. He had wounded me mortally in that respect; until the end of my life I would suffer from relapses."[29]

Perhaps these things were true, but there were also other reasons buried in the complex yin and yang dialectic of her reasoning. Han Suyin's popularity in the West was not shared by most Chinese intellectuals who survived the Cultural Revolution. Mao Zedong was apparently suspicious of her affinities and was always reluctant to meet with her. The reasons for this reluctance were explained by the Belgium-born Australian Sinologist Pierre Ryckmans (1935–2014) who wrote under the penname Simon Leys.[30] Ryckmans was struck by the "grand dialogue between Yin and Yang" that characterized her writings.[31] He referred to it variously as a "double vision," "a polyphonic coexistence of opposites," and "two different faces simultaneously, heads as well as tails." Ryckmans described fourteen contradictory points (categorized under "heads" and "tails") in Han Suyin's statements on Communist China.[32]

Han Suyin claimed that Ryckmans did not understand her perspective and felt that his account was "a highly fanciful account of meeting" her in 1972 in Beijing.[33] Ryckmans' contribution to Sinology was primarily that of an iconoclast. In his book *Chinese Shadows* (1972), written under the pen name Simon Leys in order to conceal his authorship, he was one of the first to challenge the initially favorable interpretations of the Cultural Revolution given by foreign Sinologists, and he described the wanton destruction of Beijing's ancient cultural heritage by Chinese Communists. However, the mind of an iconoclast may lack the subtlety to understand the mind of Han Suyin.

A more sympathetic reading of Han Suyin's so-called double vision would emphasize the complementary rather than opposing nature of these contrasts and see them as part of her attempt to reconcile the different aspects of her Eurasian nature. If the pieces failed to harmonize, that failure can be attributed to the life that she was dealt at birth. Like her mother Marguerite and unlike her father, Han Suyin was a restless person. However, unlike Marguerite who was very fertile, Han Suyin was subject to life-threatening ectopic (tubal) pregnancies in which the fertilized egg attached itself outside of the uterus. In 1943 in London when she was married to Tang, she suffered her first tubal pregnancy in which her fallopian tube had burst.[34] Difficulties in pregnancy led Han Suyin and her first husband to adopt their daughter Tang Yungmei. Later in 1952 in Malaya, after her second marriage, Han Suyin suffered another ectopic rupture, requiring surgery.

After divorcing her second husband Comber, she married the Indian Colonel Vincent Ratnaswamy (married 1960–2003). She, once again, explained her fluid emotional feelings in terms of a yin and yang dialectic that contrasted her love for her husband with her love for China by saying: "all my life I shall be running in two opposite directions at once; away from and towards love, away from and toward China." The nature of these yin and yang forces can be understood as complementary parts of Han Suyin's life.

Han Suyin had several cousins who were committed Communists. First Uncle's daughter Ping (Bing), the Fourth Sister in Han Suyin's generation, had run away as a teenager, going through the Nationalist lines to join the Communist base at Yenan (Yan'an). She had fought against the Japanese and had married another guerrilla, losing three of her five children. She was now a party cadre in charge of education, and she assumed the role of "teacher" to Han Suyin.[35] But Han Suyin resisted this pressure to be thought-remolded and felt she had come to learn facts and ask questions. Some of the Communists were suspicious and viewed her as being of "big landlord origin," one of the five "bad origins" (landlords, rich peasants, counter-revolutionaries, asocial elements, and bourgeois elements) who refused to be reeducated.[36]

Han Suyin was more of a Chinese chauvinist than a Communist. Her greatest concern was being accepted as Chinese. In Communist China, Eurasians had been targeted at criticism meetings because of their "mixed blood."[37] Her cousin Kung Peng (Gong Beng) claimed that was the fault of the Eurasians for not integrating, but Han Suyin argued: "How can one become anonymous and merge totally when one's nose and eyes and hair are different?" Racial bias was not only a Western problem, but also a Chinese problem. Han Suyin's intense affinity for Zhou Enlai was based, in part, on his sympathy for Eurasians in China and his condemnation of Han chauvinism throughout his lifetime.[38] It is significant that she discusses her seven meetings with Zhou Enlai, by saying "He changed my bone marrow. He was, truly, not only my teacher, but my guide for life."[39]

Han Suyin's cousin Gong Beng defended her against the Party cadres who were "infuriated by the unorthodox, non-conformist" behavior she displayed.[40] Gong Beng was more sophisticated and sympathetic than most of the Party cadres. She and her husband Chiao Kuanhua (Jiao Guanhua) both served in the Foreign Ministry under Zhou Enlai and so had access to foreign newspapers and other points of view. They lived in an austere manner in a very small flat.[41]

Han Suyin resisted the Chinese Communists' tendency to explain all problems in ideological terms. The staff of the mental hospital that she visited in Peitaiho (Beidaihe) was reluctant to refer to itself as a mental hospital.[42] The cause of all mental diseases was said to be physical exhaustion and was thought to be ideological in nature. When she asked about homosexuality, the Party cadre claimed: "There is none in China." When Han Suyin insisted that homosexuality is mentioned in the famous Chinese novel *Hongloumeng* (*Dream of the Red Mansions*), the cadre insisted homosexuality did not exist under socialism. While the physicians remained silent, the cadre explained how homosexuality was a perversion of the social system and, like most mental illnesses, of ideological origin.

Han Suyin blamed the collapse of the Chinese economy on revolutionary enthusiasm and on natural disasters like the 1961 drought of 180 days in Sichuan, the worst in a century, exacerbated by the directives of ignorant cadres.[43] She described the Great Leap Forward landscape with new tall chimneys that remained unused and emitted no smoke and with piles of machine parts that remained rusting on the ground until 1963.[44] She claims to have predicted that the lack of historical knowledge would be the major cause of the destructiveness of the Red Guards during the Cultural Revolution.[45] But she resorted to her yin-yang dialectic in claiming that she never lost faith in the Chinese Communists, telling her cousin Gong Peng she thought that "only with the system of the communes, only with the Communist Party, can China weather this period of disaster."[46]

Han Suyin's marriage to a Nationalist general caused her to be distrusted by the Communists. Zhou Enlai was one of the few Chinese leaders, other than Marshall Chen Yi, formerly the mayor of Shanghai and later China's foreign minister, who would meet with her.[47] However, Zhou, always the master diplomat, kept her at a distance. In contrast to Zhou, Han Suyin's view of the Indian leader Jawaharlal Nehru (1889–1964) was not so positive.[48] Her friendship with Malcolm MacDonald, High Commissioner of Southeast Asia, opened doors for her in India. When her publisher, Jonathan Cape, worried that the controversial nature of her novel *A Many-Splendoured Thing* would damage its reception, it was suggested that Malcolm MacDonald, then High Commissioner of Southeast Asia, write a foreword, which he did. When MacDonald moved to India in 1955, he invited Han Suyin to visit and he introduced her to Nehru.[49]

Nehru and Lady Edwina Mountbatten were then engaged in a famous extramarital love affair. Lord Louis Mountbatten, a royal naval officer and member of the British royal family, was appointed the last Viceroy of India in 1947. He was a bisexual who was said to be sexually attracted to young Asian boys with dark skin. Han Suyin noted that after dinner Lady Mountbatten sat next to Nehru and "kept patting his hand to make a point."[50] She had given him a copy of *A Many-Splendoured Thing* to read, and he immediately mentioned the book to Han Suyin with the deflating comment "I think great loves should be kept private." Han Suyin contrasted India and China by applying her yin-yang dialectic, saying India is "a totally different beauty from the untiring loveliness of China. China is pastel and nuance and discovery, and India hits you in the eye, flaunts everything. . . . Mind-jolting in its profligate splendour."[51] Consequent events did not improve Han Suyin's assessment of

Nehru. In 1955 his attempt to cultivate friendship with Zhou Enlai collapsed over the unmarked border dispute between India and China.

II.

Today it is difficult to grasp how confused the foreign understanding of Communist China was during the 1960s and 1970s and how valuable Han Suyin's writings were in providing some enlightenment. Yet in a 2021 interview posted on YouTube, the Han Suyin scholar Aamer Hussein argued that Han Suyin was more of a third-world literary figure who wrote in English than a China observer.[52] Hussein emphasized that Han Suyin's identification as a Chinese author was diminished by her residence in Singapore for twelve years. In 1959 she taught a three-month course entitled "Contemporary Asian Literature" at Nanyang University in Malaya. Nanyang University was created for Chinese students who were otherwise excluded from the educational channels open to Malays. However, she offended the Chinese students by saying the university should not exclude Malay students.[53] On the other hand, Han Suyin criticized Malays for their nationalist tendencies and for their identification with the Islamist world.

The pro-Chiang Kai-shek lobby in America became interested in cultivating Nanyang University in Singapore as a bulwark against Communism. Consequently, the well-known author Lin Yutang was chosen as an anti-Communist chancellor for Nanyang University. Prior to 1935 Lin Yutang had been a very influential anti-Communist in Chinese literary circles but after the publication of his highly successful *My Country and My People*, he moved to America and lost much of his literary influence.[54]

Han Suyin was disdainful of Lin Yutang for his intense anti-Communist positions and his affiliation with the United States. Lin had avoided living in China during the Sino-Japanese War, except for a two-week trip to Chongqing. He had gone to Taiwan in 1953 to denounce Communist China and participate in the Anti-Communist League, which was backed by the US Central Intelligence Agency. He had lived in the United States for two decades. With dripping sarcasm, Han Suyin described him as a Chinese expatriate. She claims that Lin's daughter and son-in-law were given jobs at Nanyang University and the family was "provided with a bungalow by the sea and a Cadillac or two."[55] Han Suyin criticized Lin's lack of interest in Malay. She descended to pettiness in mocking his use of the endearment "Mummy" for his wife and further mocked Mrs. Lin for asking if she would like some "cawfee," using an Americanized pronunciation. The description of her interview with the Lins was demeaning and in stark contrast to the fawning descriptions of her interviews with Zhou Enlai.

Han Suyin's relationship to Catholics was very mixed and was also characterized by a yin and yang nature. The tension began with her parents: her
mother was Catholic and her father was not. And yet in Hong Kong, she
became friends with a charismatic and fiery anti-Communist Jesuit priest
named Lazlo Ladány (1914–1990). At her wedding ceremony to Leonard
Comber in 1952, Fr. Ladány and Fr. Turner officiated at Lady of Lourdes
at Pokfulam, a small remote chapel. Fr. Ladány had insisted that she go to
confession, which was done "unsuccessfully" by an Italian priest.[56] In terms
of her greatest loyalties, her father's Chinese identity transcended any loyalty
to her mother's Catholicism. When she returned from a trip to the Chinese
mainland in 1956, Fr. Ladány criticized her for stating that religion was
free in China.[57] In fact, she claimed that she had "entirely forgotten, while
in Peking visiting her old convent school, to ask about Catholics and the
Catholic religion." When Fr. Ladány said she had a great responsibility to
state that religion was being persecuted in China, she refused.[58]

Han Suyin's bitter hostility toward the United States was partly based on
its anti-Communist policies toward China and partly on her perception of
America as alien in nature to her identity. Her sister Tiza fell in love with an
American Marine officer who was part of a contingent sent to China to assist
Chiang Kai-shek.[59] She became pregnant but was unable to marry the Marine
because of an American military non-fraternization rule. Tiza gave birth to
the child, but worried about what the Communists would do to her and the
child. She and Marguerite fled with the baby to Hong Kong, but Han Suyin
either refused or was unable to send the British Consul a guarantee for them
to live in Hong Kong. They consequently went to Italy and then to the United
States in 1956. They joined the younger daughter Marianne who had married
an American and had two children. However, Marianne's husband suddenly
died of a heart attack. For a time, Marguerite, Tiza, and the baby lived with
Marianne, but they argued and separated. When Marguerite died in Arizona
in 1966, Han Suyin grudgingly paid for her tombstone, which was hardly the
response of a filial daughter.

In Han Suyin's first interview with Zhou Enlai, he asked why she did not
go to the United States because he heard that her novel had made her popular
there.[60] She replied simply that she did not go to the United States. However,
in 1965 she began a fourteen-year series of lectures on China in the United
States, going on to Europe, Canada, Mexico, Australia, Japan, Africa, and
India.[61] She appeared numerous times on television in the United States. She
began her tour in Honolulu where her old dormitory classmates from Yanjing
University during 1933 to 1935 serenaded her with the theme song from
the film *Love Is a Many-Splendored Thing*. It was an awkward introduction
to America. On the mainland, she had come "prepared to despise, to resent

certainly," but she was drawn in by the enchantment of her engineer husband Vincent Ratnaswamy with America's human wonders.

Han Suyin rarely discussed the United States, except to criticize it in the most hostile terms.[62] She missed the crowds of Asia—the vast spaces of America by comparison seemed empty. In racially segregated Georgia, Alabama, and Tennessee, her husband's dark skin caused problems, but the foul-mouthed racists were compensated for by the African Americans who came to their hotel room to shake their hands and by the "general kindness, the real goodness" that they found everywhere.[63] And yet, despite her problematic relationship with the United States, her daughter Yungmei married (and later divorced) an American named Sidney Glazier, a Jewish film producer, and they had a daughter named Karen.[64]

III.

After her husband Tang Baohuang died in the Chinese civil war between the Nationalists and the Communists, Han Suyin went to Hong Kong to practice medicine in 1949. She lived in Hong Kong during the transformative post–World War II period when the Communist Chinese victories created a flood of refugees from the mainland and produced the increasing interracial mingling. Looking back, she wrote: "In the 1950s, intermarriage between an Englishman (or should I say Scotsman?) and a Chinese girl was regarded with animadversion, certainly in the business houses; where it led to swift demotion. . . . And yet in that year of 1949, all this was already beginning to change, and the change was due to the change in China."[65] It was during this time that she had her love affair with the Australian and *London Times* war correspondent Ian Morrison (1913–1950) that became romanticized in her famous novel.

The post–World War II view of interracial love affairs involving Chinese people and Westerners was shaped by Han Suyin's best-selling novel *A Many-Splendoured Thing* (1952). Ian Morrison was the son of the adventurer G. E. Morrison who in 1894 traveled three thousand miles from Shanghai up the Yangzi (Yangtze) River and then overland to Burma even though, in the arch style of an imperialist, he spoke no Chinese and had no interpreter.[66] The younger Morrison was married with two children, and it is unlikely that this was his first extramarital affair. Nor is it likely that the relationship would have evolved into marriage because Morrison's wife refused to give him a divorce. Morrison was later sent to the Korean War as a war correspondent and died when his vehicle hit a landmine.[67]

Han Suyin did not begin writing the story of their love affair until Morrison's last letter arrived.[68] The affair was later portrayed in the 1955 film *Love Is a Many-Splendored Thing* and in a popular US television soap opera with the same name that ran from 1967 to 1973. She sold the film rights to pay for lung surgery in London in 1954 for her daughter Yungmei.[69] After the film appeared, she corrected parts of the film in her autobiographical *My House Had Two Doors* (1980). The story had great exotic appeal for many readers and viewers throughout the world, not only because of the beautiful and remote setting in Hong Kong, but also because of the racial and cultural differences of the lovers.

Han Suyin practiced medicine but became far more famous as an interracial voice who bridged two alienated worlds and who blended her own life with Chinese history in her autobiographical trilogy.[70] She was an enthusiastic supporter of Communist China, visiting it occasionally, despite the fact that her marriage to the Nationalist officer Tang Baohuang made her suspicious in the eyes of the Communists. She was able to meet with the diplomatic Zhou Enlai seven times, but never with Mao Zedong. She had bursts of revolutionary enthusiasm, claiming "at that moment I too could have died if Zhou Enlai had asked me to die. He was China's hope, and all depended on him."[71] Her enthusiasm was steadfast, even during the years of the Cultural Revolution when most other foreign observers became disillusioned with the Chinese Communists. Afterwards she lived in Lausanne, Switzerland, for many years, dying in 2012 at the age of ninety-five. Although she paid a price for her Eurasian blood, it was the key to her great success as an author and interpreter of China to the rest of the world. Ironically, the author of the most famous novel of interracial love of the post–World War II period was for the first forty-four years of her life a sexually frigid woman who loved China with as much passion as she loved men.

NOTES

1. Han Suyin, *My House Has Two Doors* 吾宅双门 (Great Britain: Triad/Granada, 1982), 373; Frank Dikötter, *Mao's Great Famine* (London: Bloomsbury Publishing Plc., 2010), 324–34.

2. Han Suyin, *The Crippled Tree* (1965; reprinted at Frogmore: Panther Books, 1972), 166.

3. Han, *The Crippled Tree*, 182–83.

4. Han, *The Crippled Tree*, 184.

5. Han, *My House*, 149.

6. Han, *The Crippled Tree*, 197–98.

7. Han, *The Crippled Tree*, 200.

8. Han, *The Crippled Tree*, 206–07.

9. David P. T. Pong, "Li Hung-chang and Shen Pao-chen: The Politics of Modernization," in *Li Hung-chang and China's Early Modernization*, edited by Samuel C. Chu and Kwang-Ching Lu (Armonk, NY: M. E. Sharpe, 1994), 86; Yuen-sang Leung, "The Shanghai-Tientsin Connection: Li Hung-chang's Political Control over Shanghai," in *Li Hung-chang and China's Early Modernization*, edited by Samuel C. Chu and Kwang-Ching Lu (Armonk, NY: M. E. Sharpe, 1994), 109.

10. Han, *The Crippled Tree*, 268–69.

11. Han, *The Crippled Tree*, 200.

12. Han, *The Crippled Tree*, 302.

13. Han, *The Crippled Tree*, 304.

14. Han, *The Crippled Tree*, 304–05.

15. Han, *The Crippled Tree*, 335.

16. Han, *The Crippled Tree*, 334–37.

17. Han Suyin, *Birdless Summer* (Great Britain: Jonathan Cape Ltd., 1968; republished Frogmore: Panther Books Ltd, 1972), 14.

18. Han, *My House*, 193.

19. Han, *My House*, 131

20. Han, *My House*, 132.

21. Han, *My House*, 156.

22. Han, *My House*, 176.

23. Han, *Birdless Summer*, 15.

24. Han, *Birdless Summer*, 19.

25. Han, *Birdless Summer*, 21.

26. Han, *Birdless Summer*, 25.

27. Han, *Birdless Summer*, 328.

28. Han Suyin, *My House*, 60, 64.

29. Han Suyin, *My House*, 124.

30. Pierre Ryckmans and Han Suyin shared ancestral roots in Belgium. Ryckmans was born there in 1935 and visited China as part of a youth delegation. Although he lived in Australia after 1970, he returned to China in 1972 on a six-month assignment as a cultural attaché to the Belgian embassy in Beijing. Michael Forsythe, "Pierre Ryckmans" (1935–2014) obituary, *New York Times*, August 15, 2014, A21.

31. Simon Leys (Pierre Ryckman)'s "The Double Vision of Han Suyin" was originally republished as part of a collection in France under the title *La foret en feu* (Hermann, éditeurs des sciences et des arts, 1983). The English translation was published under the title *The Burning Forest: Essays on Chinese Culture and Politics* (New York: Henry Holt and Co, 1986), 177–78.

32. Simon Leys (Pierre Ryckman), *The Burning Forest*, 178–89.

33. Han, *My House*, 283.

34. Han, *My House*, 68.

35. Han, *My House*, 143–44.

36. Han, *My House*, 154.

37. Han, *My House*, 390.

38. Han, *My House*, 390–91.

39. Han, *My House*, 521.

40. Han, *My House*, 157.

41. Han, *My House*, 156–58.

42. Han, *My House*, 193–94.

43. Han, *My House*, 380.

44. Han, *My House*, 384.

45. Han, *My House*, 505.

46. Han, *My House*, 377.

47. Han, *My House*, 493.

48. Han, *My House*, 327–28.

49. Han, *My House*, 125.

50. Han, *My House*, 126.

51. Han, *My House*, 125–26.

52. Aamer Hussein, "On Not Teaching Han Suyin and Other 'Third-World' Matters," YouTube interview, June 14, 2021.

53. Han, *My House*, 291.

54. C. T. Hsia, *A History of Modern Chinese Fiction 1917–1957* (New Haven: Yale University Press, 1961), 133–34.

55. Han, *My House*, 109–12.

56. Han, *My House*, 65.

57. Han, *My House*, 227–28. Fr. Lazlo Ladany described this persecution of Catholics in his book *The Catholic Church in China* (New York: Freedom House, 1987).

58. For a discussion of Chinese Communist persecution of Catholics in the 1950s, see D. E. Mungello, *Catholic Invasion of China*, 55–69.

59. Han, *My House*, 28.

60. Han, *My House*, 212.

61. Han, *My House*, 511.

62. Han, *My House*, 512–16.

63. Han, *My House*, 513.

64. Han, *My House*, 515.

65. Han, *My House*, 15–16.

66. G. E. Morrison, *An Australian in China* (London: Horace Cox, 1895), 1.

67. Han, *My House*, 46–50.

68. Han, *My House*, 51.

69. Han, *My House*, 113.

70. Following *The Crippled Tree* (1965), Han Suyin published *A Mortal Flower* (1966; republished Frogmore: Panther Books Ltd, 1972) and *Birdless Summer* (1968; republished Frogmore: Panther Books Ltd, 1972).

71. Han, *Two Doors*, 388.

Chapter 4

The Pearl versus the Dragon

Pearl Buck and China

I.

The life of Pearl Sydenstricker Buck (1892–1973) was filled with interracial love affairs in the widest sense—for Chinese peasants, for a great Chinese poet, and for abandoned biracial children. She had a gift for storytelling that helped her become one of the most popular novelists of all time. Her fame as a novelist gave her a platform to issue highly publicized, but occasionally flawed judgments about Chinese peasants, about her parents' work as Christian missionaries in China, about Chinese history, and about the men surrounding her. She had an empathy for women, a love of children, an iron will, and a fascination with China that set her apart as an author. She was a leader of racial integration in the United States, mainly in integrating Amerasians (the abandoned children of American servicemen and East Asian mothers) into American society.

Pearl Buck was a prolific author of eighty-five books. Her most famous work, *The Good Earth* (1931), depicted the family life of a peasant named Wang Lung set in a Chinese village before World War I. The striking simplicity of the story caused it to be translated into thirty languages. It won the Pulitzer Prize for Fiction in 1932 and contributed to Buck winning the Nobel Prize in Literature in 1938, although a number of literary critics regarded her works as ponderous and banal.[1] Like Han Suyin, Buck also had a flair for the dramatic coloring of events of her life that she transformed into fiction—a transformation that was, as with Han Suyin, sometimes at odds with history. Her talents were enhanced by a remarkable early life in China where she learned Chinese as a native language.

The most influential figures in her life were her missionary parents, Absalom Sydenstricker (1852–1931) and Caroline (Carie) Stutling Sydenstricker (1857–1921). The Sydenstrickers traveled to China soon after their marriage

37

in 1880 as Southern Presbyterian missionaries, located first in Tsingkianpu (Huai'an) and then from 1896 in Chinkiang (Zhenjiang) (see China map), where they lived for twenty-seven years. Apart from home furloughs every ten years, they both remained in China for the rest of their lives. The couple quickly encountered the travails of missionary life. After crossing the Pacific Ocean and arriving in Shanghai, they were first assigned to Hangchow (Hangzhou), a city famously built around the West Lake.[2] Unlike Han Suyin, Carie was very fertile. When she was full term with their first child, because of the lack of a physician in Hangzhou, they went to Shanghai where their son Edgar was born (see figure 4.1).

Three months later, they were reassigned to Soochow (Suzhou). They returned to Shanghai in their second summer in China to be near a physician who could help Carie with her second pregnancy. While there, Absalom suffered from a severe sunstroke and for six weeks was on the point of death, but Carie nursed him back to health.[3] Back in Suzhou, Carie gave birth to their daughter Maude. Because of Maude's illness and Carie's third pregnancy, they escaped the summer heat by going to a small Japanese island. However,

Figure 4.1. American missionaries, Shanghai. Bain News Service, between ca. 1910 and ca. 1915. American Protestant Mission boards preferred to send married couples as missionaries, but by the late nineteenth century, unmarried female missionaries outnumbered male missionaries. (George Grantham Bain Collection, Library of Congress Prints and Photographs Division, Washington, DC.)

on the return voyage to China, Maude died.[4] When they briefly returned to Hangzhou, Edith was born.

Infant deaths were particularly traumatic for mothers. When Han Suyin's infant brother Sea Orchid died, Marguerite blamed her husband Zhou Wei. When Maude died, Carie seemed to blame Absalom. Buck claimed that her mother shouted at Absalom saying: "If it had not been for this other one coming too soon I could have nursed [Maudie] through the summer and saved her."[5] Since Buck was not yet born at this time, the source of this claim was apparently her mother. Certainly, it reflects long-standing grievances held by Carie which her daughter Pearl embraced. Carie's grief over the loss of Maude contributed to a breakdown in her health and she contracted tuberculosis. Instead of returning to the United States for treatment, they moved north to Chefoo (Qufu), the ancestral home of Confucius in Shandong province where the drier climate allowed her to recover. It was at this point that Carie befriended a woman whose husband had just killed her baby.[6] To the Sydenstrickers, she became Wang Amah, who, with the assistance of a man servant, helped to nurse Carie back to health and who continued to live with the Sydenstrickers until her old age.[7]

However, because Carie's health was still frail, they avoided returning to the humid climate of the lower Yangze River and moved instead to Chinkiang (Zhenjiang 鎮江), in Jiangsu, an east-central Chinese province, located at the intersection of the main thoroughfares in traditional China—the Grand Canal and the Yangzi River. Here they lived in the same bungalow for twenty-seven years although Absalom spent much of his time traveling to mission sites throughout the countryside and away from his family.[8] The Sydenstrickers devoted their lives to converting the Chinese to Christianity, but Carie was more devoted to their children than was Absalom. Eventually, both of them, along with four of their seven children (Maude, Arthur, Edith, and Clyde) were buried in China.

Buck's attitude toward her parents was more complicated than recent biographers have presented it.[9] In treating Buck as a feminist icon, these biographers have exaggerated the influence of Buck's mother Carie and slighted the influence of Buck's father Absalom. In fact, Buck identified with the subservient plight of her mother but emulated the strength of her father. Absalom was so absorbed in his attempt to produce a more accurate Chinese translation of the New Testament—which he always referred to as "the Work"—that he neglected his wife and family.[10] He sacrificed himself and diverted all the family's extra funds into producing a new Chinese translation of the New Testament, causing his children to be deprived of all but the most minimal gifts and childhood extras. He fostered a resentment in his daughter, Pearl, and yet stirred in her a drive and forcefulness that matched his own.

II.

The "pearl" in Pearl Buck's name was a revealing omen because her life was, in essence, a struggle between *yin* (female force symbolized by the pearl [*zhu* 珠 or *zhenzhu* 珍珠]) and *yang* (male force symbolized by the Chinese dragon [*long* 龍]). In this struggle, her talented and forceful female identity related in progressive stages to males who were first dominant (her father Absalom Sydenstricker and her first husband Lossing Buck), then romantic (her lover the Chinese poet Xu Zhimo 徐志摩 and her publisher-second husband Richard Walsh), and finally subservient (Tad Danielewski and Ted Harris). The significance of Pearl Buck's remarkable life lies in this turbulent interaction with the *yang* forces of both China and men. Her legacy is far more complex than the stereotypical image of a feminist icon.

In Chinese antiquity, the dragon (*long* 龍) was known as the executioner of a great god who controlled rain and drought, but in later Chinese culture the dragon evolved into a benign and auspicious force[11] (figure 4.2). It became a symbol of male sexual vigor and fertility.[12] Moreover since the time of the Han Dynasty (206 BC–220 AD), the dragon had been the imperial symbol. The pearl (*zhu* or *zhenzhu*) was by contrast a female symbol and was believed by ancient Chinese to consist of the moon's essence, created through the processes of *yin* (a female force as opposed to the male force *yang*) in the shell of the mussel.[13] In the autobiography by Shen Fu (1762–after 1809), his wife Chen Yun explains why she has given away her pearls: "Women are entirely *yin* in nature and pearls are the essence of *yin*. If you wear them in your hair, they completely overcome the spirit of *yang*. So why should I value them?"[14]

Pearl Sydenstricker Buck designed her tombstone to be inscribed solely with the Chinese characters Sai Zhenzhu 賽珍珠—*sai* for Seidenstricker and *zhenzhu* for Pearl, arranged in Chinese fashion with the surname first. She was born in West Virginia while her parents were on home leave from China. Her mother told her that they chose her name because at birth she looked like a little pearl. Buck later wrote: "It is dangerous to name a child by what she appears at birth. She changes, she grows from unknown genes, and I have never felt that Pearl was my name. Yet in Chinese it is rather pleasing, 'true gem,' one that is natural and fundamental, growing about a wound in a living organism. I like to think that perhaps there is a significance here and that somehow I did provide, however inadequately, a comforting encasement for the wound my mother carried deep inside her being when her three children died."[15] (Ultimately, four of Carie's children would die in China.)

Figure 4.2. A bronze Chinese dragon (long 龍) in the Summer Palace, Beijing, 1902. The dragon was an ancient and auspicious Chinese symbol of male sexual vigor and fertility. (Library of Congress Prints and Photographs Division, Washington, DC.)

III.

Pearl Buck's father, Absalom Sydenstricker, was far too intellectual to fit today's conventional image of an evangelical preacher. A distorted and incomplete portrait of him has been reinforced by numerous works, including the highly praised biography of Pearl Buck by Peter Conn who knew Buck personally and adopted one of the Amerasian children that Buck sponsored.[16] Conn's sympathetic treatment of Buck is based on certain comments in which Conn is too eager to accept the daughter's point of view in her differences with her father. Conn claims that her father's "cold detachment and his misogyny had wounded Pearl in ways that would never heal."[17] Buck attributed her father's misogyny to St. Paul, and this gave her greater reason to reject Pauline Christianity. Conn claims that misogyny provided the deepest roots of Buck's rejection of Christianity, but he fails to note that misogyny was pervasive in Chinese culture; this did not prevent Buck from developing a profound affinity for the Chinese. Nor does Conn discuss the widespread practice of female infanticide in China and how this failed to turn Buck against the Chinese even though her love of children was one of the most powerful passions in her life.[18]

The deficiencies of the three authors of the leading biographies of Pearl Buck—Nora Stirling (1983), Peter Conn (1996), and Hilary Spurling (2010)—led them to exaggerate the historical significance of the period of Buck's adult years in China (1914–1934). One example of this is the statement by Spurling that "Pearl's four years of isolation had occurred during a period of profound change in China. For three thousand years the country had refused to change its ways, its language or its concept of itself."[19] Conn shared this myth that exaggerated a climacteric change to an unchanging China when he wrote: "In 1911, a status quo that had lasted for over two thousand years had been knocked to rubble."[20] This widespread myth of the unchanging nature of China was based on a profound lack of familiarity with Chinese history in which there were, in fact, numerous changes, comparable in their fundamental nature to the changes in Europe.

Buck dwelt on her mother's "horror" at the bound feet of Chinese women and the need to "change" this practice.[21] However, in one of the great ironies of Buck's writing and despite her love of children, she rarely mentioned the far more destructive practice of female infanticide.[22] She had learned of this practice directly from Chinese women.[23] Female infanticide was a highly private and largely hidden act practiced by Chinese women, and the denial of infanticide was commonplace among Protestant missionaries.[24] Clearly, these selective omissions are crucial to understanding how Buck disseminated a romanticized image of the Chinese peasant that was widely accepted by readers throughout the world, a romanticized image that ironically helped to create a Cold War political movement that she opposed.

The first time Carie Sydenstricker came to China, she came for God's sake. But when she departed for their first furlough back to the United States, she left three of her children buried in Shanghai under a palm tree. When she first came to China, she was following her husband's calling, but when she returned, she was driven by her maternal feeling for needy people.[25] She had found her own mission, apart from her husband's mission. Unlike Carie, Absalom did not "feel on his own flesh and spirit the sufferings of others."[26] Unlike Carie, he was not moved by music, poetry, or nature. Despite a severe sunstroke that nearly killed him, he did not mind the heat as Carie and the children did. He had an ascetic nature, and he grew leaner and healthier as the years passed. During their years in China, their differences would become more pronounced. They were linked by only two bonds: religion and children. And their link through the children was only of the flesh because Absalom did not understand or love children as Carie did. He did not dislike children, but they were largely obscured by his "mystical union with God and with the souls of men."[27] These differences were significant for understanding Pearl Buck's religiosity because in this important aspect she absorbed the faith of her mother and not the faith of her father.

Buck's father and mother were born into very different families. Carie was born into a devout and prosperous Dutch merchant family that had emigrated from Utrecht in the Netherlands out of protest against the government's religious intolerance.[28] Prior to departing, her grandfather Hermanus Stulting married a French woman who gave birth to Carie's father Cornelius.[29] A group of three hundred Dutch merchants and artisans led by their pastor sold their property and crossed the ocean to America. They settled in the western part of Virginia on a high fertile plain surrounded by mountains and became farmers.[30] They prospered, and Hermanus and his son Cornelius built a large house much like his old house in Holland.[31] This is the house in which Carie was born and raised in a devout Protestant environment.

By contrast, Buck's father Absalom Sydenstricker was born into a Presbyterian family that had moved from Pennsylvania to the western part of Virginia. It was a quarrelsome family of seven sons and two daughters ruled by a domineering father who insisted that all of the sons work the farmland until they were twenty-one years old.[32] Four of the sons fought for the South during the Civil War, but this part of Virginia had few slaveowners and it broke off to form the separate state of West Virginia in 1863. Their farm in Greenbrier County lay on the southern border with Virginia. The Sydenstrickers were a religious family, and six of the sons became pastors (five Presbyterians and one Methodist).

Absalom was born the second to last son. All the brothers were six feet in height. They were also handsome, excerpt for Absalom. He was shy, but intense, unworldly, and deeply religious.[33] One Sunday a Chinese missionary preached at the Old Stone Church in Lewisburg and was invited to the Sydenstricker home for Sunday dinner. Absalom was deeply impressed. Soon thereafter at sixteen years of age, he first received the call to serve God in a foreign field.[34] On his twenty-first birthday, he left farming forever and enrolled in the Franklin Academy and then Washington and Lee University. School was for Absalom a liberating experience—he "loved" it.[35]

Pastor Sydenstricker was atypical of Protestant missionaries of that time in several respects. His missionary approach has been mischaracterized as "fundamentalism."[36] He belonged to a group of scholarly missionaries. Most nineteenth-century missionaries had a very low regard for indigenous Chinese culture, and their knowledge of Chinese tended to focus on preaching the gospel message rather than any study of traditional Chinese texts. Absalom Sydenstricker was different in the intensity of his approach to the Chinese language and in his respect for the intelligence of the Chinese. The Sydenstrickers allowed their servant Wang Amah to tell Pearl endless Buddhist and Daoist tales and to make her a cap decorated with little Buddhas to protect her against evil spirits.[37] In addition, they hired the scholar Mr. Kung (Kong), a refugee from foreign reprisals against the Boxers that had destroyed his home in Beijing, to teach Pearl about Confucian philosophy using classical Chinese texts.[38] Kong was a tall and dignified Chinese scholar who wore stately robes and taught Pearl using the esteemed Beijing Mandarin dialect. He came to their house for two hours every afternoon for three years. Pearl Buck developed a knowledge of Chinese that enabled her over twenty years later in 1933 to produce a vernacular translation of the Chinese classic *Shui hu chuan* 水滸傳 (Water Margins). She published the book under the title *All Men Are Brothers*.[39] Buck's choice of this novel to translate reflects her sympathy for the common people. The *Shui hu chuan* tells the story of the bandit group of picaresque heroes headed by Song Jiang 宋江 who flourished during the Northern Song dynasty (1011–1025).[40] The novel is said to have been inspired by historical events through professional storytelling.[41]

IV.

Absalom Sydenstricker's highly sophisticated knowledge of Chinese was recognized in the invitation he received to participate in the committee to produce, through revision of previous translations, a complete Mandarin translation of the Bible. This Union Version (*Heheben* 和合本) became for a time the most widespread Chinese translation of the Bible and had a great influence on the Chinese language and literature.[42] It involved a shift in translation from literary to colloquial Chinese. The new Mandarin Union Version translation committee first met in the summer of 1908 in Zhufu.[43] When the committee chairman Calvin W. Mateer suddenly died after the first meeting, there was a vacancy that Sydenstricker was invited to fill. Chauncey Goodrich (1835–1925), a Congregationalist missionary and the only remaining member of the original committee, was elevated to succeed Mateer as chairman. Sydenstricker had distinguished himself by his knowledge of Mandarin (the colloquial northern dialect of China) which he had applied in making valuable criticisms of the previously translated Mandarin Union Version New Testament.

Sydenstricker joined the committee in its second meeting which was held over a five-month period from June through October 1909. However, in a telling indication of his independent nature and inability to function as part of a team, Sydenstricker left the meeting in July and submitted his resignation in September. He wrote several letters expressing his complaints. One complaint dealt with the lack of knowledge of Hebrew by F. W. Baller which, in Sydenstricker's view, disqualified Baller from participating in a translation of the Old Testament. The situation was aggravated by Sydenstricker's claim that Baller was attempting to dominate the translation process. In part, the dispute between Sydenstricker and Baller could be viewed as a clash between two forceful personalities, but it was also true that Baller had no theological training and no training in Hebrew. Baller served in the China Inland Mission and as a Baptist held a doctrinal orientation that Sydenstricker vehemently opposed.

There were additional reasons for Sydenstricker's resignation. The new Mandarin Union Version translation committee was composed of European and American missionaries as well as Chinese Christians, but the status of the Chinese was decidedly inferior. Each Western translator had a Chinese assistant. It was the committee's low regard for these disempowered Chinese assistants that upset Sydenstricker. He had worked closely with his assistant Zhu Baohui 朱寶惠, a scholar whose abilities clearly compared well with the Western members of the committee. Zhu later studied Greek at Nanjing Seminary under the Southern Presbyterian missionary John Leighton Stuart (1867–1962) and became a teacher in the correspondence school of the seminary in which Sydenstricker was dean. Sydenstricker complained that the Chinese assistants were unable to make use of their own knowledge to contribute to the translation because they were intimidated by the foreign missionaries who were, in fact, their employers. As a result, the Chinese became mere servants and scribes to the foreigners.[44]

In making this criticism, Sydenstricker was raising one of the greatest obstacles to the development of an indigenous Chinese Christianity. This involved the Western resistance to recognizing the abilities of the Chinese and the consequent reluctance of foreign missionaries and mission boards to cede control of the churches to the Chinese. In the records of the various Bible translation projects in China, the names of Chinese contributors are rarely mentioned, reflecting the low esteem in which they were held by foreign missionaries. Sydenstricker was a notable exception to this pattern. He had an unusual degree of respect for and was remarkably prescient in terms of what needed to be done to establish Christianity on a firm basis in China.

But ultimately, the reason why Sydenstricker resigned had as much to do with his personality and manner of missionizing as disagreements with the Mandarin Union Version translation committee. The fact is that he preferred an independent path. After resigning from the committee, he returned to Zhenjiang and worked with his Chinese assistant Zhu Baohui to translate the New Testament. The first edition was published in 1913 as *Si fuyinshu* 四福音書 (The Books of the Four Gospels).[45] In its preface, Sydenstricker emphasized their primary aim of making "the Gospel more intelligible and readable to the Chinese Christians."[46] A later edition was published in 1929. Sydenstricker had to pay publication costs out of his own pocket, and his translation was not well received. His erudition in Hebrew and Greek was praised, but the style of the work was criticized as too informal and colloquial—too "common."[47] Buck defended her father's translation as being too far ahead of its time, too advanced in promoting the vernacular over the classical style of Chinese to garner the recognition it deserved.

Pearl Buck wrote complementary biographies of both her mother Carie and her father Absalom. She wrote her mother's biography, *The Exile*, shortly after her death in in 1921, but she waited until after her father's death in 1931 to publish it in 1936.[48] Because of *The Exile*'s positive reception, she published a sequel in 1936 dealing with her father's life called *Fighting Angel*. These two books are partially fictionalized, perhaps because of their negative tone toward American missionaries in China. Buck retained her mother's first name Carie; however, Absalom became Andrew. Among her children, Edgar became Edwin, Pearl became Comfort, and Grace became Faith. The children who died young—Maude, Edith, Arthur, and Clyde—all retained their own names.

Marriage for Absalom and Carie was a practical matter in which romance was secondary. Absalom probably would have gone to China unmarried if his mother had not insisted that he first find a wife before he went abroad.[49] He obeyed his mother, but his courting of Carie was perfunctory. Buck wrote: "he was singularly oblivious to the appearance of women, and even to that of his wife."[50] He felt that his marriage to Carie was not a matter of individual wills because he saw it as "providential—that is, God provided it."[51] Buck added: "the truth was that greater than the excitement of his wedding day to this young man was the realization of the young missionary that at last his dream was coming true, at last he was about to set out on his life work."[52] Later, like her mother, Pearl would marry an incompatible man. In such marriages, it often takes many years for the incompatibility to emerge. Carie, like many women with children and out of sense of duty, chose to live with the incompatibility. Pearl, with only one debilitated child and no prospects of more, chose divorce and remarriage. Unlike Carie and Absalom who had a missionary partnership that depended on one another in faraway China, Pearl was a successful individual author with a world audience of readers.

V.

Spiritual sensitivity is like musical sensitivity in the sense that not everyone's ear can hear the tonal variations. While Absalom clearly discerned the presence of the Holy Spirit, Carie had difficulty hearing the word of God.

Instead, her heart was opened by the suffering of others. Consequently, she served God, as she had served Absalom as a wife, out of a sense of duty rather than through direct revelation. Pearl absorbed her mother's sense of spiritual service but lacked her father's spiritual sensitivity. However, in other ways—energy, drive, unshakeable conviction of being right, and the refusal to compromise one's beliefs—she and her father were shaped from the same uncompromising mold.

The marriage of Absalom Sydenstricker and Caroline Stulting in 1880 was not built on romance, but rather on the practical need for a partner in the mission field. The "great romance" in Carie's life was not her husband, but her children.[53] Pearl was born on June 26, 1892, in Hillsboro, West Virginia, during their first ten-year-service home leave and three months later was taken by the family back to China.[54] She grew up speaking Chinese as a native language and had contact with Chinese children through church-related activities. From 1911 to 1914 she came back to the United States to attend Randolph-Macon Women's College in Lynchburg, Virginia.[55] In college, she had a successful academic and social life and was clearly a leader, becoming president of her class.[56] However, she found her classmates insular and parochial in their attitude toward the outside world and in their lack of interest in China, which they viewed as uncivilized.[57]

After graduating, she returned to China to care for her mother who had fallen ill with sprue or psilosis, a digestive disease occurring in tropical countries, and she assumed her mother's missionary work. She met her first husband at the Western summer retreat of Kuling (Guling) (*Guniu Ling* 牯牛嶺 or Ox Ridge) (see map) in Jiangxi province. Guling was a high valley in the Lushan Mountains. With an elevation of thirty-five hundred feet, it became a refuge from the summer heat for Westerners.[58] It was reached from Nanjing by a river boat traveling upriver on the Yangzi River. Because of the strong current, the river journey from Nanjing to Jiujiang took thirty-six hours, although the return journey downriver took only twenty-four hours.[59] Reaching Guling from the river involved an uphill climb either by foot or by sedan chair in a three-hour journey.

John Lossing Buck (1890–1975) was an agricultural economist and missionary.[60] The Sydenstricker parents disapproved of him because of his narrow focus on agriculture and lack of intellectual interests. Carie tried to convince Pearl that she and Buck were incompatible, but Pearl was firm in her intention to marry.[61] In her conviction about being right, she was like her father. She married Buck in her parents' home in 1917. They moved two hundred miles away to Nanhsüchou (Nanxuzhou), a remote town on the Huai River in Anhui province. When the church funding for Buck's agricultural projects was cut off, they moved to Nanjing where Lossing served as the head of the College of Agriculture and Forestry at the University of Nanjing.[62]

Pearl taught courses in English at the Christian University of Nanjing and at the government-run National University. Pearl was able to visit her ailing mother by way of a two-hour train journey to Zhenjiang.[63]

Nanjing had been the southern capital of China during the Ming dynasty (1368–1644) and was reestablished as the capital of the Republic of China (1912–1949), partly because of the southern orientations of Sun Yat-sen and Chiang Kai-shek. It was an old walled city near the beautiful and famous Purple Mountain, the home of many temples and monasteries. The Bucks lived close to the campus, in one of the three houses in a walled compound built for missionary teachers. An account of their neighborhood has been published by their next-door neighbor Nancy Thomson Waller (b. 1918), the daughter of Professor James Thomson, a biochemist who headed the Chemistry Department and was the Dean of Science.[64] The Thomsons at that time had three children. They lived in the three-story missionary house at 4 Ping Tsan Lane.[65]

The Bucks lived next door with a low garden wall dividing the Thomson and the Buck houses with steps built into the wall so that the families could more easily visit each other. Pearl, like her mother, cultivated flowers in the yard, and Nancy Waller remembered Pearl's beautiful rose garden. The large houses were more Westernized than the small bungalow in which Pearl had been raised in Zhenjiang. They had electricity and running water, though both ran irregularly. The Western faculty were paid missionary salaries as part of the shift in the orientation of missions from the pietistic tone to Christian social and educational endeavors. The third-story attics of the faculty homes provided temporary housing to missionaries who were newly arrived or in transit.

Pearl Buck gave birth to only one child—a girl named Carol who was born in 1920 when Pearl was twenty-eight years old. Carol appeared to be healthy, but actually suffered from phenylketonuria.[66] This was an inherited metabolic disorder, and it was not then understood that lack of treatment would lead to mental retardation, as it did in Carol's case. Carol's condition introduced a tragedy into Pearl's life that she would never fully overcome.

According to the childhood recollections of Nancy Thomson Waller, Pearl and Lossing "had never been a good match."[67] Lossing had been raised on a farm in upstate New York and graduated from Cornell University. Waller described him as a good professor of agriculture and a nice man. Unlike Absalom Sydenstricker who never played with his children, Lossing played with his daughter Carol and together they looked like "two overgrown puppies." Because of the reticence at that time over discussing intimate sexual matters, it is difficult to know the exact nature of the sexual relationship of Carie and Absalom, but their procreation of seven children indicated an active sex life that Pearl failed to reproduce with Lossing. But unlike Absalom,

Lossing did not have the chance to father healthy children. Soon after giving birth to Carol, Pearl had to undergo a hysterectomy.[68] Of course, the fertility problem was not Lossing's fault, but their inability to procreate additional children cast Pearl into a deep despair. Their incompatible relationship provided no healing compensation for the lack of children, particularly for a woman like Pearl who loved children.

When Pearl realized the severity of her child's condition, she was engulfed in despair. To deal with her feelings of guilt and shame, she blamed Lossing for Carol's problems.[69] In the late summer of 1924, to take advantage of Lossing's sabbatical, the Bucks relocated to Ithaca, New York, to enroll in Cornell University's graduate school. Lossing applied the results of his agricultural survey in China to a master's degree in agricultural economics while Pearl pursued a master's degree in English while taking Carol to a series of medical specialists.[70] To cope with her despair, she began writing articles, one of which was published in the *Nation*. Despite their lack of funds, they sought to adopt a child from a small Christian orphanage in Troy. Pearl found an underweight three-month-old little girl who had lain on her same side for so many weeks that her face was deformed. Pearl was immediately drawn to the girl, and they adopted her, naming her Janice.

The number of Pearl's adopted children would eventually total seven, ironically the same number of children that Carie had given birth to, but their racial composition was significant. The first two adopted children were white, but several of the adoptees (adopted with her second husband Richard Walsh) were biracial. Buck's concern with racism included not only Asians, but also African Americans. After returning from China in 1932, Buck joined several Black organizations and served on the board of the National Association for the Advancement of Colored People.[71] She was friendly with Paul Robeson and in 1949 coauthored a book on racism with Robeson's wife, Eslanda. Buck remained an adoption advocate throughout her life, although at the time of her death a new movement was emerging which advocated for placement of adoptees with parents of the same race and sending mixed-race children to non-white parents.[72] However, the foundations associated with Buck always focused on supporting children of mixed Asian and non-Asian (either Black or white) descent.

When the Bucks returned to Nanjing in the late summer of 1925, they encountered a rising tide of anti-foreign sentiment. The widowed Absalom joined their household while Pearl devoted herself to teaching, writing, and raising Janice. She also entertained many missionary-related visitors in her home. One of the Bucks' most traumatic memories of China occurred in 1927 during the Northern Expedition of 1926–1928. This expedition was an attempt to fulfill the lifelong dream of the father of the Republic of China, Sun Yat-sen, and it involved a northward military thrust led by Chiang

Kai-shek from Guangzhou (Canton) of Nationalist forces with the aim of defeating the northern warlord armies and reunifying China. However, when the Nationalist forces reached Nanjing and the northern warlord armies withdrew, there was a breakdown in Nationalist discipline and a pent-up xenophobia was released. On March 24, 1927, Nationalist forces began looting British, American, and Japanese consulates and attacking foreigners.[73] The Bucks were forced to flee Nanjing, going first to Unzen in Japan and later locating in Shanghai.[74] They shared a three-story house on Avenue Joffre (*Yuchanglu* 宇昌路) in the French Concession with two other families.[75] The husbands returned to Nanjing while the wives and children and servants lived in the Shanghai house. Pearl lived on the third floor with her mentally impaired daughter Carol and her adopted daughter Janice. She borrowed a typewriter and began writing. She found the names of two (or three, depending on the source) New York literary agents in a Shanghai magazine store and wrote to them.[76] One, Carol Brandt, turned her down because she claimed that American readers were not interested in China. However, another agent, David Lloyd, eagerly agreed to represent her, inaugurating a fruitful relationship that lasted from 1928 until 1955.

After returning to Nanjing, Janice attended the new Hillcrest School which was built on the site of the former American School destroyed by the looting of 1927. It was built on a hilltop overlooking the city of Nanjing and near the University of Nanjing.[77] The Hillcrest School offered classes from kindergarten through eighth or ninth grade. It was staffed by a combination of teachers, mother-teachers, and a paid principal. The small student body was international—primarily American but also included students from China, England, France, and Germany, accepting students who could speak at least a minimal amount of English. The students included the daughter and son of H. H. Kung and Soong Ailing who were described as "imperious brats."[78] The Kung children were brought to school each day by Madame Chiang Kai-shek (Soong Meiling) in a car with armed guards, although the other schoolchildren lived close enough to walk to school.

Given the limits of their missionary salaries, it was Pearl's mass-selling publications that would later provide the funding to care for Carol. Pearl felt such intense grief over Carol's condition and over her inability to conceive more children that she concealed Carol's existence for the next twenty years. She fell into the deepest despair of her life during a five-month journey back to the United States in the spring and summer of 1929. The Bucks made the trip for Lossing to secure a Rockefeller Foundation grant for his survey work in China and for Pearl to place Carol in the Vineland Training School in New Jersey.[79] Pearl borrowed two thousand dollars from the Mission Board to cover two years of Carol's expenses.

The Bucks returned to their home in Nanjing in early 1930, although Lossing was far more enthusiastic about their return than Pearl. The divergence of their lives manifested itself in their separate publications. Lossing's book *Chinese Farm Economy* was published in 1930, and it justified republication in 1982.[80] Pearl's despair over Carol reached a low point and she prayed that Carol would die.[81] However, her writing provided her with an escape from her unhappiness. She published *The Good Earth* in 1931. Its publication and remarkable reception began to lift Pearl out of her despair and transform her life.

VI.

The death of Absalom Sydenstricker in 1931 provided the impetus for a change in Pearl's life. Like her mother, Pearl had difficulty discerning the will of God, and her pain over Carol was not relieved by clear answers to her prayers. She continued to teach and draw her salary as a missionary, but she began to lose her faith.[82]

Although Pearl Buck resented her father's neglect of his wife and family for his mission, she could not escape his influence. Ultimately, she synthesized both her mother's and father's very different viewpoints. Absalom was the dominant spiritual partner of the Sydenstricker couple and Pearl absorbed the certainty of his convictions, but Carie was the emotional and compassionate core of the family. This family tension would form the background to the dramatic climax of Pearl Sydenstricker Buck's life when she gave a speech to a Presbyterian women's luncheon in New York on November 4, 1932. Her audience of two thousand in the main ballroom of the Astor Hotel included some of the most prominent clerics in the city.[83] She presented her speech "Is There a Case for Foreign Missions?" with characteristic forcefulness that lacked a shred of doubt. It was a trait she had absorbed from her missionary father, except that she had abandoned his evangelical Christian message. However, she had carried on his concern and respect for the Chinese people. She condemned evangelical missionaries in China for their narrow-minded approach that despised indigenous Chinese culture, a culture of which they were largely ignorant. When she finished speaking, she sat down to stunned silence. Applause eventually erupted, but the religious leaders seated at Buck's table were shocked.[84]

Although Buck's condemnation of missions upset the evangelical Christian community, there was a growing responsiveness to her message that had been developing in popular American culture. Even among many missionaries themselves, there had been a shift from an evangelizing Gospel-based emphasis to a Social Gospel approach emphasizing schools and medical services, an emphasis that both Lossing and Pearl cultivated. However, the ultimate failure of the Social Gospel movement in China and the eventual triumph (in Chinese transformation) of the seeds sown by Evangelicals was an ironical denouement that would contradict her argument and undermine the wisdom of the campaign she promoted. But in 1932 she was acquiring celebrity status, and celebrities excel in reflecting contemporary fashion, if not eternal verities. There is little doubt that her condemnation of the arrogance of the evangelistic missionaries was accurate, but the certainty of her convictions came more from the influence of Absalom than from her understanding of the actual situation. She failed to understand the ultimate role in Chinese history that these missionaries would play in introducing the foreign faith to the Chinese. The irony of her message is that time has proven her to be just as wrong as the missionaries she was condemning.[85]

There is another aspect of the Protestant missionary movement that Pearl Buck seemed to overlook or simply took for granted. The evangelizing of Chinese women by male missionaries was impeded by the seclusion of many Chinese women in their homes. The fact that female missionaries were more able than male missionaries to make contact with Chinese women created a ministry that attracted growing numbers of women from Europe and North America. By the 1870s in the United States and Europe, the feminist spirit was largely fused with worldwide Christian evangelization. Women were restless to break out of the narrow restraints imposed by farms and small-town milieus in Europe and North America. The numbers tell a revealing story. In China, the male numerical dominance among Protestant missionaries ended in the last half of the nineteenth century. By 1890, at about the time of Buck's birth, women missionaries outnumbered men.[86] The influence of women missionaries would be particularly important to the ministry of one of the greatest Chinese evangelists of the twentieth century: Watchman Nee (Ni Tuosheng).

VII.

The growth of indigenous forms of evangelical Christianity in China has been far beyond what Buck ever anticipated. It can be dated from 1916, but Buck left China in 1934 before it was fully developed. She had intended to return, but never did. Her remarkable firsthand knowledge of China became dated and out of touch. When Buck died in 1973, the fruits of the China mission were temporarily buried by the Cultural Revolution in China. When Peter Conn published his cultural biography of Pearl Buck in 1996, these Chinese Christians had been forced underground to survive.[87] Conn followed the then-current misinterpretation of China scholars in dismissing the fruits of the China missionaries and by minimizing those Chinese who accepted

Christianity by characterizing them as a mere "handful."[88] It may have begun as a handful, but it proliferated greatly in consequent years.

Buck criticized her father for his "spiritual imperialism."[89] She said that in one of their last conversations before he died, Absalom thanked her for a copy of *The Good Earth*, but said he would not have time to read it.[90] This was a painful rejection of her work, but it was made out of the same conviction that Pearl shared in her own work. Her father had devoted his life to translation work on the Bible and to insisting that the scholarly abilities of Chinese Christians matched those of Westerners. Pearl never recognized that his work and outlook contributed far more to the development of Christianity in China than did the Social Gospel efforts that she promoted with such conviction and which would in time be washed away by the currents of history.

Recent Chinese state-sanctioned sources estimate there to be thirty-eight million Protestants in China.[91] This is a conservative estimate complicated by the division between the officially registered and unregistered house churches. Other estimates extend beyond fifty million. The number of Catholics is estimated to be about ten million, including both the official and underground parts of the church.[92] By comparison, the prominent journalist Ian Johnson has placed the current number of Christians in China at ten million Catholics and sixty million Protestants.[93] For many years our understanding of indigenous Protestant movements in early twentieth-century China was undeveloped because historians focused on European-language materials while the documentation of these indigenous churches is almost entirely in Chinese.[94] Lian Xi's *Redeemed by Fire* shifted his attention to Chinese sources to reconstruct how distinctively Chinese forms of Protestantism emerged in 1916–1949.[95] Although almost all the leaders of indigenous churches in China began their religious careers in foreign mission churches, their attempt to separate themselves from these mission churches was a crucial part of their development. They cultivated an autonomy and independence from foreign missions that sometimes bordered on hostility.

Ni Tuosheng 倪托聲 (Watchman Nee, 1903–1972), one of the leading figures in the development of indigenous Chinese Christian movements of the 1930s and 1940s, was deeply influenced by women teachers. Ni was the founder and leader of the Christian Assembly (*Jidutu Juhuichu* 基督徒聚會處), commonly known as the Little Flock (*Xiaoqun* 小群) (after Luke 12:32), which had its headquarters in Shanghai.[96] He was one of the first indigenous Chinese church leaders to acquire a worldwide reputation and to provide inspiration to Western Christians from the 1930s. He was born into an educated family whose ancestral home was in Fujian.

Ni was more deeply influenced by Christian women than any other evangelist of his time. The first of these women was his mother, Lin Heping 林和平 (1880–1950) (figure 4.3). She was raised in an affluent Chinese family

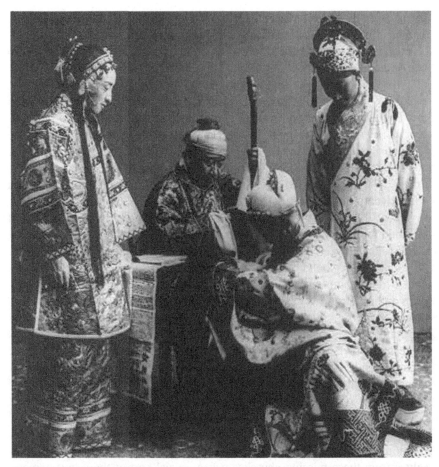

Figure 4.3. Chinese filial piety (*xiao* 孝) in the form of a mandarin worshipping his mother, Beijing. December 13, 1919. (Keystone View Co., Library of Congress Prints and Photographs Division, Washington, DC.)

and received a strict Confucian upbringing and a denominational baptism in a Methodist church. She attended two of the best girls' schools in China: the Tai-Maiu Girls' School, a Methodist school at Fuzhou, and then the McTyeire School (*Zhongxinüxue* 中新女學) in Shanghai.[97] However, her hopes for study abroad and a medical career were aborted by an arranged marriage. In Swatow, she gave birth to Shu-zu (later renamed Watchman) as her third child and eldest son. For a time, she took an interest in politics and became a supporter of Sun Yat-sen, accompanying her former McTyeire classmate Soong Qingling, who would eventually marry Sun, but then she grew disillusioned with politics and occupied herself with worldly society, theatre-going, and gambling.[98]

Then in 1920 she heard the female evangelist Dora Yu (Yu Cidu 余慈度) speak at a series of Christian revival meetings in Fuzhou, and she was transformed by a conversion experience that divided her life into before and after segments.[99] It was through his mother's influence that Watchman came to hear Dora Yu. His mother relinquished politics and mahjong and became an itinerant preacher. Watchman accompanied her to Malaya to her first leading role in a revival meeting.

In 1921, Ni attended Dora Yu's Bible school in Shanghai and at Yu's recommendation, studied with the British missionary Margaret Emma Barber (He Shouen 和受恩) (1869–1930) at Pagoda Anchorage (Baiyatan), ten miles downstream from Fuzhou. Watchman's mother Lin Heping accompanied him and his younger brother George on this visit to Barber. Lin had prayed and been convicted to ask for baptism by immersion, even though she had already been baptized as a child by sprinkling in the Methodist church.[100] Barber greeted them and on Easter Sunday Barber and the elderly Bible woman Li Aiming baptized Lin and her sons Watchman and George by immersion in the river. Lin Heping combined a belief in the need to evangelize the world in preparation for the Second Coming of Christ with the need to uplift women.

Barber served as Watchman Ni's spiritual mentor in the years after his Fuzhou conversion. Barber was born in 1866 in England and lived in Liverpool before departing for China. The Church Missionary Society (CMS) accepted her as a missionary in 1895 and sent her to the Fujian mission in 1896 at the age of thirty.[101] At that time the Anglicans did not have female priests and so Barber was unable to baptize Chinese people. Instead, she focused on teaching women with the goal of raising up Bible women, who although lowly in status, were crucial to reaching the largely secluded female population of China. Barber was always cautious in transgressing the traditional lines that separated the teaching of women and men. She taught for seven years at the CMS Fuzhou Girls Boarding School and was known for her radiant personality. While on furlough in England in 1909, she sought a full immersion baptism.[102] This second baptism severed her ties with the Anglican church which practiced only infant baptism or baptism by sprinkling. When her bishop requested that she not return to the Fujian mission, she did so as an independent faith missionary at the age of forty-eight and no longer affiliated with the CMS.

In addition to his mother Lin Heping, Dora Yu, and Margaret Barber, Ni was influenced by reading the teachings of a third woman named Jessie Penn-Lewis (1861–1927), a Welsh evangelical mystic and Holiness writer. Dora Yu, Margaret Barber, and Ni's mother indicated through their rebaptism by immersion that they were distancing themselves from denominational Christianity and from the foreign mission societies, including the China

Inland Mission.[103] They appear to have been separating themselves from a male-dominated form of Christianity and creating a Christianity adapted to females and dominated by women.[104] This gender tension in China would eventually emerge in the relationship between Barber and Ni.

In 1923, when Ni asked Barber to adjudicate his theological dispute with Leland Wang, she said he should submit to Wang because of the latter's seniority.[105] Ni submitted, but the dispute festered until 1926 when Ni and Wang parted over theological issues and Wang excluded Ni from the Assembly in Fuzhou. Ni admitted that Barber was right in forcing him to make an important correction. Although Barber could be critical of Ni, she had great hopes for his ministry. The theme of submission to God became an important theme in Ni's sermons. As Ni's views matured, he became convinced that women should not teach men in the church.[106] When he felt he could no longer submit to Barber's teaching, Barber quietly accepted his position. Gradually he spoke less of Barber as the opposition to female preachers grew.

Ni was frail in health but had a magnetic personality and a unique ability to speak in the profound end-of-time mystical language that mesmerized his followers. As Little Flock assemblies spread into major cities along the Chinese seaboard, they tended to attract a higher percentage of educated people than the other forms of popular Chinese Christianity.[107] While many Chinese evangelists, such as Wang Mingdao 王明道 (1900–1991) and John Sung (born Song Shangjie 宋尚節 [1901–1944]), were preaching in war-torn and impoverished parts of China, Ni remained in the International Settlement in Shanghai.[108]

After the Communist Liberation of 1949, the Little Flock movement fit well into the Three-Self Patriotic Movement (*Sanzi aiguo yundong* 三自愛國運動). This involved the nationwide rejection of foreign missions and the cultivation of indigenous Chinese Christian development in which churches were self-supporting, self-governing, and self-propagating.[109] However, the Little Flock movement did not share the more extreme views of the Communist Three-Self Movement that wanted a complete break from any foreign missionary influence or financial control. Moreover, the Little Flock refused the Communist demand that all congregations submit to socialist ideology. Watchman Nee and the Little Flock refused to submit to the Maoist state in the belief that they could coexist with the Communist state. Consequently, the Little Flock was attacked and driven underground during the period of Mao Zedong's leadership (1949–1976), resurfacing in 1978 after Mao's death.[110] In the 1950s, the Communist government dispersed the Christian Assembly as counter-revolutionary and their leaders were jailed. Ni died a martyr's death in prison.[111] The Little Flock survived using a pattern shared by several other Chinese Protestant churches as well as by the underground Catholic Church which remained loyal to the pope. It survived by keeping a low profile and organizing cell groups which later became the Chinese house church movement of revival.[112]

VIII.

In numerous published works, Pearl Buck became the leading force in fostering a sympathetic image of Chinese peasants as a hardworking, courageous, and peace-loving people who were victims of a terrible fate.[113] From the publication of *The Good Earth* in 1931 until the Communist victory of 1949 and even beyond, she forged a romanticized image of the Chinese. In the process, she helped to create the fantasy that was absorbed by the right-wing China Lobby and led to a political witch hunt in the 1950s to discover who was responsible for "losing" a China that had never really existed except as an American mirage.

NOTES

1. Jonathan D. Spence, "The Question of Pearl Buck," *The New York Review of Books*, October 14, 2010.
2. Pearl S. Buck, *The Exile* (New York: John Day, 1936), 98.
3. Buck, *Exile*, 110–11.
4. Buck, *Exile*, 117–19.
5. Buck, *Exile*, 120.
6. Buck, *Exile*, 136–41.
7. Buck, Exile, 136–38.
8. Buck, *Exile*, 199.
9. The three major biographies of Pearl Buck are (1) Nora Stirling, *Pearl Buck: A Woman in Conflict* (Piscataway, NJ: New Century Publishers, 1983); (2) Peter Conn, *Pearl S. Buck: A Cultural Biography* (Cambridge, England: Cambridge University Press, 1996); and (3) Hilary Spurling, *Burying the Bones: Pearl Buck in China* (London: Profile Books, Ltd, 2010). There is a partial biography by Karen J. Leong, *The China Mystique: Pearl S. Buck, Anna May Wong, Mayling Soong, and the Transformation of American Orientalism* (Berkeley: University of California Press, 2005).
10. Buck, *Exile*, 91.
11. In the *Shanhaijing* 山海經 (Classic of Mountains and Seas) (third century BC to second century AD), the dragon's functions involved punishment, travel, and the control of rain and drought. See *The Classic of Mountains and Seas*, translated by and with introduction and noted by Anne Birrell (London: Penguin, 1999), 213.
12. Wolfram Eberhard, *A Dictionary of Chinese Symbols*, translated by G. L. Campbell (London: Routledge, 1986), 83.

13. C. A. S. Williams, *Chinese Symbolism and Art Motifs*, third revised edition (Rutland, VT: Charles E. Tuttle Company, 1993), 319.

14. Shen Fu, *Six Records of a Floating Life* (*Fu sheng liu ji*), translated by Leonard Pratt and Chiang Su-hui (London: Penguin, 1983), 39.

15. Theodore F. Harris, in consultation with Pearl S. Buck, *Pearl S. Buck: A Biography* (John Day Company, 1969), 24.

16. Conn, *Pearl S. Buck*, xi.

17. Conn, *Pearl S. Buck*, 41. See also p. 20.

18. D. E. Mungello, *Drowning Girls in China: Female Infanticide since 1650* (Lanham, MD: Rowman and Littlefield, 2008).

19. Spurling, *Burying the Bones*, 60.

20. Conn, *Pearl S. Buck*, 110.

21. Buck, *Exile*, 104–05.

22. Buck, *The Exile*, 102.

23. David A. Hollinger, *Protestants Abroad: How Missionaries Tried to Change the World But Changed America* (Princeton, NJ: Princeton University Press, 2017), 34–35.

24. Mungello, *Drowning Girls in China*, 63–70.

25. Buck, *Exile*, 180.

26. Buck, *Exile*, 231.

27. Buck, *Exile*, 129.

28. Buck, *Exile*, 11–15.

29. Buck, *Exile*, 20–21.

30. Buck, *Exile*, 23.

31. Buck, *Exile*, 29–31.

32. Pearl S. Buck, *Fighting Angel* (New York: John Day Company, 1936; reprinted 1957), 6–8.

33. Buck, *Fighting Angel*, 9.

34. Buck, *Fighting Angel*, 16–17.

35. Buck, *Fighting Angel*, 18–20.

36. Conn, *Pearl S. Buck*, 1, 76, 134.

37. Lian Xi, *The Conversion of Missionaries: Liberalism in American Protestant Missions in China, 1907–1932* (University Park, PA: Pennsylvania State University Press, 1997), 103.

38. Spurling, *Burying the Bones*, 55–56.

39. Shui Hu Chuan, *All Men Are Brothers*, translated by Pearl S. Buck with an introduction by Lin Yutang and illustrations by Miguel Covarrubias (New York: The Heritage Press, 1933).

40. C. T. Hsia, *The Classic Chinese Novel: A Critical Introduction* (Bloomington, IN: Indiana University Press, 1980), 75–76.

41. Y. W. Ma and Tai-loi Ma, "Shui-hu chuan (Water Margin)," in *The Indiana Companion to Traditional Chinese Literature*, edited by William H. Nienhauser, Jr. (Bloomington, IN: Indiana University Press, 1986), 712, 716.

42. Shen Xuebin, "Die 'Union Version' der Bibel und die Sinisierung des Christentums," *China heute* 2 (210) (2021): 106–10.

43. Jost Oliver Zetzsche, *The Bible in China: The History of the* Union Version *or The Culmination of Protestant Missionary Bible Translation in China* (Nettetal, Germany: Steyler Verlag, 1999), 307–15.

44. Zetzsche, *The Bible in China*, 261.

45. A. Sydenstricker and Zu Baohui (transl.), *Si fuyinshu* 四福音書 (Shanghai: Presbyterian Mission Press, 1913).

46. Zetzsche, *The Bible in China*, 311.

47. Pearl S. Buck, *Fighting Angel: Portrait of a Soul* (New York: John Day, 1936), 196.

48. Conn, *Pearl S. Buck*, 187–88.

49. Buck, *Angel*, 23.

50. Buck, *Exile*, 93.

51. Buck, *Fighting Angel*, 25.

52. Buck, *Exile*, 91.

53. Buck, *Exile*, 147.

54. Conn, *Pearl S. Buck*, 22.

55. Stirling, *Pearl Buck*, 23.

56. Spurling, *Burying the Bones*, illustration #9 caption.

57. Spurling, *Burying the Bones*, 82.

58. Samuel Couling, *The Encyclopedia Sinica* (Shanghai: Kelly & Walsh, 1917), 227.

59. Nancy Thomson Waller, *My Nanking Home 1918–1937* (Cherry Valley, NY: Willow Hill Publications, 2010), 57–58.

60. Stirling, *Pearl Buck*, 35–43.

61. Stirling, *Pearl Buck*, 41–42.

62. Spurling, *Pearl Buck*, 130.

63. Conn, *Pearl S. Buck*, 70.

64. Waller, *My Nanking Home*, 22.

65. Waller, *My Nanking Home*, 45.

66. Conn, *Pearl S. Buck*, 71.

67. Waller, *My Nanking Home*, 45.

68. Hollinger, *Protestants Abroad*, 41.

69. Conn, *Pearl S. Buck*, 80.

70. Conn, *Pearl S. Buck*, 78.

71. Hollinger, *Protestants Abroad*, 40–41.

72. Hollinger, *Protestants Abroad*, 42–43.

73. C. Martin Wilbur, *The Nationalist Revolution in China, 1923–1928* (Cambridge, UK: Cambridge University Press, 1983), 91–94.

74. Conn, *Pearl S. Buck*, 90–92.

75. Stirling, *Pearl Buck*, 82–86.

76. Stirling, *Pearl Buck*, 85, claims Buck found two literary agents in New York while Spurling, *Pearl Buck*, 195, claims she found three.

77. Waller, *My Nanking Home*, 95–97.

78. Waller, *My Nanking Home*, 98. Waller claims there were two children of H. H. Kung (Jeanette and Louis) while Conn, *Pearl S. Buck*, 116, claims there were three.

79. Conn, *Pearl S. Buck*, 110–11.

80. John Lossing Buck, *Chinese Farm Economy* (New York: Garland Pub., 1982).

81. Conn, *Pearl S. Buck*, 121.

82. Spurling, *Pearl Buck*, 220.

83. Conn, *Pearl S. Buck*, 148–49.

84. Spurling, *Pearl Buck*, 226.

85. D. E. Mungello, *The Catholic Invasion of China: Remaking Chinese Christianity* (Lanham, MD: Rowman & Littlefield, 2015), 109–16.

86. Irwin T. Hyatt, Jr., *Our Ordered Lives Confess: Three Nineteenth-Century American Missionaries in East Shantung* (Cambridge, MA: Harvard University Press, 1976), 67–68.

87. D. E. Mungello, *This Suffering Is My Joy: The Underground Church in Eighteenth-Century China* (Lanham, MD: Rowman & Littlefield, 2021), 7–10.

88. Conn, *Pearl S. Buck*, 17.

89. Buck, *Angel*, 31.

90. Conn, *Pearl S. Buck*, 135.

91. This state-sanctioned estimate is probably based upon a study by the researchers Lu Yunfeng, Wu Yue, and Zhang Chunni of Beijing Univerity (Beida). See Katharina Wenzel-Teuber, "Statistik zu Religionen und Kirchen in der Volksrepublik China und in Singapur. Ein Update für das Jahr 2021," *China heute* 1 (213) (2022): 29.

92. According to estimates for the end of 2020 published by the Holy Spirit Study Centre of the Diocese of Hong Kong in *Tripod* 2021. See Wenzel-Teuber, "Statistik zu Religionen und Kirchen in der Volksrepublik China und in Singapur," 30.

93. Ian Johnson, "Religion in China: Zurück ins Zentrum von Politik und Gesellschaft," *China Heute* 37 (2) (2018): 110–17.

94. Daniel H. Bays, ed., *Christianity in China from the Eighteenth Century to the Present* (Stanford, CA, 1996), 309–10.

95. Lian Xi, *Redeemed by Fire: The Rise of Popular Christianity in Modern China* (New Haven: Yale University Press, 2010).

96. Lian, *Redeemed by Fire*, 155–78.

97. Grace Y. May, "Watchman Nee and the Breaking of Bread: The Missiological Forces That Contributed to an Indigenous Chinese Ecclesiology" (Doctor of Theology, Boston University, 2000), 60–61. See also Heidi A. Ross, "'Cradle of Female Talent': The McTyeire Home and School for Girls, 1892–1937," in Daniel H. Bays, ed. *Christianity in China: From the Eighteenth Century to the Present* (Stanford: Stanford University Press, 1996), 209–27.

98. May, "Watchman Nee," 65–66.

99. May, "Watchman Nee," 57–58.

100. May, "Watchman Nee," 70–71, 86; Angus Kinnear, *The Story of Watchman Nee: Against the Tide* (Wheaton, IL: Tyndale House Publishers, 1978), 62–64.

101. May, "Watchman Nee," 87–88.

102. May, "Watchman Nee," 91–93.

103. May, "Watchman Nee," 94.

104. A parallel female-dominated religious body that emerged at that time in the United States was Christian Science dominated by the American woman Mary Baker Eddy (1821–1910).

105. May, "Watchman Nee," 95–96.

106. May, "Watchman Nee," 98–99.

107. Lian, *Redeemed by Fire*, 170.

108. Lian, *Redeemed by Fire*, 176.

109. Joseph Tse-hei Lee, "Watchman Nee and the Little Flock Movement in Maoist China," *Church History* 74 (March 2005): 68.

110. Lee, "Watchman Nee," 69–70.

111. Bays, *Christianity in China*, 311–12. See Kinnear, *The Story of Watchman Nee* and the attempt to reconstruct Ni's teaching by Kinnear in Watchman Nee, *What Shall This Man Do?*

112. Lee, "Watchman Nee," 93.

113. Harold R. Isaacs, *Images of Asia: American Views of China and India* (originally published in 1958 under the title *Scratches on Our Minds*) (New York: Harper and Row, 1972), 63, 77–81.

Chapter 5

The Chinese Romantic Xu Zhimo and Pearl Buck

I.

By 1928, the Bucks' marriage was unraveling. Lossing was flirting with young Chinese women at Nanjing University where he taught, and Pearl was going through an unhappy period in which she lost forty-five pounds through stress rather than dieting.[1] She moved her bed into a separate room and began sleeping alone. As one biographer put it, "she could no longer submit to [Lossing's] sexual demands."[2] It is likely that her sexual rejection of Lossing was tied to their impaired child Carol as well as Pearl's inability to conceive other children. It was this situation that would foster her numerous adoptions of other children. It was during this low point of her life that she had a relationship with the charismatic poet Xu Zhimo 徐志摩 (1896–1931), who was four years younger than her (figure 5.1).

Xu Zhimo was the son of a wealthy banker and had been trained in the Chinese classics and later in a Western-style curriculum in Shanghai as well as a college in Beijing.[3] In 1915 he had been married in a traditional betrothal to Zhang Youyi 張幼儀 (1900–1989), the younger sister of the prominent philosopher Zhang Jiasen 張嘉森 (Carson Chang) (1887–1969). The marriage of Xu Zhimo and Zhang Youyi was important because it led to what was widely viewed as the first modern divorce in China. It began as a traditional marriage arranged between Zhang's Fourth Brother and Xu's parents. Zhang Youyi was fifteen and Xu was nineteen; in the traditional manner, they did not see each other until the wedding ceremony.

Zhang Youyi combined traditional and modern values. She was the first among the girls in her family not to have bound feet. She wanted to learn, but her father would not hire a tutor and so she was not well educated.[4] Although

63

Figure 5.1. The poet Xu Zhimo, "the Chinese Shelley." Xu was a leader during 1925–1931 of the Crescent Moon literary movement that emphasized aesthetic elements and individual expression. It was opposed by the socio-political leftist movement that promoted collectivism. (British Library, Flickr image.)

Xu had submitted to this betrothal as a filial son, he wanted an educated woman and viewed Zhang as a "country bumpkin."[5] During the first four years of their marriage, Xu spent only four months with his wife.[6] Xu had sex with his wife out of filial duty. When their son and family heir was born, Xu felt free to travel abroad. At one point, Xu told Zhang that tradition was preventing him from acting on his true feelings and that he intended to be the first man in China to get a divorce.[7] The idea was so radical that she did not take him seriously.

In 1918, Xu's father sent him to the United States with the expectation that he would eventually continue the family banking business.[8] Xu tried to pursue practically oriented subjects at Clark University in Massachusetts, majoring in history and studying economics and banking. However, he was disillusioned by the utilitarianism of American culture and inspired by the writings of the British philosopher Bertrand Russell. When he heard the rumor that Russell had died, he wept and wrote memorial poems in his honor.[9] However, when he later learned that Russell had not died, his romantic impulse caused him to leave the doctoral program at Columbia University in 1920 and travel to England in search of Russell and, eventually, discovered the aristocratic idealism of Cambridge University.

Russell, in any case, was in China in 1921 and 1922 serving as a visiting professor of philosophy at Beijing University (Beida).[10] He had been expelled from Trinity College, Cambridge, because of his pacifist views during World War I. Consequently, Xu spent the first year in England at the London School for Economics. He was befriended by the Cambridge don G. E. Dickinson who arranged for him to study at Cambridge as a special student.[11] At Kings College, Cambridge, he established lifelong relationships with the don Dalie Rylands as well as Dickinson (who he affectionately called Goldie). Both dons were homosexuals.[12] While Xu was attracted to high-Anglo homoerotic culture, Dickinson was attracted to Chinese men and had written an anonymous and sympathetic book on China in 1901.[13] He later visited China in 1913. Xu was often seen at Dickinson's living quarters on the top floor of Gibbs.[14] At London and Cambridge, Xu became friends with a number of prominent people, including members of the Bloomsbury group as well as Bertrand Russell. Xu was deeply influenced by the British Romantic poets, and he became an ardent Anglophile.

Xu also became friends with the writer H. G. Wells and the art critic and painter Roger Fry as well as the Sinologist Arthur Waley and the poet-scholar Laurence Binyon. He was enthralled by the Bloomsbury group's mixing of literary and personal freedom. As Chinese intellectuals modified their traditional culture and engaged with the modern world of the early twentieth century, they were encountering elements of individual feeling (subjectivity, self-expression, and romanticism) that were alien to traditional Chinese culture. Ironically, British culture was beginning to cast these elements aside. Julian Bell (1908–1937), son of the prominent Bloomsbury group member Vanessa Bell and a nephew of Virginia Wolf, was typical of British authors of that time in deriding this stress on feelings and subjectivity as "sentimentalism."[15]

Nevertheless, Xu was attracted to these forms of individualism that lingered in the works of the Romantic poets. When he carried them, along with the clothing and style of an English gentleman, back to China in 1923, he became known as "the Chinese Shelley."[16] When he learned that Shelley had abandoned his wife Harriet and eloped with seventeen-year-old Mary Godwin, he adopted this model in eventually abandoning his own wife Zhang Youyi and marrying Lu Xiaoman. He was one of the first writers in China to promote an emphasis on the self and on the beauty of the physical body (there were no portrayals of Western-style nudes as idealized bodies in traditional Chinese art). However, there was no room in his daring and creative lifestyle for his first wife. Even though she was a member of the prominent Zhang family and would give birth to their two sons, Xu had married her out of duty, not out of love. Now he wrote to her, asking for a divorce that would scandalize Chinese society.

Xu became infatuated with a number of women, beginning with (Phyllis) Lin Huiyin 林徽音. She was the only survivor of the children born to the concubine of Lin Changmin 林長民, whose wife was childless.[17] She was a precocious girl who became her father's favorite. The Lin family moved to Beijing in 1912 where the father took a second concubine who gave birth to four sons. However, Lin Changmin clearly favored his sole daughter over Hui's mother, and this created a difficult situation when Huiyin's mother poured out her grievances, placing her daughter in the middle of this family dispute.

Lin Changmin and the famous reformer Liang Qichao 梁啟超 had developed a close relationship. Consequently, in 1919 they initiated the arrangements for a marriage between Lin Huiyin and Liang's favorite son Liang Sicheng. In 1920 Lin Changmin went to London to serve as the director of the Chinese League of Nations Association. He took Huiyin with him and enrolled her in a girl's seminary where she became bilingual. In serving as hostess at her father's receptions, she met numerous visitors.[18] At one of these receptions, Liang Qichao introduced her to his student Xu Zhimo.[19] Xu's charm and spontaneity quickly endeared him to Lin Changmin. Xu became a frequent visitor at Lin's home, and he began to pose a threat to the arranged marriage of Lin Huiyin.

Inspired by the individualism of the British Romantic poets and seeking to break out of the constraints of his traditional marriage, Xu fell in love with the sixteen-year-old Lin Huiyin. There was a ten-year age gap between them. But while Xu was exuberant over this relationship, Lin Huiyin's feelings were more complicated. Although she was entranced by Xu's personality and his literary enthusiasms for Shelley, Keats, Byron, Kathleen Mansfield, and Virginia Woolf, she did not share his enthusiasm for marriage with him. When Xu told Lin Huiyin of his intention to divorce his wife and marry her, she remembered her father's neglect of her mother and she shrank from the thought of replacing a divorced wife.[20]

II.

Early in 1921, Xu's wife Zhang Youyi spoiled Xu's dream of independent discovery at Cambridge when she decided to come to England. The Xu family supported her visit because they wanted to remind Xu of his duties to wife and family. She came alone without their two-year-old son Xu Jigai (A-huan) who was too valuable as the Xu family heir to leave his grandparents in China. Consequently, Xu was forced to live with his wife in a cottage in the picturesque village of Swatow six miles southwest of Cambridge to which he sometimes traveled by streetcar and sometimes by bicycle.[21] He simultaneously carried on a romantic correspondence with Lin Huiyin, using the local grocery store as a *post restante* address in which letters were retained at the delivery site until picked up by the recipient. Chinese custom obliged a wife to accept a concubine without jealousy, and it is likely that Zhang Youyi would have accepted a concubine, but Xu gloried in iconoclasm and wanted a divorce. Xu consulted Bertrand Russell about his unhappy marriage and Russell, not surprisingly since he was then on the second of four wives, encouraged Xu to end his unhappy marriage. When Zhang told Xu that she was pregnant with a second child, he coldly told her to get an abortion.[22] For the first time he raised his voice toward her and shouted, "I want a divorce." About a week later, Xu disappeared, abandoning her in a foreign country where she could not speak English.

Three months pregnant, Zhang Youyi wrote to Second Brother who lived in Paris, explaining the breakup of the marriage and saying that Xu had asked her to abort the child. Second Brother told her to come to Paris and that he would take the child. Later she went to Germany where Seventh Brother Zhang Jiasen (Carson Chang) was studying philosophy at Jena. She gave birth to a second son to Xu in Berlin on February 24, 1922. She learned German and became a kindergarten teacher. Meanwhile, Xu had attained his freedom to savor Cambridge on his own.

After a year in London, Lin Changmin returned with his daughter to China in October 1921. Their return gave impetus to the earlier plans for marriage between Lin Huiyin and Liang Sicheng. By the beginning of 1923, plans for the marriage were confirmed, but the formal engagement was delayed until 1927 and the marriage postponed until 1928 in order to allow them to complete their educations and avoid the early birth of a child.[23] Meanwhile

Liang Qichao wrote a letter to his student Xu Zhimo, reprimanding him for divorcing his wife and warning him not to disrupt the marriage of his son Liang Sisheng to Lin Huiyin.[24] Xu reluctantly agreed to Liang's appeal to curb his emotion.[25]

Freed from matrimonial entanglements, Xu Zhimo and Liang Qichao were able to collaborate on cultural matters. The growth in Xu's literary reputation led to an invitation in 1924 to teach at Beijing University.[26] Liang Qichao and Lin Changmin were leaders in the attempt to introduce famous thinkers from the outside world to Chinese audiences. Xu joined with them in inviting Rabindranath Tagore (1861–1941), the Bengali polymath (mystical poet, playwright, composer, philosopher, social reformer, and painter), to China. In 1913 Tagore had been the first non-European to win the Nobel Prize in literature, and Liang and Lin believed that he could speak to China's needs. Xu met Rabindranath Tagore's boat when it arrived at Shanghai in April 1924 and accompanied him on a daily basis, acting as his interpreter for seven weeks in speaking engagements throughout China.[27] Tagore cautioned the Chinese against relinquishing their Asian culture for a materialistic and destructive Western civilization. When Tagore reached Beijing, Xu convinced Lin Huiyin to serve as co-translator and they became a famous literary trio (figure 5.2). When a party to celebrate Tagore's sixty-third birthday took place with four hundred distinguished guests, Tagore's drama *Chitra* was performed in which Lin Huiyin was cast as a princess and Xu as the god of love.

Dark clouds emerged when Tagore's lectures were criticized by organized opposition from the political left wing which distributed leaflets indicting him as a reactionary whose spirituality failed to address China's problems. This criticism coincided with the Chinese Communists' movement against Christian missionaries for their "cultural imperialism."[28] Although two thousand people attended Tagore's third lecture, he canceled the rest of the lectures because he had no heart for this sort of conflict. He withdrew to the Western Hills and shortly thereafter departed China.

III.

After Lin Huiyin returned with her father to China in the fall of 1921, Xu's restlessness increased.[29] Early in 1922 he traveled to Berlin where Zhang Youyi had given birth to their second son, Peter. He shocked his family by asking Zhang to sign the divorce papers. By signing them she became a modern woman, but Zhang was a mixture of modern and traditional values, and she regretted not getting the permission of her parents. A new divorce law in China permitted incompatible couples to divorce; however, since Xu was not yet thirty and Zhang was not yet twenty-five years old, the permission of both

Figure 5.2. The prominent Indian literary figure Rabindranath Tagore (bottom, center) visiting the Forbidden City in Beijing in May 1924. Tagore gave a series of lectures at which Xu Zhimo (top left) and Lin Huiyin (bottom left) served as translators. Isabel Ingram (bottom right), the daughter of an American missionary, served as the empress's tutor. L. K. Elmhirst, top center, was Tagore's secretary/assistant. (British Library, Flickr image.)

parents was required, but not obtained.[30] After the signing, Xu asked to see his newborn son, Peter, giving some indication of his priorities.

Zhang raised the boy with the help of a German woman named Dora Berger. In the spring of 1923, the boy fell ill with diarrhea and breathing problems. A worm was discovered in his small intestines, contracted from bad milk.[31] Apparently Zhang Youyi, who had suckled at the breast of her wet-nurse in China until she was six years old, had not breastfed her second son.[32] The Xu parents were unable to pay for the boy's treatment at an expensive Swiss clinic, and Peter died in March 1925, shortly after his third birthday. Xu wrote a memorial essay on Peter and while its artistry is moving, the depth of his feeling is questionable. Zhang Youyi said that though the memorial sounds like a man who is concerned about his family's welfare, his actions indicated a callous disregard for their basic material needs.[33]

After Xu returned to China in October 1922 and accepted the reprimand of Liang Qichao to end his romantic relationship with Lin Huaiyin, he met and fell in love with Lu Xiaoman 陸小曼, a Beijing socialite and daughter of a leading diplomat. She was skilled in the fine arts of dancing, painting, and singing, and spoke English and French.[34] Unfortunately, Lu Xiaoman was already married and Xu's affair with her so enraged her husband Wang Geng that he threatened to kill Xu.

Wang Geng was a handsome and sophisticated Princeton and West Point graduate who spoke English, French, and German. He and Lu Xiaoman had married in 1920 in Beijing; however, when Wang was appointed chief of police in Manchuria, Lu spurned its remote location as a hardship post and preferred to remain living with her parents in Beijing. When Xu Zhimo met Lu Xiaoman in the summer of 1924 in Beijing, she was twenty years old, beautiful, and a favorite at diplomatic events. In the summer of 1924, Wang asked Xu to accompany his wife to various social functions and Xu fell in love with her.[35]

In March 1925, Xu fled from the threats of an irate husband to return to Europe via the Trans-Siberian railroad across Russia (see figure 3.2). After Xu spent five months in Europe, Wang agreed to give Lu a divorce and Hu Shi wrote to Xu, saying that it was safe for him to return to China. Although Lu's divorce had been finalized, her mother would not allow her to marry Xu until his divorce to Zhang Youyi was confirmed. Consequently, the Xu family gave face to Zhang by inviting her to return to China and confirm the divorce. Upon Zhang's return, Xu's parents greeted her in their Shanghai hotel suite and asked Zhang to confirm that she and Xu were divorced and that she had no objection to her former husband remarrying. When Zhang confirmed this, Xu screamed in delight and leapt from his chair in joy.[36]

In the process of rapid modernization in Republican China, it had actually become fashionable for wealthy and Westernized couples to divorce. Xu and Lu Xiaoman were married on October 3, 1926, at the Beihai Garden in Beijing. The event was immortalized when Xu's teacher and the master of ceremonies Liang Qichao shocked the wedding guests by voicing his disapproval of Xu's actions and condemning them as immoral.[37] Xu seems to have quietly accepted this reprimand. One wonders if his rebellious nature reveled in the reprimand.

Xu Zhimo and Lu Xiaoman rented a house on the prestigious Avenue Edouard VII (Adwardi VII) in the French Concession of Shanghai. Soon, Xu's parents became disenchanted with Lu Xiaoman's behavior. They were scandalized by her having a boyfriend, the actor Weng Ruiwu, living in their house and smoking opium with Lu. Xu appeared to imitate the attitude of the Bloomsbury group in not minding Weng's presence. Xu's mother once found all three of them lying together on the hookah (*shuiyandai* 水煙袋), the opium water pipe, bed. Although Xu did not smoke opium, he had no objection to Lu and Weng smoking it.[38] Opium smoking was widespread in

Republican China. The Communists regarded it as a blight of capitalism, and when they took control in 1949, they conducted a campaign to eradicate the practice.

As Chinese artists came into greater contact with the Bloomsbury group, they joined in the Bloomsburg activity of exchanging sexual partners like musical chairs. The writer Ling Shuhua 凌叔華 (1900–1990), who was married to the prominent literary scholar Chen Yuan 陳垣 (b. 1880), fell passionately in love with Xu Zhimo but also had an affair with Julian Bell, an affair whose consummation was hindered by Bell's venereal disease.[39] Some indication of the sexual and political complexity of the Bloomsbury group is found in its overlap with The Apostles Society, a secret society of students from Kings College and Trinity College, Cambridge. Among its members was Julian Bell, who was both a homosexual lover and fellow Communist of Anthony Blunt at Cambridge in the early 1930s.[40] This setting at Cambridge produced the famous Cambridge Five Soviet spy ring that functioned from the mid-1930s until the early 1950s.[41]

When Xu returned to England in 1925, he carried a blank scroll given to him by Ling Shuhua.[42] It was a friendship scroll (3.8 meters long and 9.4 meters high) left blank for contributions from friends. Between 1925 and 1958, twenty-two entries were inscribed, drawn, or painted on it. Roger Fry painted a watercolor; the poet Wen Yiduo 聞一多 drew a sketch of Tolstoy; Bertrand Russell's wife Dora inscribed a quote from her work *Hypatia, or Woman and Knowledge* (1925), which stated "The dualism of mind and matter, is a very masculine philosophy"; and the popular woman writer of the 1920s Bing Xin 冰心 (Xie Wanying 謝婉瑩) wrote an inscription.[43] Xu carried the handscroll back to China and gave it to Ling Shuhua. Ling later preserved it and brought it to London when she left Beijing in the late 1940s. The handscroll was a concrete testament to the interaction between Chinese and British cultural figures, and more particularly, between the Crescent Moon and Bloomsbury groups.

During his five-month stay in Europe after his flight from China, Xu interviewed the British novelist and poet Thomas Hardy in London and visited the graves of famous writers in Italy and France.[44] A mark of Xu's sentimental attachment to Cambridge is found in a poem that he wrote upon departing from Cambridge for the second time. It has become one of his most famous poems "*Zai bie Kangqiao*" 再別康橋 (Goodbye Again to Cambridge). The Chinese text of the first two and last two lines of this poem have been inscribed on a memorial stone beside a walkway at Kings College, Cambridge. In translation, they read:

輕輕的我走了，　　　　　　　　　Quietly I am leaving

正如我輕輕的來；	Just as quietly I came;
...	
我揮一揮衣袖，	I shake my sleeves,
不帶走一片雲彩。	Not to bring away a patch of cloud.[45]

IV.

When Xu had returned to China in 1923, he became a leading figure in the New Culture movement which advocated for literature based on the vernacular rather than the traditional literary language. (In a parallel literary current in China, Absalom Sydenstriker was also a leading advocate of using vernacular speech rather than literary Chinese in translating the Bible.) When Hu Shi, the New Culture reformer and newly appointed president of Beijing University, invited Xu to join the faculty, he consequently attracted admirers from the literary and social elite of Beijing. Xu and Wen Yiduo (1899–1946) used British Romantic poetry to develop new stanzaic structures for Chinese poetry.[46] Together, Hu Shi, Xu Zhimo, and Chen Yuan represented a wing of Anglo-American influence among Chinese writers.[47]

When Beijing was threatened by Chiang Kai-shek's campaign against the warlords (1927–1929), Xu and many of his friends fled to Shanghai where they established the Crescent Moon Society (*Xin Yue She* 新月社) named after Rabindranath Tagore's poem "Crescent Moon." In 1928 Xu joined with Hu Shi and Shao Xunmei 邵洵美 to launch the Crescent Moon Book Company (*Xinyue shudian* 新月書店). In 1929 Hu Shi and Xu Zhimo launched the *Crescent Moon Monthly* (*Xinyue yuekan* 新月月刊), which became a leading journal in the development of modern Chinese literature.[48]

Xu's leadership of the Crescent Moon group in 1925 to 1931 was an attempt to join with likeminded Chinese writers to promote the philosophy of individualism. This represented a conservative cultural current that emphasized aesthetic and more purely literary elements. They battled with the leftist cultural current led by Lu Xun 魯迅 (Zhou Shuren 周樹人) (1881–1936) and Mao Dun 矛盾 (1896–1981) that emphasized socio-political elements. In the 1930s, the Crescent Moon movement was overwhelmed by the leftist wave of literary movements that attacked individualism and promoted collectivism, as in Lao She's famous novel *Luotuo Xiangzi* (Camel Xiangzi) (1938), which blamed "Individualism" (*gerenzhuyi* 個人主義) for China's woes.[49]

Rejecting the literary models of traditional China, Xu Zhimo's literary circle modeled their poetry on Western models. The traditional prosodic system of Chinese poetry had been based on matching the tonal qualities of monosyllabic words. However, since the modern Chinese language combined the ancient monosyllables into polysyllabic words, this system needed to be updated.[50] Xu and Wen Yiduo, who had studied in England and the United States, adopted the British stress system in prosody. Other Chinese poets adopted different forms of Western meter, such as from the French Symbolist poets. Crescent Moon writers believed that the mind and spirit of the Chinese people could only be liberated through expressive forms of the arts and poetry. Crescent school poetry was based on an aestheticism at odds with the increasing emphasis among many Chinese writers upon social and political themes.[51] The three editors of this monthly were Xu, Wen Yiduo, and Rao Mengkan 繞孟侃 (1902–1967), and they were attacked by Lu Xun and other leftists as the spokesmen of capitalism.

The group of writers led by Hu Shi, Xu Zhimo, and Chen Yuan excelled in poetry and critical erudition, but apart from Ling Shuhua, they lacked an outstanding writer of fiction until they were joined by Shen Congwen 沈從文 (1902–1988) whose innate conservatism blended well with the Crescent Moon group's aestheticism.[52] Wen Yiduo later became a professor of Chinese at Qinghua University. After the faculty and students of Qinghua University were forced to flee from the Japanese, the college was reestablished in 1938 as part of Guoli Xinan Lianhe Daxue 國立西南聯合大學 (National Southwest Associated University), abbreviated as Lianda 聯大, at the southwestern city of Kunming in Yunnan province.[53] As war conditions worsened, Wen Yiduo turned against the Nationalist government and adopted leftist politics. In the 1940s he was the most celebrated convert to the Communist cause and fostered many fledgling Communist poets. His vocal criticism of the Nationalist (Guomindang) party as fascist led to his assassination in Kunming by the secret police in 1946. After his death, Wen was elevated as a martyr whose fame for a time rivaled that of the author Lu Xun.[54]

After first returning to China in 1923, Xu wrote poems and essays in the new vernacular style and yet his command of classical Chinese caused him to become a protégé of Liang Qichao. Xu's second wife Lu Xiaoman was a talented writer and painter, and she collaborated with Xu in producing a five-act drama *Bian kungang* that was praised by critics. However, she incurred extravagant debts, forcing Xu to teach simultaneously at three different universities in order to pay the creditors. In 1929, he assumed the editorship of the Zhonghua Shuju, one of the largest publishers in China. He described the emotional battering of his second marriage as leaving him "with blood all over his head."[55]

V.

In July 1926, Chiang Kai-shek had initiated the Northern Expedition (Beifa 北伐), leading Guomindang forces northward to destroy the regional warlords occupying northern China. As the northern warlord forces poured into Nanjing to confront the Guomindang forces coming from the south, there were not only military hostilities of Chinese against Chinese, but also an explosion of a pent-up Chinese xenophobic hatred toward foreigners.[56] When on March 24, 1927, the Chinese forces began shooting white people, the 107 missionaries in Nanjing had to hide to save their lives. The next day a warship commander negotiated their release and the Chinese Red Cross drove them to the dock where they boarded a boat for Shanghai. Since Shanghai was filled with refugees, they sought refuge in Unzen, a small hot springs resort near Nagasaki in Japan.[57] The Bucks returned to China in October 1927.[58] Because of unsettled conditions in Nanjing, they chose instead to share a three-story house on Avenue Joffre in the French Concession.[59] An American family named the Bateses lived on the first floor, the Yaukeys and the elderly Pastor Sydenstricker lived on the second floor, and the Bucks and two daughters lived on the third floor. Lossing and Claude Thomson and John Reisner braved the political dangers in Nanjing to return intermittently to work in Thomson's laboratory at the university.[60]

Accounts differ as to when Pearl Buck met Xu Zhimo. The biographers Stirling and Spurling place their meeting in Nanjing in the spring of 1924 when Xu was accompanying the Indian poet and Nobel Laureate Rabindranath Tagore on a lecture tour of China as his translator.[61] However, Conn thinks it probable that their relationship began in Shanghai in 1927 and continued until Xu's death in 1931.[62] Conn suggests that Buck took Xu as a lover to retaliate for Lossing's unfaithfulness with other women. Xu was by all accounts an attractive personality possessed of grand literary ambition. He was an impulsive twentieth-century Romantic who in cultivating vernacular literature became the greatest poet of his generation.[63] At the same time, the personal relationship of Pearl Buck and Lossing was reaching a low point of disintegration.

As a love affair, the relationship of Pearl Buck and Xu Zhimo was brief, and possibly even sexually unconsummated, but it brought Buck into contact with an important literary figure whose charisma provided her with needed relief for her parched psyche. Bucks' biographers differ in their treatment of this relationship. Nora Stirling claims it was known to three of Buck's intimates, including an unnamed private secretary and close friend.[64] In addition, Buck's college friend Emma (née Edwards) White learned about it through Buck's letters. Finally, Sara Burton, who taught in the American school, learned about it through sharing the house in Shanghai, although she did not reveal it until 1978, indicating perhaps that she had been keeping an embarrassing secret. However, Peter Conn claims that there is some disagreement about whether "the affair actually took place or was invented later, either by Pearl herself or by Stirling's informants."[65] On the other hand, he concedes that Buck's sister, Grace née Sydenstricker Yaukey, confirmed the story of the affair. In a contrary claim, Hilary Spurling states that "no one in Pearl's circle at the time in China . . . knew anything about this putative affair," except for a vague assertion linking Buck and Xu fifty years after the affair by Lillieth Bates, a sympathetic campus wife at the University of Nanjing.[66]

Xu had a love affair with another Western woman, the American journalist Agnes Smedley (1892–1950). In 1929, before she became a Communist, Smedley was attracted to Xu. By this point Xu's second wife had taken a lover in a very public affair and Xu did likewise, taking Smedley on a two-week boat trip on the Yangzi River to the Xu family country estate.[67] However, Smedley's leftist sympathies soon took hold and she rejected Xu's patrician romanticism for the revolutionary excitement of authors like Mao Dun and Lu Xun.

For Pearl Buck, Xu left a lasting impression since she encountered him at a time when her marriage was failing and Xu was everything that Lossing was not: Xu personified a romantic fantasy. Buck appears to have been describing Xu in the following vivid portrait: "[One] handsome and rather distinguished and certainly much beloved young poet was proud to be called 'The Chinese Shelley.' He used to sit in my living room and talk by the hour and wave his beautiful hands in exquisite and suggestive gestures until now when I think of him, I see first his hands. He was a northern Chinese, tall and classically beautiful in looks, and his hands were big and perfectly shaped and smooth as woman's hands and guiltless, I am sure, of any real manual labor."[68]

Buck's fascination with Xu Zhimo was long-lasting; however, she came from an American Southern background and it is unclear how much of a racial impediment her cultural background was in her relationship with Xu. Consequently, she expressed her experiences by transforming them into a novel. Just as she had transformed and fictionalized her early life experiences with the Chinese in the novel *The Good Earth* (1931), so too did she transform and fictionalize her relationship with Xu into the novel *Letter from Peking* (1957), nearly thirty years after her brief affair with him ended.[69] In this novel, narrated from the point of view of a Vermonter named Elizabeth Kirke, the narrator falls in love with a biracial Harvard student named Gerald MacLeod. He is the son of an American father (a medical doctor) and a Chinese mother (Han Ai-lan) who live in Beijing. Eventually the narrator marries MacLeod and returns with him to Beijing where they spent a few idyllic years living in Beijing where MacLeod was a university professor.

This book, like other books by Buck, has a sentimental tone that enhanced its popular appeal. Eventually, the political uncertainty surrounding the Communist victory in 1949 forced Elizabeth and their newborn son to leave China. MacLeod stayed behind in China while Elizabeth made a life for herself and her son at her mother's farmstead in Vermont. Over the next few years, only twelve letters, sent surreptitiously or with deletions made out of fear of the censors, reached Elizabeth.

The last letters, written by MacLeod's Chinese wife, Mei-lan, tell of the birth to her and MacLeod of a son. Gradually, MacLeod's optimism for the new Communist government faded and he fell under increasing official suspicion. He eventually was shot and killed in an attempted escape. The character Gerald MacLeod seems to be a composite of Xu Zhimo with another unknown figure. Xu's Western affinities seem to have been transformed into MacLeod's half-Western parentage. Xu and MacLeod were both university professors. They both had skeptical attitudes toward Communism. And finally, Buck's romantic attachment to Xu was manifested in Elizabeth's love for MacLeod. The Pearl Buck biographer Hilary Spurling is skeptical and claims the suggestion that the two romantic characters in *Letter from Peking* represented Pearl Buck and Xu Zhimo was the fantasy of Buck's old age companion, Ted Harris.[70]

Today this love story seems far less daring than when it was written, but at the time of its publication in 1957, miscegenation was still illegal in twenty-seven US states and generally frowned on in the others. The love of Buck for Xu seems to have lingered for several years. Later, when she was preparing to divorce Lossing and marry Richard Walsh, she wrote to her friend Emma White, and seemed to be referring to her love affair with Xu when she said: "I once loved someone—I told you, you remember—but I beat that down, year after year. But it was no such love as this and no such man as Richard."[71]

Xu moved in elite circles in both China and Europe. He had fame and love affairs with prominent literary women, and yet he remained powerless and was unable to transform the Crescent Moon values of individualism into a dominant popular cultural force in China. Xu lived dangerously and died an early death in the manner of a Romantic. He lacked the financial means to support the extravagant spending habits of his wife, and his family refused to help him. His poetic powers were ebbing, he was disillusioned with politics, and he engaged in risky behavior. In an attempt to revive his spirits, he accepted Hu Shi's offer of a teaching position at Beijing University in 1931. To increase his income, Xu commuted between Shanghai and Beijing, traveling by air. He found the new medium of air travel exciting; however, it was dangerous. In 1931 his plane crashed in the fog near Jinan, Shandong, killing him at the age of thirty-six.[72] Without his charismatic leadership, the

Crescent Moon movement collapsed. At his death the "Chinese Shelley" was thirty-four years old, eight years older than John Keats, four years older than Percy Shelley, and two years younger than Lord Byron at the time of their deaths.

VI.

Pearl Buck's affair with Richard Walsh developed slowly. In 1933 when Lossing had completed his doctoral work in the United States and was eager to return to China, Pearl returned with him by way of Europe. Richard and Ruby Walsh joined them for the European stretch of their journey.[73] Lossing may have been insensitive, but he was not as obtuse as he is portrayed by Pearl Buck's biographers. There are conflicting accounts of who first asked for a divorce. The three main biographers all claim that Pearl initiated the divorce. Nora Stirling claims that she came to Washington in 1934 where Lossing was advising the Secretary of the Treasury Henry Morgenthau on the purchase of large amounts of silver from China.[74] Lossing is said to have made no objection to her request, but he refused to go to Reno with her to obtain the divorce. The biographer Hilary Spurling claims that Pearl asked Lossing for a divorce in Nice in 1933.[75] Peter Conn agrees that Pearl asked for a "separation" at Nice in 1933.[76] Conn claimed Lossing knew about Pearl's intimacy with Richard Walsh, but thought it was hopeless to protest.

Conn claims that Lossing may not have understood that Pearl left him because he was satisfying neither her sexual passion nor her intellect. However, the Bucks' neighbor in Nanjing, Nancy Thomson Waller, presents a more sympathetic portrayal of Lossing and claims that it was Lossing who first asked for a divorce.[77] Late in 1933, Walsh visited China in his new role as editor of *Asia* magazine. Always seeking to avoid emotional confrontation, Lossing fled to Tibet for an exploratory voyage with some soil specialists, telling Pearl's sister, Grace Yaukey, that he still loved Pearl and was upset over the prospect of losing her.[78] While Lossing was in Tibet, Pearl and Walsh traveled together, first to meet Pearl's sister Grace and then throughout southeast Asia. Finally, they went to Beijing where Buck introduced Walsh to Edgar Snow and his wife Helen Foster Snow who were both teaching at Yanjing University.[79] Helen Snow said Buck looked like a Pennsylvania farm-wife and she "loved her at once."[80] She described her as "large and matronly, not tall . . . sweet smile . . . friendly and outgoing." She had a folksy, "house-wife" quality that endeared her to woman readers. In February and March of 1934, Buck and Walsh made another long trip to Hong Kong, the Malay States, and the Philippines. Upon returning, Pearl decided to sail with Walsh to the United States. When she boarded the *Empress of Russia* for Canada in

1934, she assumed that she would be returning to China. However, circumstances in China would make that impossible.

Buck's reputation was based on popular, not high cultural, acclaim. This was partly due to male literary dominance that showed little interest in or sympathy for the lives of women.[81] But it was also due to her concern with using her writing to promote social and political causes involving the plight of Chinese peasants, racial integration, unwanted children, and women's rights. A preoccupation with aesthetic and literary elements was not her primary concern. The result was that her literary acclaim came in forms of recognition, such as the Nobel Prize for literature, that were tinged with political concerns. In addition, her works were tremendously popular and filled with a sensitivity that women, in particular, found appealing. They rewarded her with large purchases of her books which gave her wealth that enabled her to pay for her disabled daughter's care and to promote the causes dear to her heart. She also used this wealth in 1934 to purchase and renovate an old farmhouse near Perkasie in Bucks County, Pennsylvania, that was close to the New Jersey facility where her daughter Carol lived. This farmstead, called Green Hills Farm, became identified with her work for biracial children in later years.

Upon returning to the United States from China in 1934, Walsh was confronted with the bankruptcy of his publishing house, John Day Company. Buck served as a helpmate in crisis management by suspending her royalties from John Day and contributing her services as an advisory editor. She signed the Chinese expatriate scholar Lin Yutang whose book *My Country and My People* (1935) was tremendously successful. In 1936, Lin's articles attacking Chiang Kai-shek placed him in danger and led to his flight with his wife and three daughters to the United States.[82] The Lins were unable to live in Princeton because of racial prejudice against the Chinese. A professor's wife refused to rent to them, and this infuriated Buck.

Buck wanted to divorce Lossing and marry Richard Walsh, but divorce was a momentous matter in 1935 and she hesitated out of fear that it might damage her reputation.[83] When Lossing came to Washington, DC, to work with the Secretary of the Treasury Henry Mongenthau on a large purchase of China's silver, Pearl visited him and had several difficult conversations about a divorce. Although he did not oppose the divorce, he demurred when she suggested that they go together to Reno, Nevada, to obtain one. So in a bizarre scenario, Pearl and Walsh's wife Ruby traveled together to Reno where they shared lodgings during the six-week mandatory residency period required by Nevada law.[84] Finally on June 11, 1935, in a courtroom hearing lasting twenty minutes, Pearl Buck was granted a divorce on the grounds of incompatibility and two hours later Ruby Walsh in a five-minute hearing obtained a divorce on the basis of cruelty.[85] Two hours after that, Buck and

Walsh were married. The *New York Times* headline article reported a fact that is curiously ignored in the sanitized accounts by Buck's biographers, except for Nora Stirling who quoted it, namely: "The bride smoked nervously before and after divorce proceedings."[86] Since Buck would die of lung cancer, some reference to her smoking habit would seem to merit mention.[87] Perhaps this frailty conflicts with the model image that her biographies have constructed over the last twenty years. There are other omissions as well.

VII.

Buck's second marriage was far more successful than her first marriage, but a turning point in her life came on August 17, 1953, when Richard Walsh suffered a stroke in Sheridan, Wyoming. Unlike her first husband Lossing Buck, Walsh had been an intellectual and emotional soulmate. He gave her sound literary advice that she sorely missed after he was gone. He receded slowly from her life. His initially mild symptoms became more debilitating and within one year he had deteriorated into an invalid.[88] He was no longer able to contribute advice on her literary work. Ironically, the woman who so resented male domination craved male attention and acceptance to such an extent that it would darken the last chapter of her life. In an attempt to replace Walsh's flagging attention, Buck turned to younger men who gladly flattered her with attention in order to advance their personal fortunes. Consequently, the woman who had been so discerning of people became, in her need for flattery and attention, oblivious to their exploitation of her.

The first of these male flatterers was Tad Danielewski. The treatment of Danielewski by Buck's biographers parallels and reflects their development of her exemplary model image. Like Buck's smoking habit, these exploitive male flatterers are minimized or deleted from their sanitized versions. Whereas Hilary Stirling's *Pearl Buck: Woman in Conflict* (1983), perhaps the most objective of the three biographies, devoted thirty pages to Buck's embarrassing relationship with Danielewski, Peter's Conn's more sympathetic *Pearl S. Buck: A Cultural Biography* (1996) devotes only four pages to him.[89] Karen J. Leong's book on the trio of Buck, Anna May Wong, and Maying Soong omits any mention of Danielewski.[90] The most recent and most hagiographical of the biographies, Hilary Spurling's *Burying the Bones* (2010), also omits mention of him.[91] In the arc of ascent of Pearl Buck's reputation in these three books, we can follow her transformation from a remarkably talented and compassionate but flawed woman into a feminist icon.

Tad Danielewski (1921–1993) was born in Poland and had worked with Allied Occupation Forces in theatre productions in Poland and Germany.

After training for the theatre in England, he emigrated to the United States, coaching and teaching theatre in various colleges. He shifted to television and directed the "Omnibus" show. He and Buck met during their collaboration on an "Omnibus" segment, after the publication of her *My Several Worlds*. Danielewski drove, with his pregnant Polish-born wife, to Green Hills Farm to consult with Buck. The series was televised in May 1954. After switching from CBS to NBC, Danielewski contacted Buck in June 1955 and arranged for an interview out of which several collaborations occurred

Figure 5.3. Director Tad Danielewski and author Pearl S. Buck in rehearsals for the stage production "A Desert Incident," 1959. (Friedman-Abeles photographs. Permission of the New York Public Library.)

in which they formed a team of author and director. After Danielewski was forced out at NBC, he exploited Buck's fascination with composing dramas—she had little skill or talent as a dramatist—to fulfill his own dream of producing a Broadway play. Consequently, Buck became a vehicle to realize Danielewski's aspirations (figure 5.3).

Rumors about the relationship between Buck and Danielewski were fed by her financing of his projects, by his married status, and by the twenty-five-year age difference between them. Richard Walsh's son, Dick Walsh, Jr., who now headed the John Day Publishing Company, and his wife Tsuta were concerned enough for Tsuta to visit Buck's sister Grace Yaukey in 1959 and convey their anxiety. Danielewski was aware of Buck's loneliness and would visit her, bringing flowers and fawning attention. He catered to her and together they launched Stratton Productions. Although Buck's talents as a playwright were mediocre, any doubts about the wisdom of producing her dramas were countered by her conviction that Danielewski was brilliant and had star quality. Critics of her plays were not so kind, but she dismissed them. Danielewski had enormous energy and was a great promoter, but his projects failed to attain success. He and Buck were in Japan making a film when news of Richard Walsh's death arrived.

Buck's romantic hopes were built on the fantasies of an aging woman. When Danielewski's marriage disintegrated, Buck hoped that he would propose marriage to her, but he married a young actress instead. In June of 1964, Buck attended their wedding but asked to be taken home early. She wondered out loud what the look Danielewski had given to her at the wedding meant, clearly hoping that it conveyed some lingering romantic import.[92] In comparison with Buck's later relationship with Ted Harris, the Danielewski affair was mild, but it was important to signify the growing desperation of her emotional needs.

VIII.

The last twenty-five years of Pearl Buck's life were a contradictory blend of her benevolent impulse and her vulnerability to exploitation by self-serving men. Her benevolent effort involved helping biracial children of Americans and Asians whom she termed "Amerasians."[93] These children of mainly Japanese, Korean, Okinawan, and Vietnamese women and American servicemen were rejected by both Asian and American societies. The eminent Japan historian Edwin Reischauer wrote in 1977 that "the Japanese today are the most thoroughly unified and culturally homogeneous large block of people in the whole world."[94] Consequently, mixed blood children produced by the interbreeding of Japanese women and American servicemen were referred to as *konketsuji* 溫血兒, which had negative connotations of half-breed or mongrel.[95] They were discriminated against and rejected by Japanese society and even attacked and sexually mutilated. Similar discriminatory situations emerged where American troops served in South Korea, Taiwan, the Philippines, and Okinawa.

Because of racially restrictive attitudes in the United States, established adoption agencies normally did not place biracial children. Out of her compassion for these children, in 1947 Buck organized a new adoption agency called Welcome House. She began working alone out of her home at Green Hills Farm, but gradually enrolled prominent Bucks County neighbors in the project, including the lyricist and playwright Oscar Hammerstein II, the philanthropist Lois Burpee, and the novelist James Michener. Clearly, she was a civil rights activist and a leader in promoting the end of racial segregation. Welcome House placed over five thousand biracial and foreign-born children for adoption.[96]

Unfortunately, as Pearl Buck grew older, her vulnerability to exploitive types of men grew. The wealth generated by the royalties on her books bought by her large and loyal audience of mainly female readers made her a target for exploiters. Whereas her relationship with Tad Danielewski was collaborative and romantic in nature, her later relationship with Ted Harris was more complicated. It was a complex mix of collaborative, exploitive, romantic, and maternal elements. Their age difference, Buck's emotional needs, and Harris' material ambitions helped to define their relationship.[97] Only the Stirling biography fully captures this complicated denouement to Pearl Buck's life with the subtitle "Woman in Conflict," devoting two and a half chapters to this relationship.[98] By contrast, the Conn and Spurling biographies devote much less attention to Buck's relationship with Harris. Actually, the life of Ted Harris was just as uniquely American as the life of Pearl Buck.

In 1931 when Fred Leon Hair, Jr., was born, Pearl Buck was thirty-nine years old and attaining fame as the author of *The Good Earth*.[99] Hair was born into a poor family in Bamberg County, South Carolina. His father, an insurance salesman, suffered an early stroke, and his mother worked as a domestic servant. Hair left school in the eighth grade to work as a dance instructor. He had charm and a mind that was focused on escaping from poverty. In 1964 he changed his name to Theodore Findley Harris. Like many ambitious poor people, he underwent a self-creation in which he sought to re-create himself in movement and speech. Stirling aptly described Harris' studied personal re-creation by saying he had "a dancer's walk and an actor's precise diction."[100] He had a particular talent for cultivating older women who were flattered by his attention.

When Buck suspected that her affair with Danielewski was drawing to a close, she began to move on psychologically. She told a friend that she wanted to learn how to dance and to do it well.[101] Early in 1963 she arranged for Harris, a dance instructor at the Arthur Murray Studio in nearby Jenkintown, to come to Green Hills Farm to give her younger daughters (a German-American Black and three Japanese-Americans) dancing lessons. Soon she was taking lessons from him as well. Harris knew from his humble background that subservience to the right people was a sure means of advancing. While Spurling claimed that Buck found Harris both handsome and fascinating, Stirling claimed Buck did not find his red hair romantic.[102] The key to Buck's affection for Harris lay in his intelligence, his creativity, and—above all—his devotion to Buck. After several sessions, Harris had gained her confidence and she was sharing her plans to help several thousand Amerasian children. She was particularly concerned with children born to Korean mothers and American G.I.s who were regarded as outcasts in their own country. The plight of these children was made worse by the refusal of the American government or veterans' organizations to recognize any responsibility for them.[103] Unlike the Welcome House adoptees, these children could not be adopted because they were not orphans.

When Buck proposed in the fall of 1963 that Harris be appointed administrative head of a new project aimed at helping these Korean children, the Welcome House board refused because of his lack of qualifications or experience. The board was somewhat stodgy. When Harris had suggested the idea of a Welcome House Ball as a fundraiser, the board had not been enthusiastic. There were rumors that Harris and James Johns (Jimmy) Pauls were homosexuals.[104] One board member told Buck that Harris had a seventeen-year relationship with James Johns (Jimmy) Pauls who had been arrested the previous year in the men's room of the Jenkintown station of the Reading Railroad for sodomy.[105] Given the sensitivity of the charge and the involvement of minors in the proposed Pearl S. Buck Foundation project, a more cautious person might have treaded carefully, but Absalom's Sydenstriker's daughter (like father, like daughter) did not shirk from doing what she thought was right. She responded to the charge of homosexuality by dismissing it. Harris had already told her about his unusual sexual habits and how they had been corrected through psychiatric treatment. Anyway, she cited the names of two distinguished homosexuals and said sexuality was a private matter. Buck's attitude was not only tolerant but also advanced in anticipating the gay liberation movement that began six years later.

In 1964, Buck circumvented the Welcome House board by establishing the Pearl S. Buck Foundation to provide one-on-one sponsorship of Korean American children who had been abandoned in their homeland after the Korean War. Harris was named president. Previously, Buck had begun

Welcome House modestly out of her home at Green Hills Farm, but now her judgment was affected by her feelings for Harris and she began to indulge his ambitious tendencies. The foundation was housed in one of the most elegant townhouses in Philadelphia—a five-story building at 2019 Delancey Place. Harris lived on the fourth floor and Jimmy Pauls lived on the fifth floor. A full-time cook and houseboy were on the staff. Harris spent lavishly for personal items and automobiles, such that in the year 1964, less than 4 percent of the funds collected through private contributions to the foundations actually went to helping Amerasian children.

Drawing upon Pearl Buck's name, a cross-country tour of balls in twenty-one cities from coast to coast with carefully planned media coverage involving newspapers, television stations, and local dignitaries took place as part of a fundraising campaign for the Pearl S. Buck Foundation.[106] At each ball Buck arrived in a limousine, wearing an elaborate evening dress. The band played a fanfare and Harris led her out onto the dance floor to the strains of a waltz. Buck's memories of her missionary childhood deprivation imposed by the austerity of her father's missionary work in China were now obliterated by the fulfillment of a long-delayed dream. But the dream was built on an exaggerated reality. Although Buck had claimed in one article that fifty thousand Amerasian children were starving on the streets of Korea, a Korean government official claimed that their numbers were between five thousand and eight thousand.[107] Harris staffed the foundation with former Arthur Murray dance instructors who also served as foundation board members, providing Buck with majority support on any board decisions. Harris' imperious manner alienated donors, but his attentiveness to Buck was devotedly deferential and she continued to support him. In a sense, it would be her last dance.

The Pearl S. Buck Foundation was accused of two forms of immorality: financial and sexual. These accusations involving corruption and the sexual abuse of minors were aired in a fifteen-thousand-word article that appeared in the *Philadelphia Magazine* in July 1969. The *Philadelphia Magazine* provided several hints of Harris' sexual attraction toward very young men, as when it referred to a second dance tour in which Buck and Harris were "chauffeured in a Chrysler Imperial driven by a lithe and handsome young waif from the streets of South Philadelphia."[108] However, the specific accusations were based on more than hints and innuendo. Four Korean youths made tape-recorded interviews with the WIP Radio News Director Paul Rust in November 1967.[109] While the Stirling biography discusses the sexual charges against Harris, Conn barely mentions them. Conn, the normally meticulous researcher, writes only: "There was gossip that [Harris] had molested several young boys, Ameriasians brought to the foundation from Korea," and cites the Stirling biography as his source![110]

Buck's sense of unreality grew, and she regarded the attacks as a campaign of hatred against Harris and her.[111] When Harris fled to Maryland to avoid possible prosecution in Pennsylvania, she followed him, leaving Green Hills Farm in 1968, just prior to her seventy-seventh birthday.[112] She would never return, except for one brief visit. At first, she and Harris lived in the summer house built by her sons in the Green Mountains of Vermont, which reminded her of her family's missionary resort in Guling, China. Later, she bought property in the economically depressed town of Danby, Vermont, seeking to revive it. Her listing by UN Educational, Scientific and Cultural Organization as one of the most-translated authors in the world reinforced the conviction of her own stature.[113] Also, the woman's magazine *Good Housekeeping* once again placed her on the list (1972) of the most admired women (in third place after Rose Kennedy and Mamie Eisenhower).[114]

After leaving China in 1934 at the age of forty-two, never to return, her sympathy for the Chinese peasants continued to grow and her compassion for biracial children left behind by American occupying forces throughout East Asia transformed her into a highly admired figure. At least it did until the corrosive effects of power and prestige and a weakness for young male flatterers in her old age caused her reputation to take a tumble. Since her death, there have been further pendulum swings caused by changes in the cultural atmosphere. While some evaluate her in terms of the literary quality of her work, others do so in terms of her contribution to racial equality while still others regard her as a feminist icon. The Chinese themselves have had a low regard for her novels. The writer Shao Xunmei (1906–1968), Emily Hahn's lover, punned on Buck's name and reputation. Grassy Western-style cemeteries in China made them attractive night-time assignation sites for Chinese lovers and Shao penned this epitaph: "Villagers, please don't fuck. Here lies Pearl Buck."[115]

The end of Pearl Buck's life was marked by disappointment. Previously in 1943 the Communist leader Zhou Enlai, now premier of the People's Republic of China, had invited Buck to visit China.[116] Unable to accept the invitation because of wartime conditions, she filed it away in her mind. In February 1972 when the American President Richard Nixon made his historic visit with Henry Kissinger to China, she wanted to accompany him, but her request was refused. She asked for the intervention of John S. Service, who had been dismissed from the State Department for excessive sympathy for the Chinese Communists. Service passed her request on to the Chinese authorities.[117] The shock was great when a letter from the Canadian embassy of the Peoples' Republic of China arrived in May of 1972 rejecting her visa application because of the anti-Communist tone she had taken in her works. One explanation for the rejected visa application is traced to internal Chinese politics and the need for Zhou Enlai to appease Jiang Qing, Mao's wife who was then very much in the running to succeed Mao as part of the Gang of Four. Presumably Jiang Qing's enmity toward Pearl Buck was caused by Buck's long-ago friendship with a rival actress to Jiang Qing named Wang Ying.[118] Another source of Chinese Communist hostility toward Buck can be traced to Lu Xun's claim that her novel *The Good Earth* demonstrated a superficial knowledge of China. The Chinese leaders were Marxists who probably did not share Buck's romantic view of the peasantry.

The month after the visa rejection, Buck briefly returned to Green Hills Farm to celebrate her eightieth birthday with her family of seven children and fourteen grandchildren.[119] However, the event was marked by tension between her family and Ted Harris, who had become her constant and trusted companion. A few days later she returned to Vermont and entered a Rutland hospital for treatment of lung cancer, followed by ten months of illness until her death on March 6, 1973. She was buried at Green Hills Farm. Her 1971 will left most of her wealth to Creativity, Inc. and the Pearl Sydenstriker Buck trust, which Harris controlled.[120] The family contested the will, accusing Harris of "undue influence" to increase his wealth at their expense. A jury ruled in favor of the family, but Harris and his allies appealed and countersued. After seven years, a secret settlement was negotiated.[121]

NOTES

1. Peter Conn, *Pearl S. Buck: A Cultural Biography.* (Cambridge, England: Cambridge University Press, 1996), 90–92; Nora Stirling, *Pearl Buck: A Woman in Conflict* (Piscataway, NJ: New Century Publishers, 1983), 1–5, 77–79.

2. Hilary Spurling, *Burying the Bones: Pearl Buck in China* (London: Profile Books, Ltd, 2010), 211.

3. Howard L. Boorman, ed., *Biographical Dictionary of Republican China*, five volumes (New York: Columbia University Press, 1967–1971), II, 122–24.

4. Pang-Mei Natasha Chang, *Bound Feet and Western Dress* (New York: Anchor Books, 1997), 55–57.

5. Chang, *Bound Feet and Western Dress*, 67.

6. Chang, *Bound Feet and Western Dress*, 98.

7. Chang, *Bound Feet and Western Dress*, 100.

8. Leo Ou-fan Lee, *The Romantic Generation of Modern Chinese Writers* (Cambridge, MA: Harvard University Press, 1973), 127.

9. Jonathan D. Spence, *The Gate of Heavenly Peace: The Chinese and Their Revolution, 1895–1980* (New York: Viking Press, 1981), 154.

10. Upon returning from China, Bertrand Russell published *The Problem of China* 中國問題 (London: George Allen & Unwin, Ltd., 1922; second edition Taibei: 虹橋 書店 [Rainbow-Bridge Book Co.], 1966).

11. Chang, *Bound Feet and Western Dress*, 106.

12. Leslie Mitchell, *Maurice Bowra: A Life* (Oxford: Oxford University Press, 2009), 124, 128; D. E. Mungello, *Western Queers in China: Flight to the Land of Oz* (Lanham, MD: Rowman & Littlefield, 2012), 80, 84–85, 138.

13. G. Lowes Dickinson, *Letters from John Chinaman* (London: Brimley Johnson, 1901).

14. Patricia Laurence, *Lily Briscoe's Chinese Eyes: Bloomsbury, Modernism, and China* (Columbia, SC: University of South Carolina Press, 2003), 132–33.

15. Laurence, *Lily Briscoe's Chinese Eyes*, 55.

16. Percy Bysshe Shelley (1792–1822) was a famous Romantic poet who cultivated a radical lifestyle.

17. Wilma Fairbank, *Liang and Lin: Partners in Exploring China's Architectural Past* (Philadelphia: University of Pennsylvania Press, 1994), 10–11.

18. Fairbank, *Liang and Lin*, 11–12.

19. Chang, *Bound Feet and Western Dress*, 129.

20. Fairbank, *Liang and Lin*, 12–14.

21. Lee, *Romantic Generation*, 132–33.

22. Chang, *Bound Feet and Western Dress*, 126.

23. Fairbank, *Liang and Lin*, 16.

24. Fairbank, *Liang and Lin*, 17.

25. Spence, *Gate of Heavenly Peace*, 162.

26. Fairbank, *Liang and Lin*, 20–21.

27. Spence, *Gate of Heavenly Peace*, 174.

28. Fairbank, *Liang and Lin*, 21–22.

29. Gaylord Kai Loh Leung, "Hsü Chih-mo and Bertrand Russell," *Renditions* 14 (autumn 1980): 29.

30. Chang, *Bound Feet and Western Dress*, 148.

31. Chang, *Bound Feet and Western Dress*, 151–58.

32. Chang, *Bound Feet and Western Dress*, 7.

33. Chang, *Bound Feet and Western Dress*, 162–64.

34. Chang, *Bound Feet and Western Dress*, 164–66.

35. Chang, *Bound Feet and Western Dress*, 164–66.

36. Chang, *Bound Feet and Western Dress*, 168–69.

37. Chang, *Bound Feet and Western Dress*, 175–76.

38. Chang, *Bound Feet and Western Dress*, 184–85.

39. Laurence, *Lily Briscoe's Chinese Eyes*, 70–72.

40. Andrew Lownie, *Stalin's Englishman: Guy Burgess, the Cold War, and the Cambridge Spy Ring* (New York: St. Martin's Press, 2015), 34, photograph caption of the Apostles Society, between 50 and 51.

41. The Cambridge Five Spy Ring included Anthony Blunt (1907–1983), Guy Burgess (1911–1963), Harold "Kim" Philby (1912–1988), Donald McLean (1913–1983), and John Cairncross (1913–1995).

42. Michael Sullivan, "A Small Token of Friendship," *Oriental Art* 35 (2) (summer 1989): 76–85.

43. C. T. Hsia, *A History of Modern Chinese Fiction 1917–1957* (New Haven: Yale University Press, 1961), 71–77.

44. Boorman, *Biographical Dictionary of Republican China*, II, 122; Chang, *Bound Feet and Western Dress*, 164–65.

45. Xu Zhimo, "On the China Sea, November 6, 1925," *The Crescent Monthly* I (10), translated by Kai-yu Hsu, *Twentieth Century Chinese Poetry: An Anthology* (Garden City, NY: Doubleday, 1963), 83–84.

46. C. T. Hsia, *A History of Modern Chinese Fiction*, 26.

47. C. T. Hsia, *A History of Modern Chinese Fiction*, 194.

48. C. T. Hsia, *A History of Modern Chinese Fiction*, 121; Howard L. Boorman, ed., *Biographical Dictionary of Repubican China* (New York: Columbia University Press), II, 122–24.

49. Lao She [Shu Qingchun], *Rickshaw* [*Luotuo xiangzi*], translated by Jean M. James (Honolulu: University of Hawaii Press, 1979), 237, 247, 249.

50. C. T. Hsia, *A History of Modern Chinese Fiction*, 26.

51. Hsu, *Twentieth Century Chinese Poetry*, 49–50.

52. C. T. Hsia, *A History of Modern Chinese Fiction*, 194–95.

53. Bert Stern, *Winter in China: An Amerian Life* (Xlibris, 2014) p. 137f.

54. C. T. Hsia, *A History of Modern Chinese Fiction*, 314.

55. Gaylord Kai Loh Leung, "Hsü Chih-mo and Bertrand Russell," *Renditions* 14 (autumn 1980): 31.

56. Stirling, *Pearl Buck*, 78–79.

57. Stirling, *Pearl Buck*, 80–81.

58. Conn, *Pearl S. Buck*, 100.

59. Stirling, *Pearl Buck*, 82; Conn, *Pearl S. Buck*, 100.

60. Stirling, *Pearl Buck*, 82–83.

61. Stirling, *Pearl Buck*, 87; Spurling, *Burying the Bones*, 192.

62. Conn, *Pearl S. Buck*, 103.

63. Kai-yu Hsu, ed., trans., *Twentieth Century Chinese Poetry: An Anthology* (Garden City, NY: Anchor Books, 1964), 69–77.

64. Stirling, *Pearl Buck*, 86.

65. Conn, *Pearl S. Buck*, 397.

66. Spurling, *Burying the Bones*, 194.

67. Janice R. MacKinnon and Stephan R. MacKinnon, *Agnes Smedley: the Life and Times of an American Radical* (Berkeley: University of California Press, 1988), 143, 149–50.

68. Pearl Buck, *My Several Worlds* (New York: John Day Company, 1954), 178–79.

69. Pearl S. Buck, *Letter from Peking* (New York: John Day Company, 1957).

70. Spurling, *Burying the Bones*, 194.

71. Pearl S. Buck to Emma Edmunds White (September 17, 1933), transcribed by Nora Stirling and cited in Conn, 159.

72. Kai-yu Hsu, *Twentieth Century Chinese Poetry*, 75–77.

73. Conn, *Pearl S. Buck*, 156.

74. Stirling, *Pearl Buck*, 161.

75. Spurling, *Burying the Bones*, 235.

76. Conn, *Pearl S. Buck*, 158.

77. Nancy Thomson Waller, *My Nanking Home 1918–1937* (Cherry Valley, NY: Willow Hill Publications, 2010), 45.

78. Stirling, *Pearl Buck*, 149–52.

79. Conn, *Pearl S. Buck*, 160–62.

80. Stirling, *Pearl Buck*, 152–53.

81. Conn, *Pearl S. Buck*, 163–64.

82. Stirling, *Pearl Buck*, 177.

83. Stirling, *Pearl Buck*, 161.

84. Conn, *Pearl S. Buck*, 182.

85. "Pearl Buck Weds After Reno Divorce," *New York Times*, June 12, 1935, 19.

86. Stirling, *Pearl Buck*, 164.

87. Conn, *Pearl S. Buck*, 376, and Spurling, *Burying the Bones*, 279, both state that Buck died of "lung cancer," but neither makes any reference to her smoking habit.

88. Conn, *Pearl S. Buck*, 332–33.

89. Conn, *Pearl S. Buck*, 242–44, 352.

90. Karen J. Leong, *The China Mystique: Pearl S. Buck, Anna May Wong, Maylong Soong, and the Transformation of American Orientalism* (Berkeley: University of California Press, 2005).

91. Stirling, *Pearl Buck*, 241–70; Conn, *Pearl S. Buck*, 342.

92. Stirling, *Pearl Buck*, 270–71.

93. Conn, *Pearl S. Buck*, 313.

94. Edwin O. Reischauer, *The Japanese* (Cambridge, MA: Harvard University Press, 1977, 1981), 34–36.

95. Conn, *Pearl S. Buck*, 360.

96. Conn, *Pearl S. Buck*, xi, 313–14, 327.

97. Stirling, *Pearl Buck*, 289.

98. Stirling, *Pearl Buck*, 278–312.

99. Greg Walter, "The Dancing Master," *Philadelphia Magazine*, July 1969, 55–126.

100. Stirling, *Pearl Buck*, 280.

101. Stirling, *Pearl Buck*, 269.

102. Spurling, *Burying the Bones*, 272; Stirling, *Pearl Buck*, 288–89.

103. Conn, *Pearl S. Buck*, 354.

104. Stirling, *Pearl Buck*, 289.

105. Walter, "The Dancing Master," 57–58.

106. Stirling, *Pearl Buck*, 286.

107. Walter, "The Dancing Master," 59.

108. Walter, "The Dancing Master," 114.

109. Walter, "The Dancing Master," 120–22.

110. Stirling, *Pearl Buck*, 296–301; Conn, *Pearl S. Buck*, 362.

111. Stirling, *Pearl Buck*, 308.

112. Spurling, *Burying the Bones*, 275–76, 306.

113. Stirling, *Pearl Buck*, 313.

114. Stirling, *Pearl Buck*, 318.

115. Ken Cuthbertson, *Nobody Said Not to Go: The Life, Lovers, and Adventures of Emily Hahn* (Boston: Faber and Faber, 1998), 140.

116. Xi Lian, *The Conversion of Missionaries: Liberalism in American Protestant Missions in China, 1907–1932* (University Park, PA: Pennsylvania State University Press, 1997), 127.

117. David A. Hollinger, *Protestants Abroad: How Missionaries Tried to Change the World But Changed America* (Princeton, NJ: Princeton University Press, 2017), 45–46.

118. Ross Terrill, *The White-Boned Demon: Biography of Madame Mao Zedong* (New York: William Morrow, 1984), 103, 263.

119. Conn, *Pearl S. Buck*, 375.

120. Conn, *Pearl S. Buck*, 376.

121. Conn, *Pearl S. Buck*, 450.

Chapter 6

A Love Bypassed by Time

Emily Hahn and Shao Xunmei

I.

In the period before the series of forced unequal treaties imposed on China by Western nations, beginning with the Treaty of Nanjing (1842), Western women were largely excluded from China. Those few women who did accompany Western traders to China remained in the Portuguese colony of Macau during the annual trading season while their male companions went to Guangzhou (Canton). The main impetus for opening China to Western women came with the arrival of the Protestant missionaries after 1842. However, these missionaries sought to penetrate the interior of China rather than remain in the treaty port enclaves of Canton, Xiamen (Amoy), Fuzhou, Ningbo, and Shanghai. Catholic women missionaries from Europe did not arrive in China until 1891 when the first six sisters of the Canossian order came to Shaanxi and dedicated themselves to caring for unwanted children, mostly girls.[1] As a result, the Western population of trading centers like Shanghai remained predominantly male where a unique China coast culture emerged. Large trading firms hired young unmarried men and although some of them eventually married, the foreign population of Shanghai (and other treaty ports) remained largely bachelor societies with all-men's clubs that barred women, except for an annual ladies' night[2] (figure 6.1). A distinctive part of this segment of society was the bachelor mess of small residential clubs where bachelors planned their own meals and where new residents were admitted only by the unanimous consent of the members.[3] While Western women in Shanghai were few in number, Chinese women were more numerous, but those from wealthier classes were secluded.

The American businessman Carl Crow (born in Missouri in 1883) lived in Shanghai from 1911 until his forcible eviction in 1937. His book, originally entitled *400 Million Customers* (1937), but later reprinted as *Foreign Devils*

Figure 6.1. Foreign passengers claiming baggage on the waterfront at Shanghai in 1907. At that time, the overwhelming number of foreign entrepreneurs coming to Shanghai were men. The number of women from Europe and North America in Shanghai increased by the 1930s. (Copyright 1907 by H. C. White Co. Library of Congress Prints and Photographs Division, Washington, DC.)

in the Flowery Kingdom (1940), is a record of the commercial perspective of foreigners in Shanghai during this period. It also reflects the racial biases that Americans brought to Shanghai. Crow described marriages of Western men with lower-class Chinese women as producing "the unfortunate Eurasian" who was "generally looked on as a social outcast, a stigma that he must pass on to his children."[4] The fathers of most first-generation Eurasians in Shanghai were British and, to a lesser extent, Americans.

Prior to the 1930s, anti-foreign feelings among the Chinese combined with the colonialist mentalities among Europeans and Americans to impede the development of interracial relationships in East Asia. The two groups remained largely separate, with the Chinese known as Shanghainese and the foreigners as Shanghailanders.⁵ While traditional Chinese culture continued and was manifested in the great Buddhist temple of Loong Wah (figure 6.2), other Shanghainese were introduced to foreign culture through the orphanages and schools established by the Christian missionaries (figure 6.3). However, the large number of unmarried Western males on the China coast eventually attracted unmarried women from Europe and North America. Young women came to the cites on China's coast, particularly as tourists or in search of work as nurses, secretaries, or beauticians, and many of them found husbands. A 1925 census indicated that in a total Shanghai population of over

Figure 6.2. The Longhua (*Loong Wah*) 龍華 Buddhist Pagoda and Temple in southwest Shanghai. This Pagoda is an octagonal, seven-story structure of wood and brick that dates from the Three Dynasties period (238–251). The temple is famous for its peaches whose blossoms attract visitors in the spring. 1900. (Library of Congress Prints and Photographs Division, Washington, DC.)

Figure 6.3. Orphans and teachers at Jesuit Orphanage, T'ou-se-we at Zi-ka-wei (Xujiahui) (see Shanghai map). B. W. Kilburn Company, ca. 1901. (Library of Congress Prints and Photographs Division, Washington, DC.)

2.5 million people, 1.1 million lived under foreign administration in the foreign settlements, although only 3.3 percent of the residents were foreigners.[6]

As colonialism began to fade, some of the more daring people began to cross color lines and challenge social barriers. Although miscegenation still had negative connotations in America and Europe as well as in China, China became an exciting place and adventurous people on both sides of this racial divide in East Asia were falling in love in new ways that were considered scandalous, if not illegal, in their native lands. The 1930s were a breakthrough period for these new relationships and no Chinese city was more open to racial blending than Shanghai. However, while historical circumstances brought some interracial couples together, these same circumstances also worked to divide other couples. In the case of Emily Hahn and Zau

Sinmay (Shao Xunmei 邵洵美), the cultural excitement, the sexual attraction, and the romantic love that united them eventually faded in the face of the momentous historical events that separated them.

II.

Emily Hahn (Ding Meili 頂美麗) (1905–1997) was a woman who thrived on being a daring eccentric, on meeting socially marginalized types of people, and writing witty essays about her visits to faraway places. She was a prolific author of over fifty works in a range of genres, from fiction and nonfiction to children's and travel literature. She was born in St. Louis to Isaac and Hannah Hahn, a family of nonobservant Jews with six children whose ancestors had immigrated from Germany in the mid-nineteenth century. Apart from her businessman father and one brother, it was a family of six independent women who frequently disagreed with one another. Hahn was nicknamed "Mickey" because of her resemblance to an Irish comic book character.[7] In her youth she was described as "not boy-minded, and well-padded with puppy fat" and the "chubby and serious" girl in the family. However, in other ways she was a fairly typical young girl who was very conscious of her appearance, and she later grew into an attractive woman.[8] She delighted in breaking social barriers and scandalizing people, but she was independent in the bourgeois rather than revolutionary sense. She was an independent woman who rejected the feminist label. Like her mother Hannah and her sisters, she was headstrong and prone to go her own way.[9]

Although St. Louis was a very Southern town, the family's Jewish roots made them less inclined to engage in Southern racial prejudice. When the family moved to Chicago, she became interested in art, but her parents forced her to go to the University of Wisconsin at Madison where she could have a more practical major. Mickey displayed her individuality by being the first woman to enroll in the mining engineering program, although she later showed little occupational interest in working as an engineer.[10] She was an attractive and gregarious exhibitionist who had a passion for traveling to faraway places and in meeting unusual people.[11] While still an undergraduate, Mickey and a female housemate made an adventuresome trip to the American Southwest in 1924. Her housemate's father bought them a Model T Ford for $290.[12] After a sixteen-hundred-mile trip lasting for seventeen days, they reached Albuquerque where Mickey's uncle lived.[13] From July 11 to 24 they visited Los Angeles, but then returned to Albuquerque and finally went back to Chicago.

The trip stoked her interest in socially marginal types of people like writers, actors, and homosexuals. Travel provided escape from her misery working at an engineering job in St. Louis. She returned to Santa Fe to work as a part-time "Harvey Girl" tour guide. These were the early twentieth-century versions of "Hooters Girls" who were chosen for their looks as much as for their other skills.[14] She appears to have been a "fag hag" (a heterosexual woman whose closest friends include male homosexuals) in Santa Fe. When she later was living in New York and becoming disillusioned and considering a return to Santa Fe, a reporter friend dissuaded her and argued that it would be better for her to concentrate on her writing because: "What would I do out there [in New Mexico] anyway but play around with a lot of fairies?"[15]

When her parents offered to pay for graduate school, she moved to New York where her sister Helen lived. She enrolled at Columbia University and for two semesters taught geology part-time at the Hunter College for Women. Hahn had mixed feelings about New York. She thrived on meeting socially marginal types of people, but she was frustrated by her failure to gain traction as a writer, and she worried about her precarious financial situation. The presence of her sister Helen in New York helped, although Helen was in the process of divorcing her husband and Hahn became involved in that domestic drama by testifying at the divorce proceedings. She became friends with a number of artists as well as writers and editors who encouraged her to write and helped her to sell a few pieces, but she was skeptical about surviving on her writing.[16]

III.

Hahn became excited by the Harlem Renaissance (Black cultural awakening) which in 1925 was in full swing.[17] Interest in Black culture grew and being Black (or even slightly colored) became fashionable. The white impresario Carl Van Vechten (1880–1964) was a great patron of the Harlem Renaissance who promoted the image of negroes as "exotic" people. He took numerous photographic portraits of Black entertainers and cultural figures, particularly of Black men with whom he had numerous homosexual relationships, although he was twice married to women.[18] Hahn had met Van Vechten in Taos and she attended several of his celebrated mixed race parties at his apartment in New York.[19] She participated in "Harlemania" by following the white crowd that took the "A" train uptown to Harlem, visiting the Jim Crow speakeasies along 133rd Street and dancing the Charleston. The Cotton Club at 142nd St and Lennox Avenue offered a scene of tribal rites in an imitation jungle clearing with African drums and sculpture and vegetation.[20] While the patrons were white, the dancers and jazz musicians who entertained the patrons were Black.

Van Vechten became a white impresario of Black art who fueled the Harlem Renaissance as a publicist and dealmaker. He helped struggling Black workers find employment and helped Black artists such as the poet Langston Hughes and the singer Paul Robeson to get publicity and sometimes he helped them financially.[21] There was another side to the Harlem Renaissance. The Black historian Henry Louis Gates, Jr., famously said that it "was surely as gay as it was black."[22] Some Blacks were suspicious of Van Vechten's motives. The poet Countee Cullen thought he was interested in Black people for sex and music and to promote his own profile. These suspicious grew when Van Vechten published the melodramatic novel *Nigger Heaven* (1925). The term was commonly used for the Black balcony seating section of a racially segregated theater, but the term was loaded with emotional meaning and many Blacks felt Van Vechten's use of it crossed a line in offensiveness.[23]

Hahn, encouraged by her brother-in-law Mitchell Dawson, began submitting articles to a new literary magazine called the *New Yorker* that had been founded in 1925 by the editor Harold Ross. Hahn's first article appeared in 1929 in the form of a 550-word piece entitled "Lovely Lady" which related a lunchtime conversation between two women in New York.[24] It was the beginning of Hahn's lifetime relationship with the *New Yorker*. Over the years, Ross became not only a mentor and employer, but also one of Hahn's best friends.[25]

In 1928, Hahn made her first trip to Europe as a research assistant to a date-turned-roommate named Davey Loth who was doing research on the poets Robert and Elizabeth Barrett Browning.[26] After spending time in Florence, Hahn went alone to Paris to see John Gunther. She had known Gunther since he had visited her family home in Chicago in 1923 in an unsuccessful effort to marry Hahn's sister Helen.[27] He later became a foreign correspondent in Europe and wrote the best-seller *Inside Europe*.

The stock market crash of October 1929 did not affect Hahn as much as her professional frustration and personal unhappiness depressed her. There was a history of depression and suicide in her family, which contributed to her attempted suicide with an overdose of sleeping pills.[28] She made a second trip to Europe with David Low, this time to London where, once again, her fag-hag sympathies emerged and she associated with a group of homosexual art students and ballet dancers.[29] Restless and unwilling to live in the United States, she again departed for London, borrowing enough money to fulfill her dream of visiting Africa in 1931. She was exhilarated by the challenge of visiting Africa as a single woman. A friend named Patrick Putnam, who worked for the Red Cross in the Belgium Congo, invited her to visit him. She bought a third-class ticket, departing from the French port of Bordeaux and going to

Dakar, the capital of Senegal on the west coast of Africa.[30] She traveled in a steamboat to Stanleyville (now Kisangani). The Belgian consul informed her that Putnam had been transferred to Penge, a village two hundred miles northeast of Stanleyville.[31]

She finally found Putnam and enjoyed his hospitality, helping him at the clinic and learning a local dialect of Swahili. However, her simplistic and romanticized images of Africa were shaken when she realized that he had three African wives.[32] Miscegenation was common in the Belgian Congo where African woman were eager for the social status and economic benefits of living with a white man. Hahn was naïve and shocked when she found Putnam brutally punishing one of his wives for infidelity. She revised her opinion of him, now seeing him as "an opportunist in an altruist's clothing."[33] She soon departed in disgust with a pigmy guide, her pet baboon Angelique, and twelve porters, walking 250 miles over eighteen days in an easterly direction toward Uganda.[34] After arriving at the eastern shore of Lake Tanganyika, she was able to take a train six hundred miles to Dar es Salaam on the Indian Ocean where in January of 1933 she boarded a ship to London. Before publishing the journal of her journey, she had to rewrite part of *Congo Solo: Misadventures Two Degrees North* (1933) to obscure the identity of Patrick Putnam.[35] However, in the novel *With Naked Foot* (1934), she criticized the exploitive nature of Black-white and male-female relationships in colonial Africa by writing about an African concubine who was dominated by several white "masters" including Putnam who was thinly disguised as a well-intentioned American schoolteacher.

In London, Hahn began a doomed relationship with Edwin (Eddie) Mayer, a playwright and Hollywood screenwriter who had once dated Hahn's sister Helen.[36] Mayer later contacted Hahn in New York. He was a thirty-seven-year-old New Yorker with only a grade-school education, but an ambition to succeed as a writer. He was gregarious, dapper, and liked to party. He drank too much and was estranged from his first wife. Initially, Hahn was not attracted to him, but as he spent money on her and bought her gifts, she fell in love. It was a turbulent relationship. When they moved together to England, Hahn enrolled in a graduate-level program in anthropology at Oxford. Her informal American ways clashed with British formality. She befriended an African student and together they were referred to on campus as "the woman and the nigger."[37] After returning to the United States, Mickey flew from New York to Los Angeles to attempt a reconciliation with Mayer, but the relationship disintegrated.

IV.

In 1935 while Han Suyin was traveling from Beijing to Brussels via the Trans-Siberian railway, Hahn crossed the Pacific Ocean to Asia. She was on the rebound from the soured love affair with Mayer. In an effort to recapture an earlier period of happiness, she decided to return by way of the Pacific Ocean to the Belgian Congo where she had lived in 1930 to 1932.[38] She joined her sister Helen, whose marriage was disintegrating, in booking first-class passage on a passenger liner, the *Chichibu Maru*, out of San Francisco bound for Shanghai. However, after two weeks at sea, the Japanese captain announced that the ship would not be going to Shanghai. Instead, it docked in Yokohama, Japan, and after three weeks they proceeded on to Shanghai in far less glamorous style on "a dirty little tub of a mail carrier."[39]

Because of the silt, they disembarked in April onto a steamer several miles downriver from Shanghai and navigated between junks and houseboats on the Whangpoo (*Huangpu* 黃浦) River to arrive at a dock near the Bund (*Huangpunan lu* 黃浦灘路). The foreign-inspired architecture of the Bund stood in stark contrast to the native architecture of Shanghai (figures 6.4, 6.5, and 6.6). The origins of the term "Bund" (quay) was an Anglo-Indian word and reflected the strong foreign presence.[40] Although in the 1930s Shanghai was one of the most exciting and sophisticated cities in the world, Hahn did not arrive with any romantic images of China. She had left orderly

Figure 6.4. View of the center portion of the "Bund," Shanghai, with its strikingly Westernized structures, including the Palace Hotel, the Chartered Bank of India, Australia & China, and the North China Daily News, ca. 1915. (Library of Congress Prints and Photographs Division, Washington, DC.)

Figure 6.5. North end of the Bund, Shanghai, ca. 1915, linking to the Garden Bridge (Waibaidu Bridge) over Suzhou Creek into the Hongkew (Hongkou) district. (Carpenter Collection. Library of Congress Prints and Photographs Division, Washington, DC.)

Japan with reluctance and her first impression of Shanghai was that it was "vulgar" and "loud." She said: "China is garish, China is red and gold and big, everything I don't like."[41] Initially, she was only indulging her sister's wish to visit Shanghai before returning to Africa. However, she soon became enamored of the city and when her sister left a few weeks later to return to the United States, Hahn stayed because, as she said: "Of all the cities of the world [Shanghai] is the town for me."[42] Another reason for staying was her relationship with a charismatic and handsome Chinese author named Zao Sinmay (Shao Xunmei 邵洵美) (1906–1968).

Hahn had a gregarious nature that soon warmed to the intense socializing of Shanghai life. She arrived at a transition point in Shanghai's history when Chinese and foreigners began to mix on a much greater scale. She found work writing feature stories on women's affairs at the *North-China Daily News*, although she left it after a year because she hated office jobs with regular hours.[43] In contrast to the American newspapers, this British-owned newspaper focused almost entirely on the social life of "Caucasian groups who could be considered sufficiently upper-class."[44] With her outgoing American exuberance and informality, she cultivated friendships with a wide range of foreigners and Chinese. She "loved" garden parties at the wealthy estates on Hungjao (Hongzhao) Road where they kept horses, and she could be photographed wearing a long dress and wide-brimmed hat.[45]

She enjoyed sitting in the box of the fabulously wealthy Sir Victor Sassoon at the Shanghai Race Club. The Sassoons were the most famous family in

Figure 6.6. Chinese native quarter, Shanghai. Bain News Service, between ca. 1920 and ca. 1925. (Library of Congress Prints and Photographs Division, Washington, DC.)

the Sephardic Jewish community of Shanghai.[46] Elias David Sassoon had been the first member of this community to go to Shanghai in 1844 where he expanded his father's trading network beyond Baghdad and Bombay to include Hong Kong, Shanghai, and other Asian ports, dealing with silk, tea, and opium. His descendant Victor Sassoon had been educated at Cambridge and arrived in Shanghai in 1931.[47] He became very wealthy through international commerce, particularly from the opium trade from India to China. He later diversified into industry and real estate, becoming highly respectable. He was extravagant und unpredictable. He had flown in the Royal Air Force in World War I until a plane crash left him with a limp. The war-time poet Siegfried Sassoon was his cousin. Victor Sassoon lived a very active social life and was one of the few wealthy Shanghai foreigners who enjoyed mixing socially with Chinese women.

Hahn's social consciousness was very middle-class American in the sense of having an awareness of class differences but feeling confident about her ability to maneuver through them. She worried about money, but she somehow found the sums she needed to travel and reside abroad. She was not filled with revolutionary resentment or fervor to change the class structure. She distinguished in the foreign population in Shanghai between the *taipans* (wealthy foreign merchants, such as Victor Sassoon), on one hand, who were knowledgeable about China and whose "brains" enabled them to be successful and, on the other hand, the middlemen who drove her "nuts" with their colonialist attitudes and their nearsighted obsession with profit.[48] She gave a classic characterization of a typical member of the latter group: "He was the one who talked a little too loud, ate a little too much, and knew nothing."

Hahn grew to know Shanghai by accompanying the peripatetic Shao Xunmei on his many activities. Her relationship with Shao led her to try to speak Chinese, an effort that distinguished her from most expatriates then living in Shanghai. Most expatriates avoided trying to speak Chinese because it exposed their deficiencies. But like other expatriates, she relied on a foreign currency that enabled her to live a lifestyle far beyond what would have been possible in the United States. The Chinese currency was undergoing hyperinflation and rice was very cheap in Shanghai in 1935, and that meant cheap labor.[49]

V.

Shao Xunmei was born into a nouveau riche family that had only recently gained prominence. He described his grandfather as a late nineteenth-century ambassador to the court of the Russian czar.[50] His father, said to have been a former governor of Taiwan and a mayor of Shanghai, smoked opium and squandered large amounts of money on poor investments. Shao was a favored son who had an indulgent upbringing. In 1923, at the age of seventeen, he was wearing a purple tweed suit, driving a red sports car, and enjoying Shanghai's nightlife with a beautiful actress. He inherited a fortune but lost most of it a few years later.[51] Gangsters saw opportunity and had him jailed until his family paid a ransom.

In an attempt to change Shao's ways, his family sent him to Europe where he enrolled at the University of Cambridge and met the poet Xu Zhimo, apparently in 1923 just before Xu returned to China. Instead of studying political economy, he polished his English and absorbed current trends in Western literature. Although he never engaged in politics, he was very knowledgeable about it and he broadened Hahn's interests from purely artistic concerns and high culture—at that time Hahn proudly claimed that she had "never voted"—to become informed about the political situation in contemporary China.[52] When Shao returned from England to China in 1926, a marriage was arranged with his cousin Zoa and together they gave birth to nine children. Shao retained his extravagant ways, and his good looks made him a highly attractive figure to both Chinese and foreign women in Shanghai. According to the famous writer Lu Xun, Shao was "renowned for his manly beauty."[53]

Part of the Shanghai sophisticated culture of the 1930s included opium smoking, and Shao became the medium of Hahn's addiction. Shao and Hahn seem to have met at a dinner party given by Bernadine Fritz, an American patron of drama whose parties were known settings where foreigners could meet intriguing Chinese people.[54] There was some outrage when Hahn and Shao left abruptly after the meal ended. In an adventure with long-term consequences, Hahn and several Chinese climbed into Shao's brown Nash automobile which he drove to his home. The house was located in an unstylish neighborhood in Yangtszepoo (*Yangzipu* 楊樹浦), north of Soochow (*Suzhou*) Creek and across the Garden Bridge (*Waibaidujiao* 外白渡橋), several miles to the east out in an area near the Japanese shipping wharves on the Whangpoo (Huangpu) River. Shao lived there with his wife in a Victorian redbrick house filled with relatives, children, and servants.

Upstairs, Shao and his guests settled into a comfortable bedroom with sofas, chairs, and pillows on the floor. On one of the sofas was a silver tray with an oil lamp, small boxes, and utensils. Hahn watched as Shao prepared the lumpy brown opium in a pipe which he smoked, producing a caramel-like odor. When he offered the pipe to Hahn, she took it without hesitation. Although hundreds of drug traffickers had been executed in the years 1932 to 1935, foreigners were largely exempt from Chinese law. Soon several pipes of opium became part of Hahn's daily routine. As she spent increasing amounts of time with the Shaos, her opium consumption increased, depressing her appetite and causing a loss of weight.[55] Her dress size sixteen dropped precipitously. She suffered from jaundice, her stomach cramps increased, and she stopped menstruating.

Shao was intimately familiar with a wide range of people in Shanghai. He was a writer with a broad circle of Westernized Chinese literary friends in the

Shanghai-Nanjing area which included Lin Yutang. He followed Xu Zhimo in rejecting the classical literary tradition for new verse forms in the vernacular.[56] Shao was also a publisher who had invested a large part of his inherited wealth in purchasing an elaborate printing press that included a rotogravure (photogravure).[57] This press was commonly used in newspaper photo features and in printing magazines, postcards, and stamps. Shao printed a wide range of materials, including obscure collections of poems written by him and his friends, Chinese translations of pirated Western novels and nonfiction works, innovative magazines, the famous humor magazine *Analects* which played on the works of Confucius, and pornography.

Shao and Hahn collaborated in producing a bilingual Chinese-English magazine called *Vox*, which they were forced to discontinue after three issues in 1936.[58] This was followed by a second collaborative effort in which they produced a magazine with separate Chinese and English editions. The English edition was called *Candid Comment*, while the Chinese edition was given a title that meant "Free Speech."[59] Their original plan to produce identical editions in translation had to be adapted to the practical realities of technical and economic factors and consequently the two editions were limited to using the same chief leader and many of the same articles, but differed in format, illustrations, and other ways. Hahn noticed that educated Chinese tended to be good draftsmen because Chinese training in calligraphy developed a manual dexterity that Westerners lacked. Hahn depended on Shao to make English translations of the Chinese articles.

As someone who saw no reason "why white people should not marry Negroes," Hahn was slow to realize that similar racial prejudice existed in China toward "Eurasians."[60] In Shanghai she met Grace Brady, a woman who reflected a widespread negative attitude toward racial intermarriage. Her brother had married a Chinese woman, and Grace was embarrassed by the mixed blood of their children. Hahn was surprised to find that "the China Coaster attitude toward Eurasians" was similar to American attitudes toward Negroes. They "feel about Eurasians as our own Southerners do about mulattoes."[61] Since Hahn was having an affair with Shao and would marry him as his second wife, she clearly did not share those attitudes, although she admitted that most people felt differently.

There were degrees of Westernization among Shanghai Chinese, and Shao clearly remained grounded on the Chinese side. According to Hahn, the British were more frightened of the Communists than of the Chinese. Japanese, on the other hand, were viewed by the British as more reliable. Japanese were allowed in the Shanghai Club while the Chinese were excluded. Lao She had noted in the *Two Ma's* that "among the yellow race, the Japanese are a tad more esteemed."[62] Except for short trips, Shao never left Shanghai, even when it later fell to the Communists in 1949. His politics were somewhat ambiguous. Hahn described him as a "fire-eater" who wrote editorials for radical newspapers and yet he was slow to turn on Chiang Kai-shek until he finally grew disgusted with the Generalissimo's appeasement of the Japanese.[63] Shao's cultural loyalties were revealed in his attitude toward dancing. While many young Chinese joined the dancing crowd at the newly built, glamorous Park Hotel on Bubbling Well Road (Jingansilu靜安 寺路) and aped Westerners in giving parties in the open rather than in hired private dining rooms of restaurants, Shao would not join them. He refused to dance—he only did things that he could do well and he was "too short for dancing."[64] It is probably not coincidental to their compatibility that Hahn was herself relatively small by Western standards and quite similar in height to most Chinese women.

Shao liked Hahn's flat because of its convenient location in the heart of Shanghai where he could meet friends and use the phone. Sometimes he brought his favorite brother, Huan, who had been educated in Paris. Huan was sweet but not very bright and later became a good "guerrilla general."[65] Shao had hundreds of friends, and Hahn became close with some of them who spoke English and were fond of America or England. Among them was Lin Yutang who was editing the Chinese humorous weekly called the *Lunyu* 論語 (*Analects*), a title that played on the famous work of the same name by Confucius. Lin was popular among the Chinese literati, and Pearl Buck was encouraging him to write his first book in English.[66] This group of writers was engaged in a new project to produce a monthly magazine in English entitled *Tian Hsia*天下 (Everything under the Sky). Shao contributed some pieces, and Hahn wrote articles and book reviews for the magazine.

When the Japanese invasion of Shanghai began in 1937, Shao and his wife Zoa and their children stubbornly remained in their house in Yangtzepoo until the violence made that area dangerous.[67] They hastily evacuated in an old Ford belonging to Shao's father and drove to his ancestral home in the French Concession and then moved into a cramped one-room apartment. The Japanese allowed Hahn as a white expatriate to make several trips to Shao's house in Yangtzepoo to retrieve household goods, some of which had been looted and needlessly smashed. Although Hahn was not allowed to bring Chinese coolies to help, ten Russian workmen were permitted. They loaded Shao's furniture into a truck and transported them to Shao's family in Frenchtown (the French Concession). On a second trip they removed Shao's collection of books, most of which were valuable Ming editions. The Japanese stopped her at Garden Bridge, but with the help of a British police interpreter, she was able to pass through. In order to avoid the Japanese confiscation of Shao's printing press, Hahn became the official owner. To avoid the bombing of Japanese planes, Hahn moved to a bungalow on Avenue Joffre (*Yuchanglu*

宇昌路) in the French Concession and was joined by the Shaos who found an empty cottage in the same group of houses.

Hahn was eccentric in several ways. She became famous for keeping gibbons as household pets—a practice she acquired in Africa. When Shao suggested that she marry him as a second wife, she demurred but only for a while. The idea had presumably come from Shao's wife Zoa who said it would legalize the question of Hahn's ownership of Shao's press.[68] A relationship to the Shao family would also strengthen her expatriate legal status. But the offer also seems to have been based on genuine affection between Shao and Hahn, affection which at some point had become a love affair. The Chinese legal status of marriage was somewhat ambiguous and, according to foreign law, Shao and his first wife Zoa were not even married. Shao's children already referred to Hahn as "Foreign Mother," and he proposed that she legally adopt one of his children, other than his favorite son. Shao promised that at her death, she would be buried in the family graveyard at Yuyao. After thinking about Shao's offer, she signed an agreement in his attorney's office declaring her his wife "according to Chinese law." Other collaborations followed. For a time, Shao and his brother Huan, who was active in the anti-Japanese resistance, set up a transmitter in Hahn's back bedroom. As a foreigner, she provided excellent cover, although the danger was great and the transmitter was moved after a month or two.[69]

Wartime conditions and the effects of the Japanese occupation on Shanghai are described in a journal by the British authors W. H. Auden and Christopher Isherwood who were in Shanghai from May 25 to June 12, 1938. They described the impressive warships in the Huangpu River and the large buildings on the Bund as the mere "façade of a great city."[70] While international businessmen were able to find everything to satisfy their desires, most of the native populace suffered. The International Settlement and the French Concession formed an isolated island in the middle of the Japanese-occupied city.[71] In the makeshift factories that relocated from Hongkew to two or three rooms in the International Settlement, the child workers already had the blue line in their gums that was symptomatic of lead poisoning.[72]

VI.

Shao Xunmei played an important role in the creation of Hahn's most famous book *The Soong Sisters* (1941). In 1938 her friend John Gunther, who had written the best-selling *Inside Asia* (1936), recommended her to a publisher as a potential author of a biography of the Soong sisters.[73] Hahn was interested, but not very knowledgeable about the Soongs. Nevertheless, her financial situation was becoming desperate because of a dispute with an editor at the *New Yorker* which disrupted the payments for her contributions to the magazine. She had her own house to pay for and she was lending money to the Shaos. Shao was churning out three detective novels each month, but the income from them did not cover his extravagant spending habits. His wife Zoa was reduced to selling her jade and diamond jewelry. As a result, the advance payment and royalties from writing a biography on the Soongs were attractive.

Hahn had met Soong Ailing 宋靄齡 (1888–1973), one of the three Soong (Song) sisters, at a reception at the Shanghai house of Ailing and her husband Dr. H. H. Kung (Kong Xiangxi 孔祥熙, 1881–1967), the American-educated finance minister to Chiang Kai-shek. She had also met Agnes Smedley who was rumored to be the private secretary of the second sister Soong Qingling 宋清齡 (1893–1981) (Madame Sun Yat-sen), but she had never had any contact with the third sister Soong Meiling 宋美齡 (1898–2003) (Madame Chiang Kai-shek).[74] Because Hahn felt she needed to obtain the Soong sisters' permission before writing the book, she sent individual letters to each of the Soong sisters. Both Madame Sun and Madame Chiang were too busy to get involved, but Madame Kung was attracted to Hahn's desire to write a "truthful book."[75] Her willingness to consider the project had been fostered by her wish to set the record straight after John Gunther's unfavorable portrait of her in *Inside Asia*. Gunther had described her as "a hard-willed creature, possessed of demonic energy and great will-to-power, violently able, cunning, and ambitious."[76]

Shao was enthusiastic about the project and provided crucial guidance by suggesting that she focus on making initial contact with Soong Ailing. He spoke with his aunt who was a long-time friend of Ailing and who made inquiries. Because of the war with Japan, Soong Ailing was then living in Hong Kong. In June of 1939, Shao and Hahn traveled together by boat to Hong Kong where Shao had many Chinese friends. Although Shao had spent two years studying at Cambridge and felt a strong sense of loyalty to the institution of Cambridge, he disliked the British colonialists.[77] They stayed in the Hong Kong Hotel where Shao startled the Westernized Chinese as he moved through the lobby in his traditional long brown Chinese robe, chatting with Hahn.[78]

Hong Kong was filled with friends and former classmates of Zhao who had left Shanghai.[79] The Chinese viewed Hong Kong as a nicer but more expensive version of Shanghai. However, waiting for Madame Kung and partying with Shao's friends did not fill enough of Hahn's time, particularly since her Chinese language skills often could not keep up with their conversations. Consequently, she started contacting some of the English-speaking people who populated the British colony.

Unlike "delightful and wicked" Shanghai, Hong Kong was "slow and peaceful."[80] In Hong Kong the Brits played a lot of golf and spent vacuous evenings drinking and playing bridge. They staged amateur plays two or three times a year. For the most part, they did not mix with the Chinese, and Hahn found them boring. However, wartime conditions had caused an influx of more interesting Chinese and foreigners fleeing from northern places like Shanghai and Beijing. It was among this group that Hahn met some fascinating people, such as the young Australian Ian Morrison, a correspondent for the London *Times* who later had an affair with Han Suyin. Morrison's father was an old China hand who was said to have had a street in Beijing named after him. The young Morrison had worked as a secretary to the British ambassador to Tokyo and had walked on the Burma Road prior to its completion. Hahn teased him about his mysteriousness and believed that his contacts amounted to work in British intelligence. A second significant contact was Captain Charles Boxer who Morrison said had been one of the best Japanese language students in Japan. Hahn wanted to meet Boxer and his wife.

Shao became annoyed at Hahn's socializing with the British and felt left out. He hated the British despite fond memories of his two years at Cambridge.[81] He had never expressed those hostile views in Shanghai, and Hahn suspected it was because of the way the British colonialists in Hong Kong shunned the Chinese. In any case, Hahn and Shao suddenly had two sought-after engagements. One was a long-awaited meeting with Madame Kung. The second was a luncheon hosted by Captain Boxer at the Café de Chine, the newest restaurant in Hong Kong. Boxer wanted to introduce his young wife who had made Boxer read all Hahn's articles. At the luncheon Boxer was very sociable and went back and forth between the two tables shouting "*Ganbei!*" 乾杯 (bottoms up) and proceeded to get drunk.[82] He told Hahn that anyone who lived in Hong Kong for more than four years either became an alcoholic or married, and he did both. Shao said Boxer was a "real gentleman" and that he had a wonderful collection of books. One wonders when the attraction between Hahn and Boxer began that would eventually lead to their marriage.

Finally, the day of Hahn's appointment with Soong Ailing arrived and Shao helped Hahn overcome an anxiety attack, accompanying her to the meeting. Madame Kung's house was located on Sassoon Road and built in the grand Hong Kong style on a steep bluff overlooking the ocean, surrounded by terraces and tennis courts. At the entrance, they were met by a smiling houseboy and two husky bodyguards.[83] The meeting went well, and Shao's aunt was present and had been able to cultivate a favorable attitude in Soong Ailing prior to the meeting. It was agreed that Hahn would come back to Hong Kong in the autumn to begin work on the book. After the meeting, Shao assured the much-relieved Hahn that Madame Kung liked her. Hahn blurted out impulsively "well I love her" and said she never changed her mind about that.[84] Hahn and Shao returned to Shanghai in August 1939. Later Hahn came back on a second trip to Hong Kong during which she saw Madame Kung only twice.[85] The rest of their contacts were made through mail.

After returning to Shanghai with Shao, Hahn realized that she would have to cure her opium addiction in order to undertake a book on the Soongs. When she saw a physician, she confessed that she was smoking twelve pipes of opium each day.[86] The physician advised her to check into a clinic. She was particularly upset when he told her that her addiction would prevent her from ever having a child. When she learned about a German doctor who ran a clinic for opium addicts, Shao urged her to check into it. She entered the clinic in late 1939 and suffered withdrawal symptoms that included severe cramping in her legs. When Shao visited her, she was struck for the first time how the opium smoking had stained his teeth and clouded his eyes. She was amazed at how she had regained the ability to taste and smell her food. Shao also expressed the desire to stop using opium but was unsuccessful. When Hahn left Shanghai in the fall of 1939, she thought she would be back in three months. Shao was reluctantly overseeing the care of her pet gibbons in her house on Avenue Joffre. In fact, she would not see Shao for several years and she would never return to Shanghai again.

VII.

Time would show that the love affair between Emily Hahn and Shao Xunmei was inseparable from the period and setting of Shanghai in the 1930s. The unique conditions of Shanghai brought Hahn and Shao together in 1935 and later caused their love affair to languish after 1939. During their first visit to Hong Kong in the spring of 1939 to discuss a book on the Soong sisters, it had been agreed with Soong Ailing that Hahn would return in the fall to Hong Kong for an extended stay and for a visit to Soong Meiling (Madame Chiang Kai-shek) in the wartime capital of Chongqing. In her preparation for writing the book, Hahn collected information on the scandals associated with the Soong family. The scandals were difficult to trace because although they were vast, they were also "nebulous" and based on rumors that were difficult to document.[87] When she returned to Hong Kong, she found Soong Ailing "generous" with sharing information both in conversations and in allowing her to make abstracts of family documents.[88] Unfortunately, numerous documents had become inaccessible after the Japanese took over the Kung estate in Shanxi province.

As for the other two Soong sisters, Meiling sent an informal invitation to Hahn for a future visit to Chongqing.[89] However, Qingling would not make a similar commitment. She was distressed in receiving the "highly colored details" of Hahn's life because she was modest about sexual matters.[90] Nevertheless, her mind was not completely closed to assisting Hahn.

Ailing gave Hahn a helpful tip, suggesting that she book a table at the dining room of the Hong Kong Hotel to watch the three Soong sisters having a rare dinner together. Qingling was still suspicious of Hahn, whose nickname was Mickey. When Hahn was dancing with her escort, Qingling commented to Ailing: "There's Mickey Hahn. I suppose that's Mickey Mouse she's with?"[91]

In order to interview Madame Chiang Kai-shek (Soong Meiling), Ailing arranged for Hahn to take the seven-hundred-mile flight to Chongqing. Chongqing was the site of the Chinese wartime capital where the Nationalists had withdrawn in order to move beyond the reach of the Japanese army, though not the Japanese warplanes which attempted to bomb the city on a daily basis. The most secure form of travel between Hong Kong and Chongqing was by air on DC-3 aircraft, and Madame Kung secured a precious ticket for Hahn on one of the flights, despite a long waiting list. Finally in December 1939 one of Madame Kung's burly detectives accompanied Hahn to the plane which departed from Kai Tak Airport at night in order to avoid Japanese anti-aircraft shelling.[92]

The plane landed unceremoniously in Chongqing on a "sandspit," a runway of sand projecting into a body of water from which a wooden pathway led them to sedan chairs to go through customs.[93] Chongqing was a makeshift wartime capital, seemingly composed of cardboard buildings. The city was wet, muddy, dark, and foggy, and the buildings were insufficiently heated.[94] The surrounding countryside was lush and green and very fertile. During most of the year it was beset by fog which, fortuitously, helped to keep Japanese bombers away.[95] It was a place where flowers proliferated, including roses that grew all year round.

Soong Meiling made contact with Hahn through her advisor, W. H. Donald (1875–1946), the Australian journalist and well-known advisor to the Generalissimo and Madame Chiang Kai-shek. Hahn had been forewarned that Meiling was less "human" than Ailing, but Hahn found her to be very fond of Ailing and indignant about John Gunther's criticism of her sister.[96] Although she claimed no need for a gushing book about herself, she was quite willing to help counteract "the malicious stories that were being spread over the Kung name."[97] The reference here was to Soong Ailing and her husband Dr. H. H. Kung (Kong Xiangxi), a descendant of Confucius, banker, and politician who together with his brother-in-law T. V. Soong (Song Ziwen 宋子文) were the leading Nationalist economic advisors.

It was during this time that Hahn's relationship with Shao began to unravel.[98] The personalities of Hahn and Shao differed in the sense that she was an American with moveable affiliations while Shao's Chinese personality was anchored in Shanghai. He had not felt comfortable in Hong Kong, and it is doubtful that he would have felt comfortable in Chongqing. He had been instrumental in putting Hahn in contact with the Soongs, but when she wanted him to come with her to Chongqing and help as an interpreter, he refused. His letters lament that she was abandoning Shanghai and her Chinese family, but Hahn was ready to leave Shanghai. In Hong Kong she was able to relax, unlike in Shanghai where after the Japanese took over, a terrorist atmosphere took hold in which people were shot on the street or in restaurants in broad daylight because of any suspected actions against the Nationalist government or the Japanese Army or even a private feud.[99]

After returning from Chongqing to Hong Kong, Hahn bought a return ticket by sea to Shanghai and packed her bags. On the day of her departure, she was saying her goodbyes when Soong Ailing appeared. Ailing surprised Hahn by speaking in a very personal way. She had spoken with Shao's aunt, who was fond of Hahn, and she expressed her concern about her being exploited by Shao. Soong Ailing cautioned that Shao might be taking advantage of her in an unconscious Chinese way. She convinced her not to return to Shanghai, but rather to remain in Hong Kong and return to Chongqing where all three sisters would be gathering. Hahn was so shaken by Madame Kung's suggestion and felt that for once in her life, she had been "knocked off [her] feet."[100] Hahn allowed herself to be persuaded by Madame Kung's "greatness," but one might also wonder if Soong Ailing was also taking advantage of her in an unconscious Chinese way by keeping her in Hong Kong to write a book redeeming her. Perhaps Hahn's decision to stay in Hong Kong was based ultimately on her dawning realization that Shanghai's moment in history had passed.[101]

VIII.

The Soong Sisters was published in 1941 to good reviews and commercial success. At the same time, Hahn was falling in love with Capt. Charles Boxer (1904–2000), a British army intelligence officer stationed in Hong Kong who later became a notable historian of Portuguese and Dutch overseas expansion. When they first met, Boxer was married, but the childless marriage disintegrated and Hahn and Boxer had an affair out of which Hahn gave birth to a daughter, Carola, in October 1941. When the Japanese occupied Hong Kong, Boxer was incarcerated as a war prisoner and Hahn had difficulty surviving, although her situation was ironically improved by claiming marriage to a Chinese national, namely, Shao. She and Carola were finally able to leave Hong Kong in September 1943 and return to the United States.

Hahn's memoir of her experiences in Shanghai, Chongqing, and Hong Kong during the years 1935 to 1943 was published as *China to Me* in 1944. It offended many readers because of her sexual candor in describing her interracial love affair with Shao and adulterous relationship with Boxer as well as her opium addiction. It was also offensive to leftist sympathizers such as Agnes Smedley and Edgar Snow who were trying to present the Chinese Communists in a favorable light and to contrast them with the corrupt and inept Nationalist followers of Chiang Kai-shek.

Hahn believed that this campaign of leftist sympathizers had filled Americans "full of hooey" about the Chinese Communists.[102] She believed that this misinformation was "due to the peculiarity of most American news-papermen in China, who are nearly all of them inclined to be leftist, out of a frustrated sense of guilt, a superior viewpoint of things as they are, and a tendency to follow the crowd—of newspapermen." Journalists had access to Zhou Enlai, who was based in Chongqing, but as a Communist leader, he naturally withheld some information. In fact, Hahn believed that these journalists were as uninformed about the Communists as she was, except that she admitted it. In *China to Me*, Hahn made a mocking reference to the leftist sympathizer Smedley as "the picturesque Agnes."[103] Smedley was incensed about Hahn's comments and was particularly aggressive in criticizing both *The Soong Sisters* and *China to Me*. She ceased speaking to "the bitch Emily Hahn" who had previously befriended her in Hong Kong.[104] *China to Me* was a publishing success, selling twenty-four thousand copies in the first two months after publication and continuing to sell well in 1945.

Soon after the publication of *China to Me*, Shao wrote a nostalgic letter, asking for a copy of the book. He and Zoa had survived the war, although he had aged far beyond his years and "no longer kissed young women."[105] It was a bittersweet attempt to restart their relationship, but the positions of patron and patronized were now reversed as Hahn had moved on. At that moment Hahn was more concerned about whether Boxer had survived the war. Shortly thereafter Boxer surfaced and arrived at Hahn's residence in New York to great publicity. Hahn was a friend of Clare Booth Luce whose husband, Henry Luce, was the publisher of Time-Life publications. Soon after Boxer arrived at Hahn's Manhattan apartment, a *Life* magazine photographer arrived to record the happy reunion of Boxer, Hahn, and their daughter Carola.[106] Boxer and Hahn were married soon thereafter, although the marriage had its ups and downs. Hahn was vulnerable to drugs and a rogue domestic servant helped her become temporarily addicted to morphine.

In 1953 Hahn traveled to East Asia but was unable to obtain a visa for a visit to Shanghai.[107] Shao and his family were still living in the same house on Avenue Joffre (*Yuchanglu* 宇昌路). The Communists had imprisoned him because of his opium addiction. After his rehabilitation, he survived by translating English-language novels and poetry for government publishers. In 1948 he was allowed to travel to New York where he tried, once again, to get Hahn to invest in his business schemes, including a Chinese version of *Life* magazine. In New York in 1948 he appeared much diminished and no longer the charismatic figure of the 1930s. In 1961 he began to suffer from heart problems, and he died in poverty in 1968.

Hahn lived to be ninety-four years of age and died in 1997. It is difficult to know if the relationship between Shao and Hahn might have developed differently if the Sino-Japanese War and Chinese Civil War between the Communists and Nationalists had not intervened. Those wars cast Shanghai into a half-century of obscurity. As late as the 1980s, most of the old buildings remained, but in dilapidated condition and new buildings were only starting to be constructed. Today Shanghai is a revived city and its surviving fragments from the 1930s provide only a shadowy background to the love affair that once existed between Emily Hahn and Shao Xunmei.

NOTES

1. D. E. Mungello, *The Catholic Invasion of China: Remaking Chinese Christianity* (Lanham, MD: Rowman & Littlefield, 2015), 77–87.

2. Carl Crow, *400 Million Customers* (New York: Harper & Brothers, 1937), reprinted as *Foreign Devils in the Flowery Kingdom* (1940; Hong Kong: Earnshaw Books, 2007), 248.

3. Crow, *400 Million Customers*, 249.

4. Crow, *400 Million Customers*, 249–50.

5. Betty Peh-T'i Wei, *Shanghai Crucible of Modern China* (Oxford: Oxford University Press, 1987), 104.

6. Nicholas R. Clifford, *Spoilt Children of Empire: Westerners in Shanghai and the Chinese Revolution of the 1920s* (Hanover, NH: University Press of New England, 1991), 41.

7. Ken Cuthbertson, *Nobody Said Not to Go: The Life, Loves, and Adventures of Emily Hahn* (Boston: Faber and Faber, 1998), 15.

8. Cuthbertson, *Nobody Said Not to Go*, 22.

9. Cuthbertson, *Nobody Said Not to Go*, 26.

10. Cuthbertson, *Nobody Said Not to Go*, 32–33.

11. Cuthbertson, *Nobody Said Not to Go*, 119.

12. Cuthbertson, *Nobody Said Not to Go*, 39.

13. Cuthbertson, *Nobody Said Not to Go*, 40–41.

14. Cuthbertson, *Nobody Said Not to Go*, 49–50.

15. Emily Hahn to Hannah Hahn, July 1, 1928, cited in Cuthbertson, *Nobody Said Not to Go*, 60.

16. Cuthbertson, *Nobody Said Not to Go*, 59.

17. Richard Bruce Nugent, *Gay Rebel of the Harlem Renaissance*, edited by Thomas H. Wirth (Durham, NC: Duke University Press, 2002), 1–2.

18. Nugent, *Gay Rebel of the Harlem Renaissance*, 148.

19. Cuthbertson, *Nobody Said Not to Go*, 57.

20. Edward White, *The Tastemaker: Carl van Vechten and the Birth of Modern America* (New York: Farrar, Straus and Giroux, 2014), 173–74.

21. White, *The Tastemaker*, 186–89.

22. White, *The Tastemaker*, 177.

23. White, *The Tastemaker*, 198–201; Emily Bernard, *Carl von Vechten & the Harlem Renaissance* (New Haven, CN: Yale University Press, 2012), 107–90.

24. Cuthbertson, *Nobody Said Not to Go*, 67–69.

25. Cuthbertson, *Nobody Said Not to Go*, 70–71.

26. Cuthbertson, *Nobody Said Not to Go*, 62–64.

27. Cuthbertson, *Nobody Said Not to Go*, 27–28.

28. Cuthbertson, *Nobody Said Not to Go*, 73–75.

29. Cuthbertson, *Nobody Said Not to Go*, 76.

30. Cuthbertson, *Nobody Said Not to Go*, 85.

31. Cuthbertson, *Nobody Said Not to Go*, 98.

32. Cuthbertson, *Nobody Said Not to Go*, 103.

33. Cuthbertson, *Nobody Said Not to Go*, 106–07.

34. Cuthbertson, *Nobody Said Not to Go*, 114–17.

35. Cuthbertson, *Nobody Said Not to Go*, 121–23.

36. Cuthbertson, *Nobody Said Not to Go*, 120–21.

37. Cuthbertson, *Nobody Said Not to Go*, 127–28.

38. Cuthbertson, *Nobody Said Not to Go*, 127–32.

39. Emily Hahn, *China to Me: A Partial Autobiography* (Garden City, NY: Country Life Press, 1944), 2–3.

40. Clifford, *Spoilt Children of Empire*, 37.

41. Hahn, *China to Me*, 2.

42. Hahn, *China to Me*, 1.

43. Hahn, *China to Me*, 12–13.

44. Hahn, *China to Me*, 6, 8.

45. Hahn, *China to Me*, 13.

46. Wei, 106.

47. Harriet Sergeant, *Shanghai Collision Point of Cultures 1918/1939* (New York: Crown Publishers, 1990), 129–35.

48. Hahn, *China to Me*, 14.

49. Hahn, *China to Me*, 12.

50. Cuthbertson, *Nobody Said Not to Go*, 140–43.

51. Sergeant, *Shanghai Collision Point of Cultures*, 294.

52. Hahn, *China to Me*, 10–11.

53. Lu Xun [Zhou Shuren], "On Seeing Shaw and Those Who Saw Shaw," in *Selected Works*, third edition, translated by Yang Xianyi and Gladys Yang (Beijing: Foreign Language Press, 1980), volume 3, 252.

54. Sergeant, *Shanghai Collision Point of Cultures*, 292.

55. Cuthbertson, *Nobody Said Not to Go*, 165, 175–76.

56. Hahn, *China to Me*, 20, refers to Xi Zhimo as "Hsu Tse-mo" as a famous poet who brought revolutionary ideas to China from France, by which she mistakenly means England.

57. Hahn, *China to Me*, 23.

58. Hahn, *China to Me*, 23–24.

59. Hahn, *China to Me*, 27–28.

60. Hahn, *China to Me*, 28–30.

61. Hahn, *China to Me*, 29.

62. Lao She, *Mr. Ma & Son a Sojourn in London* 二馬。 Bilingual Chinese-English edition, translated by Julie Jimmerson (Beijing: Foreign Language Press, 2001), 127.

63. Hahn, *China to Me*, 17.

64. Hahn, *China to Me*, 41.

65. Hahn, *China to Me*, 15.

66. Hahn, *China to Me*, 16; Hsia, *History of Chinese Fiction*, 132.

67. Hahn, *China to Me*, 47–51.

68. Hahn, *China to Me*, 55–57.

69. Hahn, *China to Me*, 61–63.

70. W. H. Auden and Christopher Isherwood, *Journey to a War* (1939; New York: Paragon House, 1967), 237.

71. Auden and Isherwood, *Journey to a War*, 240.

72. Auden and Isherwood, *Journey to a War*, 245–46.

73. Cuthberston, *Nobody Said Not to Go*, 167–71.

74. Hahn, *China to Me*, 81–82.

75. Hahn, *China to Me*, 83.

76. John Gunther, *Inside Asia* (New York: Harper & Brothers, 1939), 202.

77. Hahn, *China to Me*, 82–87.

78. Hahn, *China to Me*, 84.

79. Hahn, *China to Me*, 84–85.

80. Hahn, *China to Me*, 86.

81. Hahn, *China to Me*, 87.

82. Hahn, *China to Me*, 87–88.

83. Hahn, *China to Me*, 88–91.

84. Hahn, *China to Me*, 91.

85. Hahn, *China to Me*, 94.

86. Cuthbertson, *Nobody Said Not to Go*, 175–76.

87. Hahn, *China to Me*, 95.

88. Hahn, *China to Me*, 99.

89. Hahn, *China to Me*, 100.

90. Hahn, *China to Me*, 101.

91. Hahn, *China to Me*, 154.

92. Hahn, *China to Me*, 110.

93. Hahn, *China to Me*, 113.

94. Hahn, *China to Me*, 113.

95. Hahn, *China to Me*, 130.

96. Hahn, *China to Me*, 122.

97. Hahn, *China to Me*, 123.

98. Hahn, *China to Me*, 136–39.

99. Hahn, *China to Me*, 96.

100. Hahn, *China to Me*, 156.

101. Hahn, *China to Me*, 144, 154–58.

102. Hahn, *China to Me*, 199–200.

103. Hahn, *China to Me*, 82.

104. Cuthbertson, *Nobody Said Not to Go*, 286.

105. Cuthbertson, *Nobody Said Not to Go*, 290–92.

106. Cuthbertson, *Nobody Said Not to Go*, 302–04.

107. Cuthbertson, *Nobody Said Not to Go*, 329–30.

Chapter 7

Interracial Homoeroticism

Robert Winter

I.

After Emily Hahn arrived in Hong Kong on her second visit, Madame Kung (Soong Ailing) promised to get her to the wartime Chinese capital Chongqing without a long delay, although there was a long list of people waiting to fly on the limited number of flights to Sichuan province. Hong Kong was a waystation for expatriates from many lands and during her long wait, Hahn encountered many of them. She had a re-encounter with Ian Morrison, who had just completed a trip through Indochina. She also spent a lot of time with Robert (Bob) Winter (Wen Te 溫特) (1890–1988).[1] Winter was a classic American expatriate who had fled an unhappy life in the United States to become a resident of Beijing and evolved into a member of the "aristocracy of old-timers."[2] He was a knowledgeable but obscure figure who had lived in China since 1923.[3] Hahn described him as "a big man with freakish glands or some other accident of physiology that has prevented him from showing any signs of advancing age."[4]

Winter grew up in Crawfordsville, Indiana, as the ninth child in a family of seven sisters and only one brother. Soon after his birth, his carpenter father died, leaving a struggling family headed by a widow.[5] He grew up fatherless and, later in life, he complained of being surrounded by women in his youth and spoke about wanting to escape them. He attended the local Wabash University where he was deeply influenced by a bright and eccentric teacher, the young poet Ezra Pound, who was only two years older than him. Pound taught Greek at Wabash for a few months before being terminated and replaced as the instructor of the Greek class by Winter himself.[6] After earning a master's degree at Wabash, his restlessness and an emerging homosexuality led to a familiar pattern of escape—in this case to England, to classes at the Sorbonne, and to studies at the University of Naples. He returned to the

United States in 1912 where he felt estranged, in part, because of his "disillusionment" with the acquisitive and materialistic nature of American culture and, in part, because of his hidden homosexual feelings.[7] He taught French and Spanish at a high school in Evanston, Illinois, for three years.

By 1920 Winter had obtained a full-time teaching position at the University of Chicago. He became troubled by American racism in the spring of 1923 when the head of his department told him to "mark down" the examination papers of the Jewish and Black students in his class in order to limit their enrollment numbers.[8] At the Art Institute in Chicago, Winter met and became friends with the poet Wen Yiduo 聞一多.[9] At that point Wen Yiduo was, along with Xu Zhimo, a member of the Chinese literary movement of aesthetes called the Crescent Moon Society. (Later Wen became a Communist supporter and was assassinated by the Nationalist secret police in 1946.)[10] Wen described a China that appealed to Winter. In 1923 when Winter faced a crisis, possibly due to a same-sex relationship, he fled the United States and arrived in Nanjing where he would remain teaching for two years.[11] On the basis of Wen Yiduo's letter to a colleague in China, asking him to use his influence with the president of Qinghua (Tsinghua) University in Beijing, Winter obtained a position at Qinghua and arrived there in 1925.[12] He had a small house where he cultivated an elaborate flower and vegetable garden with pet deer.[13] He returned briefly to the United States in 1928.[14]

At Qinghua Winter became part of the Basic English project led by two scholars from Cambridge University named I. A. Richards and C. K. Ogden.[15] In their attempt to create a universal language of 850 words, Ogdon reduced four thousand verbs to eighteen common verbs and condensed the entire vocabulary and grammatical rules of English to one sheet of paper. In the globalist reaction against the caustic nationalism of World War I, Basic English initially met with enthusiastic success as part of Ogden's and Richard's world federalist vision. It was financially supported by the Rockefeller Foundation as part of an effort to standardize scientific methodology throughout the world.[16] Winter also assisted the scholar R. D. Jameson in his related effort to use Basic English to reorganize China along Western lines. Basic English penetrated Qinghua's teaching of English while Basic texts were accepted for the elementary English classes at Yanjing University, at Catholic University, and at Marist brother institutions in Beijing. However, Basic English met increasing resistance from many Chinese who regarded the vocabulary as a childish form of expression (baby talk).[17]

II.

Beijing in the 1930s was a welcoming and idyllic city for foreign visitors, and it fostered a vibrant small community of expatriates, many of whom knew Bob Winter. One of these was the British scholar John Blofeld (1913–1987) who arrived in Beijing in 1934 after having lived elsewhere in China and having acquired a basic fluency in speaking and reading Chinese. At the youthful age of twenty-two years, Blofeld devoted himself to the city's "countless sensuous, aesthetic and intellectual charms."[18] After an initial phase of wine and womanizing, Blofeld turned to moral and spiritual development before leaving Beijing in 1937. He devoted a long passage in his book on old Beijing to Winter, whom he referred to under the pseudonym of Professor Bill Luton.[19] A student in Winter's class on European literature told Blofeld that Winter was trying to make the students appreciate the French homosexual author Marcel Proust's *A la recherche du temps perdu* (*Remembrance of Things Past*). Winter was a challenging lecturer who sometimes offended the Chinese with his comments, but then apologized and won their sympathy.[20]

Blofeld described his initial visit to Winter's home in the Western part of Beijing, located off a typical Beijing *hutong* 胡同 (alley), in a house with flowers and shrubs reflecting a mixture of East-West tastes. A heavily built, bearded Winter greeted him along with his friend and guided them into a small room in which "six or seven scholarly-looking old gentlemen dressed in gowns of dark-coloured silk" were listening to the famous Wu Guantian play the ancient seven-stringed lute.[21] Blofeld had heard gossip about this eccentric American and was struck by Winter's imitation of the manner of his Chinese friends. In contrast to their pale, delicate bodies in silk gowns, Winter seemed grotesque as a "large, red-faced, bearded Westerner" who was too awkward to perform the proper bows.[22]

Winter may have been physically awkward, but his fluency in Chinese surpassed most expatriates in Beijing. During the 1930s in Beijing, there was a homosexual subculture of expatriates from Europe and North America. Its members were foreign aesthetes who included the Briton Harold Acton (1904–1994) and the American art historians George Kates (1895–1990) and Laurence Sickman (1907–1988).[23] The inclusion of four pieces of Winter's furniture in Kates' illustrated book on Chinese furniture indicates that Winter was part of this group.[24] This idyllic period for Beijing ended in 1937 when the Japanese took control of the city. Most expatriates departed, but Winter stayed three years longer, using his protected status as an American to try and continue the work of the Orthological Institute Project with continued funding from the Rockefeller Institute.

Winter thrived on espionage and in helping refugees. Although he denied ever being a Communist, he supported the revolutionary activities of his language students at Qinghua University at great personal danger by carrying letters and parcels of guns and ammunition to Tianjin.[25] In the summer of 1938 he met and befriended Delewa Gegen—the Living Buddha of Outer Mongolia (Uliassutai).[26] This Living Buddha had fled Outer Mongolia when the Russians took control of that territory and had spent the last twenty years as a refugee in Beijing. The Japanese wanted to exploit him by returning him to Uliassutai and gaining legitimacy for their control of Outer Mongolia. The Living Buddha wanted instead to go to Tibet which he regarded as his spiritual homeland where he had been reborn in previous reincarnations. To achieve this, he hoped to go to Chongqing to gain the support of the Nationalist Generalissimo Chiang Kai-shek and then to proceed on to India and Tibet. Winter helped him by arranging for them to travel separately to Shanghai and then onward together to Hong Kong.

During her Hong Kong stopover late in 1939, Emily Hahn met the Living Buddha. She described him as "a man between fifty and sixty, with charming manners and a pock-marked face."[27] Winter flew with the Living Buddha to Chongqing where they met with the Generalissimo. Afterwards they were separated and Winter later discovered that the Nationalists had held the Living Buddha prisoner in Chongqing throughout the war. Hahn was able to visit him and share a Christmas Eve dinner in Chongqing with Winter and the Living Buddha.[28] Twenty years later in 1959, Winter's association with Delewa Gegen would cause Winter to be interrogated by the Communists on the suspicion that he was secretly serving the Nationalist cause.

When Japanese forces occupied Beida and Qinghua Universities in Beijing and destroyed Nankai University in Tianjian in 1937, the faculty and students fled to Hunan. However, Japanese bombs forced nearly three hundred students and a dozen faculty members to make a further sixty-eight-day journey across China to Kunming in southwest China. Here on a sixty-five-hundred-foot plateau in Yunnan province they established the National Southwest Associated University, known as Lianda 聯大 (Combined University).[29] Winter's support of the anti-Japanese resistance worried the Rockefeller Foundation, which pressured Winter to leave Beijing by the late summer of 1940. After arriving in Kunming in November 1940, he remained there for almost six years.[30] When the director of the Orthological Institute died, Winter was named to replace him. The school's building was destroyed by air raids in January 1941, but Winter managed to have it replaced with a modern three-storied building and to continue the operations of the Orthological Institute.[31] However, the continued air raids combined with the hyperinflation of Chinese currency made life very difficult.

III.

The prominent China historian John King Fairbank and his wife and colleague Wilma Fairbank supported appointing Winter as a cultural affairs specialist in China under the auspices of either the Rockefeller Foundation or the US State Department.[32] This led to the suggestion of Winter making a trip back to the United States for consultation. However, Winter was reluctant to return to the United States for several reasons. He had a strong sense of loyalty to his Chinese colleagues and to Lianda, which was very short of teachers.[33] He also liked being the center of attention. His weekly lectures on poetry at Lianda had to be moved to larger and larger halls to accommodate all the interested students.[34] Winter had a theatrical flair and liked to act out roles as diverse as a demon or nun and recite portions of Shakespeare's dramas from memory, changing the intonation to match each character and entertaining the students. Finally, he had the reluctance of a closeted homosexual returning to his American homeland that was hostile to his sexuality.

Winter finally returned to the United States in 1942/1943 and went to New York for consultation with the Rockefeller Foundation over the plight of Chinese intellectuals. In part, the problem was twofold, consisting of their malnutrition due to an imbalanced diet and, in part, to the danger produced by their resistance as Western-trained faculty, mainly at Qinghua University, to the Nationalists' efforts to regiment intellectual life in China.[35] Fairbank wanted to bring some of these scholars to America for their protection. However, American support of these Chinese intellectuals who favored American ideals conflicted with American anti-Communist support for the Nationalists who opposed a free professoriate. Although the Rockefeller Foundation tried to keep Winter in the United States and arranged for interviews with leading Sinologists at several American universities, no job offers were forthcoming and Winter was eager to return to China. In any case, it is questionable whether Winter would have accepted a job offer in the United States where he no longer felt comfortable. He boarded a military transport in September 1944 and flew to India where after four months he returned to Kunming.

The end of the war against the Japanese in 1945 was followed by a civil war between the Nationalists and the Communists, concluding with the latter's victory in Liberation (1949). Winter returned to Beijing from Kunming in the summer of 1946, but for him there was no personal liberation.[36] China under the Communists was no longer a refuge for queers. Although the new Chinese government tolerated certain high-level foreign homosexuals, such as Rewi Alley (1897–1987), homosexuality was generally prohibited and punished until 1992.[37]

In 1947, John Blofeld returned to Beijing in search of his old friends. He was now married to a Chinese woman and the father of two children. At one of many banquets held in his honor, he encountered Bob Winter (a.k.a. Bill Luton) whose idiomatic Mandarin made him a congenial companion in that group of Chinese men.[38] Later they went to Bei Hai (North Lake) just west of the Forbidden City where a professional flower girl sang. Blofeld remarked how the fragrance of Turkish tobacco from Bob Winter's pipe united them in a cloud of happiness.[39] However, as midnight approached and they were parting, Blofeld asked Winter if he might be the next one to receive a farewell party if the Communists forced him to leave Beijing. Winter denied that he would ever leave Beijing because he did not believe it was in the Chinese nature to be ungrateful to an old teacher.[40]

Winter was faced with few options. When asked in a 1980 interview why he had not followed his fellow nationals in leaving China and returning to the United States, he replied that he "couldn't face living there again."[41] To him, Americans seemed very materialistic and acquisitive. He had heard that America was even more sexually permissive than it had been during his last visit there in the 1940s. He said it was possible in China to "escape the obsession with sex" that was part of the West.[42] Affluent Americans who he expected to be cultured were invariably ignorant and coarse. "The women were the worst," he said, because "they were so loud and vulgar." The Chinese, by comparison, had a certain refinement even though most of them were desperately poor. Clearly, Winter had become Sinified during his long residence in China.[43]

Of course, it remained unspoken that if he had returned to the United States, he would also have faced a hostile environment to his sexuality. In post–World War II America, a national obsession with homosexuality emerged as newspapers throughout the country began to fill with stories of sex crimes. Homosexuality was not seen as an inborn characteristic, but rather as a temptation to which one succumbed.[44] In order to better prosecute homosexual offenses, the head of the Federal Bureau of Investigation, J. Edgar Hoover, claimed in 1947 that homosexuality was second only to Communism as a threat to the nation. In 1947, the US Park Police in the District of Columbia inaugurated a "Pervert Elimination Campaign" which targeted men in cruising areas for arrest.[45] Between 1947 and 1955, twenty-one states and the District of Columbia introduced sexual psychopath laws targeting homosexuals.[46]

IV.

In the initial social elation following victory in the Communists' Liberation in 1949, the Chinese commonly distinguished between the watershed of "before Liberation" (*jiefang yiqian* 解放以前) and "after Liberation" (*jiefang yihou* 解放以後). In the relaxed atmosphere following Liberation, Winter rode his bicycle daily during the summer the two or three miles to the Summer Palace where he swam in the Kunming Lake and helped Chinese children learn to swim.[47] However, the political atmosphere in China soon turned grim. In his 1980 interview, Winter claimed that Mao Zedong's "major shortcoming was that he was a ladies' man."[48] But Winter also said Mao was too impatient in his wish to change people and that his impatience caused problems.

Winter's initial support for the Chinese Communist government and his opposition to the US role in the Korean conflict gave way to disillusionment with the new government and he applied for an exit permit in 1952.[49] By 1954 he was prohibited from teaching. His relationships with Wen Yiduo, Richards, the Orthological Institute, and the Rockefeller Foundation were investigated. His income became precarious. He was protected from the early Red Guard violence by Zhou Enlai, but in 1969 thirty youths stormed his house and knocked the eighty-two-year old professor to the floor, pinning him with their feet on his chest.[50] A fellow lecturer in Spanish named Zhao Deming led a group of cadres in raiding his house and seizing much of his personal property, including his turntable and classical records, lecture notes, and correspondence.[51] Zhao demanded that Winter "lend" him money and imprisoned him in a university building for three months in 1969 while he was compelled to write confessions of his so-called crimes. This included his relationship to the Nationalists in the case of the Living Buddha Delewa Gegen and his meeting with Chiang Kai-shek. The Red Guards had apparently gained access to the Public Security Bureau file on him. From this file he learned that a fellow American who had spent four years in jail in the 1950s as a counter-revolutionary had accused Winter of being a spy.[52] He was watched, and his visitors were restricted. One of his few frequent visitors was Gladys Yang, who with Yang Xianyi formed the famous husband and wife team of translators based at the Foreign Language Institute in Beijing (see chapter 9).[53] After Winter broke his hip in 1982, he became bedridden and delusional.[54]

In September 1984, Professor Bert Stern of Wabash University made the first of several visits to Winter during a one-year teaching position at Beida and found him confined to his house in cramped, near-squalid conditions while his mind was filled with reminiscences and clouded with hallucinations. Winter's life-long preference for living in China rather than America or Europe was shaped by the sexual freedom that China allowed him earlier in the twentieth century and by his sexual preference for East Asian males. His preference for living abroad in China rather than Europe indicates that he might have been, in queer jargon, a "rice queen" (a homosexual attracted to younger Asian men). His desire for interracial love lasted until the end of his life although the oppressive attitude of Communist China toward same-sex love in 1984 made it difficult to know details. A member of the English Department conveyed that late in Winter's life, they had to stop sending male students to help care for him because although he was bedridden, he made sexual advances to them.[55]

Among Winter's possessions was a painting of a young fisherman holding a seahorse.[56] The seahorse is a homoerotic symbol because the male of the species carries the eggs to birth. Stern concluded from the stories related in interviews in Beijing that Winter and this fisherman were lovers in Qingdao.[57] Winter frequently insisted to Stern that he had grown up in a household of women and he did not like women although his friendship with Emily Hahn indicates that he was not entirely misogynous.[58] In his senility, Winter believed his end-of-life confinement to his small room and his subjugation to the care of a woman were punishment for his sexual preference for men over women. The woman was actually his longtime servant. She had once been a prostitute and been attacked by a crowd with stones and sticks. Winter saved her by using his walking stick to drive the crowd away, and he took her in.

Winter's caution toward women appears to have reinforced his Sinification in terms of his belief in fox fairies (*huxian* 狐仙) and fox demons (*huliqing* 狐狸精).[59] When Blofeld first visited Winter's home in the 1930s, Winter was holding the bloody severed tail of an unidentified animal. Later, Winter showed Blofeld his collection of animals, including three caged wolves.[60] The bloody, severed tail had been found on the floor of the wolf cage. When Blofeld asked if he could explain it, Winter hesitated, but then connected it to the fox tower at the bottom of his garden where his gatekeeper burned incense.[61] There had been a widespread traditional belief among many Chinese in the ability of spirits to assume the form of foxes. The fox fairies (*huxian*) were benign, but the fox demons (*huliqing*) who took the form of seductive women were thought to cause destruction and death. In north China for two thousand years the fox had been associated with venereal diseases in which a fox in the form of a beautiful young girl appears to a scholar while he is studying and leads him to make love to her. She reappears regularly at night until the fox has drained him of his essence and he dies.[62]

Winter told Blofeld a frightening story about a fox demon. Ten years before when he had been living out in the country, near Qinghua University, a student died suddenly of tuberculosis. Because of his infatuation with a beautiful, but mysterious prostitute, he had neglected eating healthy food and getting enough sleep. One night when he arrived early at the temple to meet her, he saw how she was transformed from a fox. He tried to get away, but she ran to him and embraced him. He was powerless to get away because the fox demon's beauty and seductive smile hid a powerful desire to suck the energy out of her victim's body. Underlying the belief in fox demons was the Chinese Daoist philosophy that taught males to engage in sex while minimizing the male's seminal emission. It was thought that the female, on the contrary, sought to absorb the male's sperm. Consequently, many Chinese males have traditionally sought to retain their seminal fluids because detumescence of the penis was associated with death.[63]

Stern's last visit to Winter was in December 1987 on the occasion of Winter's one-hundredth birthday (counting in the Chinese manner). This formal and rather sad event sponsored by Beida and the Foreign Affairs Office brought a crowd of people into Winter's small house, including professors from Beida and reporters from both the Chinese and American press.[64] Winter was bewildered and not fully conscious of the significance of the event. It was an anticlimax to his remarkable life. He died a few days after the party. Two hundred people came to his funeral in the Ba Bao Shan Cemetery.

NOTES

1. A gatekeeper on the campus of Beida where Winter lived referred to Winter as "Professor Wen-de." See David Finkelstein and Beverly Hooper, "57 Years Inside China: An American's Odyssey," *Asia* (Asia Society) 2 (Jan/Feb 1980): 10.

2. Emily Hahn, *China to Me: A Partial Autobiography* (Garden City, NY: Country Life Press, 1944), 106.

3. Bert Stern, *Winter in China: An American Life* (Xlibris LLC, 2014), 9. This book has been translated into Chinese as *Wente xian sheng: qin li Zhongguo liu shi nian de chuan qi jiao shou* 溫特先生：親歷中國六十年的傳奇教授 (Mr. Winter: the long poetic drama of his sixty-year personal experience as a professor in China) by Bote Site'en zhu 伯特。斯特恩著 (Bert Stern 1930–), Ma Xiaowu 馬小悟 (translator) amd Yu Wanhui 余婉卉 (translator) (Hong Kong: Xianggang Zhonghe Chuban Youxian Gongsi 中和出版有限公司, 2016).

4. Hahn, *China to Me*, 106.

5. Stern, *Winter in China*, 28.

6. Stern, *Winter in China*, 35.

7. The habits of the closet were hard to break. In the 1980 interview that he gave to two *Asia* journalists, Winter spoke of his disenchantment with American greed and racism but omitted mention of his homosexuality. See Finkelstein and Hooper, "57 Years Inside China," 10.

8. Finkelstein and Hooper, "57 Years Inside China," 10. This article contains the only pictorial image of Winter that I have found. Finkelstein and Hooper claim that they interviewed Winter when he was ninety-three years old; however, since Winter was born in 1890 and since the interview was published in *Asia* in 1980, Winter could not have been more than ninety years old at the time of the interview.

9. Stern, *Winter in China*, 39–42.

10. C. T. Hsia, *A History of Modern Chinese Fiction 1917–1957* (New Haven, CT: Yale University Press, 1961), 314; Stern, *Winter in China*, 302.

11. Stern, *Winter in China*, 43. Finkelstein and Hooper, "57 Years Inside China," 10, differs from Stern in stating that Winter taught at Nanjing for four years.

12. Stern, *Winter in China*, 64.

13. Hahn, *China to Me*, 106.

14. Finkelstein and Hooper, "57 Years Inside China," 11.

15. Stern, *Winter in China*, 89–90.

16. Stern, *Winter in China*, 92–93.

17. Stern, *Winter in China*, 138.

18. John Blofeld, *City of Lingering Splendour: A Frank Account of Old Peking's Exotic Pleasures* (London: Hutchinson, 1961), 14–15.

19. Blofeld, *City of Lingering Splendour*, 73–86, 174.

20. Blofeld, *City of Lingering Splendour*, 73–74.

21. Blofeld, *City of Lingering Splendour*, 75–76.

22. Blofeld, *City of Lingering Splendour*, 76–77.

23. D. E. Mungello, *Western Queers in China* (Lanham, MD: Rowman & Littlefield Publishers, 2012), 18–22, 89–100.

24. George N. Kates, *Chinese Household Furniture* (London: Harper & Brothers, 1948). Winter's game table appears as plate #33 with text on page 80; a lute table appears as plate #36 with text on page 81; a large wooden *kang* appears as plate #69 with text on page 98; and a small couch appears as plate #73 on pages 100–01.

25. Finkelstein and Hooper, "57 Years Inside China," 11.

26. Stern, *Winter in China*, 129–31; Hahn, 109.

27. Hahn, *China to Me*, 108.

28. Hahn, *China to Me*, 140.

29. John Israel, *Lianda: A Chinese University in War and Revolution* (Stanford: Stanford University Press, 1999), 1–2.

30. Stern, *Winter in China*, 145, 148.

31. Stern, *Winter in China*, 152, 161.

32. Stern, *Winter in China*, 186–89.

33. Stern, *Winter in China*, 187.

34. Personal correspondence from Bert Stern, August 5, 2012.

35. Stern, *Winter in China*, 198–99.

36. Stern, *Winter in China*, 274.

37. Mungello, *Western Queers in China*, 5, 64–69.

38. Blofeld, *City of Lingering Splendour*, 246, 248.

39. Blofeld, *City of Lingering Splendour*, 250–51.

40. Blofeld, *City of Lingering Splendour*, 252.

41. Finkelstein and Hooper, "57 Years Inside China," 11.

42. Finkelstein and Hooper, "57 Years Inside China," 11.

43. Finkelstein and Hooper, "57 Years Inside China," 11.

44. David K. Johnson, *The Lavender Scare: The Cold War Persecution of Gays and Lesbians in the Federal Government* (Chicago: The University of Chicago, 2004), 12.

45. Johnson, *The Lavender Scare*, 59.

46. Edward White, *Tastemaker* (New York: Farrar, Straus and Giroux, 2014), 291.

47. Finkelstein and Hooper, "57 Years Inside China," 10.

48. Finkelstein and Hooper, "57 Years Inside China," 46.

49. Stern, *Winter in China*, 327–28.

50. Finkelstein and Hooper, "57 Years Inside China," 11.

51. Stern, *Winter in China*, 329–30.

52. Finkelstein and Hooper, "57 Years Inside China," 47.

53. Stern, *Winter in China*, 338, misspells Gladys Yang's name as Gladys Wang.

54. Stern, *Winter in China*, 334.

55. Bert Stern email to the author dated August 5, 2012.

56. Winter's painting of a fisherman holding a seahorse is reproduced on the cover of Stern's book *Winter in China* (2014).

57. Bert Stern email to the author, August 3, 2012.

58. Stern, *Winter in China*, 338–39.

59. On the origin of love stories and fox lore in Chinese history, see R. H. Van Gulik, *Sexual Life in Ancient China* (Leiden: Brill, 1961), 210–11, 314–17.

60. Blofeld, *City of Lingering Splendour*, 80–82.

61. Blofeld, *City of Lingering Splendour*, 84–85.

62. Wolfram Eberhard, *A Dictionary of Chinese Symbols*, translated by G. L. Campbell (London: Routledge, 1986), 117–18.

63. Pu Songling, *Strange Tales from a Chinese Studio*, translated and edited by John Minford (London: Penguin Books, 2006), xxi–xxiv, 143–49, 524–25.

64. Stern, *Winter in China*, 343–44.

Chapter 8

A Love Affair as Concubinage

Joseph Needham and Lu Gwei-djen

I.

The love affair of Joseph Needham (Li Yuese 李約瑟) (1900–1995) and Lu Gwei-djen (Lu Guizhen 魯桂珍) (1904–1991) was inseparable from Lu Gwei-djen's plight as a refugee from the Japanese invasion of China, from their collaborative work as historians of Chinese science, and from Needham's raging libido. Needham was a polymath who combined the work of a scientist, Sinologist, and historian. He came from a high church Anglican background in England and remained a practicing, politically left-wing, Anglo-Catholic throughout his life.[1] He had initially planned to follow his father in becoming a physician, but after entering Gonville and Caius College at Cambridge, he turned to biochemistry. In a Cambridge biochemical laboratory, he met a fellow student named Dorothy Moyle who would become his future wife.[2] The marriage would last for sixty-three years (1924–1987), although Needham's "roving eye" repeatedly disrupted its fidelity.[3]

The most significant disruption began in 1937 when Lu Gwei-djen and two other young scientists departed from Shanghai on a ship that would arrive in London two months later.[4] They escaped the ferocious Japanese attacks on Chinese coastal cities, including the notorious "Rape of Nanjing" that began in the following year. Lu was born into a Christian family in Nanjing in which her father was a respected apothecary. She studied at the American-run Ginling College for Girls in Nanjing and developed an intense interest in biochemistry, sharing coincidentally with Dorothy Moyle Needham a research focus on the biochemistry of muscles. She was attracted to Cambridge because of the academic reputations of both Needhams, but particularly Joseph Needham's published work on embryology, and because she shared his leftist politics.

At Cambridge, Lu became Needham's assistant in investigating the compelling question of why China had so successfully developed the natural sciences prior to 1500 but failed to develop modern science after 1500. This contradiction would become the animating question of the research leading to the publication of the multivolume *Science and Civilisation in China*. Needham had been trained in biochemistry, but not in Sinology and Chinese history. He and Lu soon became lovers, but what sustained their love affair from 1937 until Lu's death in 1991 was the role Lu played in helping Needham, first as his as tutor in introducing him to the Chinese language and history and later as a close intellectual associate in the study of Chinese science. After Lu's initial tutoring, Needham progressed to more advanced study of the Chinese language under the guidance of the Cambridge professor of Chinese Gustav Haloun.[5]

Lu was assigned a room across the corridor from Needham and during the fall and winter of 1937 and 1938 they fell deeply in love.[6] Needham and Lu spent increasing amounts of time together—in the laboratory, on walks, in restaurants, at the movies, and in bed. There was a tradition among numerous Sinologists to have Chinese mistresses or wives in order to develop their fluency in Chinese, and Lu fulfilled this role for Needham. Both Needham and Lu were heavy smokers. Drawing from Needham's university diary, the biographer Simon Winchester claims that their relationship became intimate probably in February 1938, roughly six months after they met.[7] While they were lying together in a small bed in a sixteenth-century gaslit room in Caius College, in a romantic postcoital gesture Needham lit two cigarettes and handed one to Gwei-djen. Then he asked her how to write the name for cigarette in Chinese. After she wrote the characters *xiangyan* 香煙 (fragrant smoke), he looked at it and said he must learn this language. She would be his first teacher.

II.

Needham's biographer claims that his wife Dorothy was aware of the love affair between her husband and Lu, but that she withdrew into her own studies and pretended not to mind (figure 8.1). He explains the lack of scandal in terms of the standards of Cambridge in the 1930s which were more "socially progressive and sexually tolerant."[8] And yet certain near-contemporaries at Cambridge, such as Bertrand Russell and Xu Zhimo, had preferred the purity of divorce over infidelity.

But perhaps there was another reason that gave Dorothy Needham grounds to welcome this form of concubinage. The Needhams were a childless couple, although it is difficult to know whether this was caused by the infertility of

Figure 8.1. At lunchtime in the Common Room, about the time when the ménage à trois between Lu Gwei-djen, Joseph Needham, and Dorothy M. Needham (all to the right side) was developing. A colleague V. Booth is seated on the left, 1937–1938. (Photograph from the archives of The Department of Biochemistry, University of Cambridge, United Kingdom, reproduced with permission.)

the partners or the frigidity of the wife or even by choice. In any case, her husband's affair with Lu might have provided Dorothy Needham with a form of release from a frustrating and unhappy sex life fostered by their conjugal inability to conceive children. Lu would have been aware of this sort of situation from her life in China where concubinage frequently occurred as a result of the wife's inability to conceive children (particularly sons). In a sense, Needham's fidelity to his marriage rather than divorce in the manner of Russell or Xu Zhimo was an act of kindness to his wife, particularly in her later years when she fell ill with Alzheimer's disease. This fidelity may have been a reflection of Needham's Christian values, which Russell and Xu did not share.

In 1939 their affair continued at long distance when Lu accepted a position at the University of California at Berkeley. Needham's growing knowledge of the Chinese language and culture and his opposition to the Japanese military campaign against China, albeit in a controversial politically leftist form, garnered him an invitation to make his first trip to China under the auspices of the British Council, an arm of the British Foreign Office.[9] In 1942, before leaving for China, Needham made a trip to New York where he met with Lu and together they generated their plan to study China's unrecognized contributions to science and technology.[10] This was the genesis of the multi-volume work *Science and Civilisation in China.*

Although there was some British opposition to the appointment of someone with Needham's Communist sympathies, he departed England in 1943. After a long trip via India, he arrived in Kunming, the home of China's refugee university Lianda (Southwest Consolidated University) which had relocated from Japanese-occupied territory. Needham remained in China for two years, visiting 296 Chinese educational and research facilities.[11] He fostered the development of science in China by facilitating the delivery of equipment and scientific journals while reading voraciously and laying the groundwork for *Science and Civilisation in China.* Although he had his wife Dorothy with him, he missed his mistress Gwei-djen. In order to see her, he arranged in 1945 for Gwei-djen to be brought from New York to China as a staff nutritionist.[12] This arrangement was criticized by Needham's colleagues as blatantly nepotistic. When one colleague, a senior Cambridge biologist named Laurence Picken, submitted a memorandum highly critical of Gwei-djen's appointment, Needham responded with a vicious critique of Picken.[13]

III.

Needham's trips to China served to inspire his work and to convince Zhou Enlai that he shared the Communists' economic views.[14] Zhou Enlai assured Mao Zedong of Needham's affinity to the Communists. Unlike Han Suyin, Needham was able to meet with Mao Zedong several times. Han Suyin defended the Chinese Communists, but she was never a Communist. She defended the Chinese Communists to the world, although her ultimate defense was of China. However, within China she refused to silence her questions. Needham, by contrast, rarely asked skeptical questions and was later duped by a disinformation effort that claimed the Americans had engaged in biological warfare against the Chinese people in northeast China. In 1951 during the stalemated Korean War, accusations were made that Americans were poisoning Korean water wells with cholera and infecting cattle with anthrax.[15] In the spring of 1952, infected voles (small rodents) were reported to have been dropped from the sky in Korea and Manchuria followed by outbreaks of cholera. Zhou Enlai, who had befriended Needham during his stay in China, accused the United States of dropping the voles and employing bacteriological weapons.[16] When the head of the Chinese Academy of Sciences invited Needham to come to China to join the investigation, Needham readily accepted.

Needham took a leading role in conducting the investigation and in issuing a 665-page report which fully supported the biological warfare claims of Mao and Zhou against the Americans. (Later it was learned that the incidents that had given rise to the accusations of biological warfare were the products of Soviet disinformation.) The report was issued on September 15, 1952, and the evidence for the claims was so weak that the reaction in Europe and the United States was highly hostile and threatened to severely damage Needham's reputation as a scientist. He was banned from traveling to the Unites States for twenty-seven years. As a "fellow traveller" (Communist), Needham suffered from a lack of objectivity in regard to the Chinese Communists. He confined his criticism to his private diaries. He never made public criticisms of Chinese Communist actions like the disastrous Great Leap Forward or the persecution of fellow scientists during the Cultural Revolution or the Tiananmen military massacre of Chinese citizens in June 1989.[17]

Needham's reputation for posterity was redeemed with the publication of the series of volumes under the title *Science and Civilisation in China*. Lu Gwei-djen was a crucial helpmate in that redemption. The first volume *Introductory Orientations* appeared in 1954 followed by volume 2 *History of Scientific Thought* in 1956 and subsequent volumes.[18] By 2004, twenty-seven volumes had been published. Lu Gwei-djen is listed as a collaborator in the four volumes (1974, 1976, 1980, and 1983) that deal with spagyrical (alchemical) discovery and invention, with a volume on botany (1986), and with a volume on medicine (2000).

IV.

The ménage à trois took full form in 1957 when Lu Gwei-djen moved into a residence at 28 Owlstone Road, just down the street from the Needhams who lived at 1 Owlstone Road in Cambridge.[19] The half-hour walk across the campus to their offices was idyllic in its beauty. Even with two women, Needham's eye continued to roam and in the mid-1970s he had a romantic interlude with a Canadian Chinese woman named H. Y. Shih who had been the director of the National Gallery of Canada.[20] After leaving the mastership of Caius College at the age of seventy-six, he and Lu engaged in a program of fundraising involving travel to Asia, dinners, and speeches. Meanwhile Dorothy Needham published her *Machina Carnis* in 1972 but soon after began to exhibit symptoms of Alzheimer's disease.[21] She died at home in 1987 at the age of ninety-two.

Gwei-djen, who had chain-smoked since her youth, began to suffer from bronchial problems. Despite her failing health, she and Needham married in 1989. She fell and broke her hip in a Cambridge restaurant in 1991 and died shortly afterwards of bronchial pneumonia. Needham became terribly lonely and in consequent months proposed to three East Asian women, including the aforesaid Ms. Shih of Toronto, all of whom declined. In 1992 at Buckingham Palace Queen Elizabeth awarded him the prestigious Companionship of Honour. One of his caregivers dressed him in a black silk Chinese robe for the occasion.[22] His physical decline continued slowly in the form of scoliosis and Parkinson's disease, which forced him to use a wheelchair. His wasp-ish streak intensified. He became a revered but lonely figure surrounded by much younger and generationally remote associates. He continued to work but dozed more and more. His energy diminished gradually and one day he stopped breathing and died quietly at the age of ninety-four.

NOTES

1. Simon Winchester, *The Man Who Loved China* (New York: HarperCollins, 2008), 17.

2. Winchester, *The Man Who Loved China*, 20–21.

3. Winchester, *The Man Who Loved China*, 239.

4. Winchester, *The Man Who Loved China*, 36–37.

5. Winchester, *The Man Who Loved China*, 44.

6. Winchester, *The Man Who Loved China*, 38.

7. Winchester, *The Man Who Loved China*, 38–40.

8. Winchester, *The Man Who Loved China*, 43.

9. Winchester, *The Man Who Loved China*, 51–53.

10. Winchester, *The Man Who Loved China*, 56–57.

11. Winchester, *The Man Who Loved China*, 157.

12. Winchester, *The Man Who Loved China*, 159.

13. On Picken's distinguished career as a scientist with interests in music and musical instruments of Asia, see Richard Widdess, "Obituary: Laurence Picken," *Ethnomusicology Forum* 17 (29) (November 2008): 269–74. Winchester's bias in favor of Needham is evident in his description of this incident. Although Lu Gwei-djen lacked training for the position of a nutritionist, Picken's criticisms of the appointment caused Winchester to describe him as a man with a "mean streak" and characterized his complaint "as vitriolic in tone" while Needham's vicious response is justified by saying "The venom was diluted, the vitriol repelled" (159–62).

14. Winchester, *The Man Who Loved China*, 96.

15. Winchester, *The Man Who Loved China*, 200.

16. Winchester, *The Man Who Loved China*, 202.

17. Charles Burton, "Loved China. Maybe Too Much. Also Loved Women," *Globe and Mail*, May 31, 2008.

18. Joseph Needham and Wang Ling, *Science and Civilisation in China. Volume 1 Introductory Orientations* (Cambridge, England: Cambridge University Press, 1954); *Volume 2 History of Scientific Thought* (Cambridge England: Cambridge University Press, 1956).

19. Winchester, *The Man Who Loved China*, 244.
20. Winchester, *The Man Who Loved China*, 239.
21. Winchester, *The Man Who Loved China*, 245.
22. Winchester, *The Man Who Loved China*, 250.

Chapter 9

A Love That Lasted

Yang Xianyi and Gladys Yang

I.

One of the most remarkable literary couples of modern Sino-Western history was Yang Xianyi 楊憲益 (1915–2009) and Gladys (née Tayler) Yang Dai Naidie 戴乃迭 (1919–1999). While historical events caused the romantic love of Emily Hahn and Shao Xunmei to fade, the romantic love of Yang Xianyi and Gladys Yang endured despite the chaos of civil war and revolution in China. They became in the 1950s and 1960s the most celebrated team of English translators of Chinese literature. In addition to classical Chinese literature, they translated Western classics, such as Homer's *Iliad*, Aristophanes' *Birds*, and the medieval French epic *Le Chanson de Roland*. Their devotion to one another over a sixty-year period stands out as a steady counter-current of romantic love in the midst of waves of East-West hatred and violence.

Yang Xianyi's January 10th birth fell auspiciously into the last phase of the previous lunar year, which was a Year of the Tiger. Before giving birth to him, Yang's mother dreamt that a white tiger leapt into her lap. A fortune teller interpreted this dream to mean that he would have no brothers and that while his life would be distinguished, it would be filled with misfortunes and danger.[1] The fortune teller's interpretation was largely fulfilled. Yang's father had three wives. When the first wife produced two daughters but no sons, his father took a concubine. After giving birth to Yang Xianyi, this concubine was elevated to spousal status and Xianyi called both of his father's wives "mother." Yang's mother gave birth to two girls, but no more sons. Yang's father also took a third wife who gave birth to a daughter.

Yang's grandfather came to live with the family in the large mansion in the Japanese concession of Tianjin. After his death, his much younger concubine lived in a rear courtyard until her death in the 1930s.[2] She had given birth to a son who was called "young uncle" because he was several years older than Yang. After 1949 he fled with his family to Hong Kong and became a photographer and film producer. Yang had no more contact with him, but his son, John Dragon Young (Yang Yilong 楊意龍) (1949–1996), became an American-trained historian who was active in Hong Kong politics until his untimely death.[3]

Yang Xianyi's ancestral home was in Sizhou (now Sixian) in northern Anhui province. It was a prosperous and successful family. Yang's grandfather and three granduncles had passed the imperial palace examination as Hanlin Academicians and served as high-ranking Qing provincial officials.[4] His grandfather was governor of Huainan in northern Jiangsu province.[5] Several of his granduncles were close colleagues of the military strongman and reactionary political leader Yuan Shikai. Yang's father was the eldest of eight sons. All eight sons were sent to study abroad in England, France, the United States, and Japan. Yang's father went to Japan, but he was profligate, becoming addicted to opium and geisha girls. Upon returning to China, he reformed and became an astute financier and eventually president of the Bank of China in Tianjin. Working with northern warlords, he became wealthy. He died of typhoid in his fifties, leaving a large estate to his family in the form of bank deposits and landed estates in Tianjin. However, his two wives mishandled the wealth, two uncles lost much of it through speculation, and family servants stole many items. The family continued to spend lavishly to maintain their high standard of living. When the Japanese occupied Tianjin during the late 1930s, most of the Yang family bank deposits were converted into Japanese puppet government currency. When the war ended, the Japanese currency was worthless. By the time of the Communist Liberation of 1949, most of the family wealth was gone.

The Yang family home in Tianjin was a large, ugly mansion on Garden Street in the Japanese concession. The property was surrounded by a wall and divided by several courtyards. At the front was a garden with two large pomegranate trees and flowerpots. When the Japanese armies moved into Manchuria in 1931 and encroached on Tianjin, the family sold the large house and moved into the French concession of Tianjin. Later, when the Second Sino-Japanese War broke out in 1937, they moved yet again into the British concession.

Because Yang was the only son, Number One Mother did not allow him to leave the family home to attend school for fear that he might be kidnapped or harmed in an accident.[6] From the age of six until twelve, he studied at home under the guidance of private tutors, the best of whom was a good but impoverished scholar named Wei. Mr. Wei taught Yang the Confucian classics, works by important Chinese classical writers, and how to write poetry. Yang's wealthy family background and traditional education made him reluctant to accept the value of literary reform by Hu Shi, although he was quick to appreciate the literary works of Zhou Zuoren 周作人 and Lu Xun. At the age of twelve or thirteen, Yang was sent to the Tianjin Anglo-Chinese College (TACC), a British missionary school in the French concession not far from his home. He studied at the TACC for seven years and developed his proficiency in English. The school had been founded by the London Missionary Society, and its teachers were Christian missionaries with degrees from English universities. The school had a half-hour Christian service each morning. Prior to his arrival at the TACC, one of the teachers had been J. B. Tayler, the father of Yang's future wife, who had since moved on to teach at Yanjing University in Beijing.

On May 30, 1925, in Shanghai, British police opened fire and killed several students and workers involved in a political protest. Yang became a ringleader, twice leading student strikes at TACC to commemorate this incident. The protesting students refused to attend classes of British teachers in order to honor May 30 as a day of national shame.[7] Although the British principal, Dr. Hart, was furious and threatened to expel the student protesters, Yang's family prestige and wealth saved them. Clearly Yang was a child of privilege. He graduated from TACC in 1934 and prepared to enter one of the three most prestigious Chinese universities in Beijing: Qinghua (Tsinghua) University, Beijing University (Beida), or Yanjing (Yenching) University.[8]

However, a former English teacher at TACC, C. H. B. Longman, was returning on holiday to England and offered to take Yang with him. Longman proposed that he find a Greek and Latin tutor in London for Yang and then enroll him in an English university. At the age of nineteen, Yang left Tianjin for the first time in his life and traveled with his family to Shanghai where he boarded one of the Empress liners bound for the United States by way of Japan and Hawaii. Although Longman and his wife were very fond of Yang, Yang objected to Longman's strict sense of guardianship. In his autobiography, Yang expressed regret for his harsh reaction to the Longmans' supervision, but attributed it to his headstrong nature, nurtured by the fact that he was the spoiled first-born son in a wealthy and powerful family.[9]

After touring the United States, they arrived in London where Longman found Greek and Latin tutors for Yang,[10] At that time, Asian and African students had difficulty entering Oxford because of a quota system that limited their numbers to one or two in each college. Yang passed the written admission exam, but because another Asian student had already been admitted, Yang had to wait until the Michaelmas term in the autumn of 1936 to enter Merton College. At Oxford he met the less than a dozen Chinese students, most of whom had come to study for a B. Litt. (Bachelor of Letters) degree, which took only one or two years. Most of them were older than Yang. The closest friend he made was the Chinese historian Xiang Da 向達 who had

come to study the ancient manuscripts found in the Dunhuang caves by Aurel
Stein and housed in the British Museum in London. Yang pursued an Honours
B.A. degree, which with Greek and Latin took four years.[11] He spent the first
two years studying Greek and Latin literature, concluding with a final examination for Hon. Mods. Following that, he studied English literature before
taking final examinations for the Honours B.A. degree. He was bright, but not
studious. He ended up getting a fourth, the lowest of the four grading levels.
The degree was simply not very important to him.

II.

With the beginning of the Sino-Japanese War, Yang lost all interest in aca-
demics and spent most of his time in the summer of 1937 and early spring of
1938 doing anti-Japanese propaganda work. During a brief period of studying
medieval French, he met his future wife, Gladys Tayler, who was also studying French before becoming the first student to enroll in the Honours School
in Chinese literature.[12] She was born in 1919 in Beijing to missionary teachers
of the London Missionary Society, but returned to Britain with her mother,
Selina Tayler, and an older sister when she was four or five. The two sisters
attended school in Seven Oaks, Kent, and after graduating from high school,
Gladys received a scholarship at Oxford where she studied from 1937 until
1940, graduating from St. Anne's College with a bachelor's degree in Chinese
literature. Her Chinese tutor was E. R. Hughes, a former missionary in south
China whose interest was in Confucianism.[13] He taught Gladys to read the
Confucian Four books, but his spoken Chinese was poor.

Yang held a breakfast party in his rooms at Oxford to announce his wedding engagement to Gladys[14] (figure 9.1). Their mothers were both upset by
the news. Gladys' mother predicted that the marriage would disintegrate after
four years, but Yang's mother was eventually reconciled to it. The couple
departed wartime England in 1940, just before the Germans began to bomb
London, traveling by ship across the Atlantic Ocean to Montreal, across
the continent to Vancouver, and then across the Pacific Ocean to Japanese-
occupied Shanghai. They went on to Hong Kong, seeking to go to Chongqing
where Yang's mother and younger sister had relocated.[15] However, the overland journey to Chongqing was dangerous and the Yangs were penniless.
They found an old family friend of Gladys' father named Dr. Chen Hansheng
who was working on a leftist program with Soong Qingling, the widow of
Sun Yat-sen. Before the Sino-Japanese War, Yang Xianyi's future father-in-
law, J. B. Tayler, left his teaching post at Yanjing University and went to
economically depressed Gansu province in northwest China to help found
the Chinese Industrial Cooperatives or Gongye Hezuoshe 工業合作社.[16] The

Figure 9.1. Yang Xianyi and Gladys Tayler Yang, at the time of their marriage, ca. 1940. They met as students at Oxford University where Yang was a bright but indifferent student in Merton College and Gladys Tayler was a more serious student of Chinese literature in St. Anne's College. (British Library, Flickr image.)

founders of the Chinese Industrial Cooperatives were British socialists of the Fabian Society who believed in the need for poor, undeveloped people like the Chinese to organize into cooperatives and learn industrial arts. One of the participants of this effort was the New Zealander Rewi Alley.[17] Dr. Chen lent the Yangs the money to pay their hotel bill and also bought them tickets on the weekly (sometimes twice-weekly) air flight to Chongqing. This flight traveled at night to avoid Japanese interception. It was the same flight that Emily Hahn used when she traveled to Chongqing to interview Soong Mei-ling (Madame Chiang Kai-shek) for her famous book on the Soong sisters.

The couple arrived in Chongqing in the fall of 1940, and Yang was reunited with his mother.[18] During the Sino-Japanese War many Chinese intellectuals and artists fled to the safety of southwest China, settling in Beibei, Chengdu, and Leshan in Sichuan province; Kunming in Yunnan province; and Guilin in Guangxi province. The Yangs signed a contract to teach at Lianda (Southwest Consolidated University) in Kunming, but Yang's mother felt Kunming was too vulnerable to Japanese bombing and convinced them to stay in Chongqing where they taught at Central University. However, Central University was dominated by Nationalist (Guomindang) sympathizers, and the Yangs got entangled in the tensions between the Nationalists and Communists. After one year, they were pushed out.

Before they left Chongqing, Yang's mother arranged a double wedding ceremony for Yang and Gladys and Yang's sister Amy and her fiancé Luo Peilin, the son of a prominent Tianjin commercial family.[19] Yang's mother designed a Chinese satin gown for Gladys that was embroidered with dragons and phoenixes. It was short-sleeved, tight-fitting, uncomfortable, and impractical in the chilly March weather in Chongqing. Gladys submitted, but she never enjoyed living under her mother-in-law's roof and tried to avoid it.[20] Gladys' British passport was suspended when the British declared war on Japan, leaving her stateless. Her attempt to apply for Chinese citizenship was fruitless, and her British passport was later reinstated. After the Communist Liberation of 1949, she never reapplied for Chinese citizenship and remained a British citizen until her death.

After the birth of their son, Gladys suffered from poor health, including malaria, fever, and chronic diarrhea. In order to find a healthier location in Sichuan, the Yangs moved in late 1943 to Beibei where they worked at the Institute of Translation and Compilation. During Yang's trips from Beibei to Chongqing, he stayed with English friends who worked at the British Embassy. One of the most eccentric was John Blofeld (mentioned in the chapter on Robert Winter), who had also studied at Cambridge.[21] Yang and Blofeld shared a fondness for heavy drinking and during Yang's visits to Chongqing, Blofeld regaled him with stories about his time as a Buddhist monk at Wutai Mountain, about opium smoking and prostitutes in Vietnam.[22] While he was Second Secretary of the British Embassy, he invited the British ambassador to his wedding to a Chinese woman, but Blofeld failed to appear at his ceremony and caused such a scandal that he resigned from the embassy. However, he did eventually marry a Chinese woman and they had two children. Later, Blofeld would live in Bangkok and write books about popular Buddhism and Daoism.

As the war was ending, Yang decided to join the anti-Nationalist forces.[23] During his stay in southwest China, he had become disgusted with the Guomindang and its resumption of the war against the Chinese Communists. In the spring of 1946, he and several younger colleagues in the Institute of Translation and Compilation joined one of the anti-Guomindang parties which were organized in various universities and governmental organizations. Late in 1945 the Yangs traveled with their son and daughter on a crowded junk down the Yangzi River to Nanjing. The Nationalist capital along with the Institute of Translation and Compilation was being reestablished there.[24] As the Nationalist government was collapsing, inflation was rampant and US dollars were in demand. Yang's friend, the novelist Lao She (pen name for Shu Qingchun) introduced him to people who helped him join an underground political organization called the *Minlian* 民聯 (Comrades of Dr. Sun Yat-sen's "Three People's Principles").[25] It was, in fact, a secret party linked to the Communists and filled with former Guomindang officials who had turned against the Chiang Kai-shek regime.

While in Nanjing, the Yangs spent a good bit of time socializing with Adrian Conway Evans, a military attaché at the British Embassy, who they had met in Beibei.[26] Evans was a young bachelor who often visited the Yangs, driving them in his German Volkswagen to scenic spots along the Yangzi River. Evans was likeable, but naïve, and had contacts with Guomindang generals. Yang was able to get bits of information from him about the civil war between the Nationalists and Communists, including the disposition of Communist troops in north China, which he passed on to his Communist contacts. Because of his friendship with Evans, Yang later came under suspicion by the Communist government of being a counter-revolutionary. This led to interrogations in the 1950s and culminated in the Cultural Revolution with the incarceration of both Yang and Gladys in 1968 to 1972.

Communist forces captured Nanjing in April 1949. Gladys gave birth to their third child, a second daughter, in November 1949. She was invited by Nanjing University (formerly Central University) to become a professor in the English Department. When the Korean War broke out in 1950, strong xenophobic and anti-imperialist feelings against Americans and Britons were voiced, especially by the young people at universities. After the initial hysteria receded, British nationals were regarded as second-class citizens. In 1952, the Yangs were transferred to Beijing to work as translators in the new government's Soviet-style Foreign Languages Press where they participated in the project to translate the primary works of Chinese literature into English. During their time at the Foreign Languages Press, they worked as a team to translate more than sixty works.[27] In addition to teamwork with Xianyi, Gladys also did her own translations as well as polished the translations of others.[28] After sharing a house in the center of Beijing with several foreign workers, the Yangs moved in 1954 when the press was relocated to a new building. They lived in this western suburb of Beijing, Baiwanzhuang 百万庄, near the zoo, for nearly forty years.[29] Their home became a welcoming center for newly arrived teachers and translators from abroad.[30]

Yang described Beijing in the early days of the Communist regime as an attractive place. The dust and dirt of pre-Liberation days had been cleaned up, and the old city with its massive city walls and quiet lanes (*hutongs*) had not yet been demolished. There was a mass movement against corruption, and the people were filled with hope for the future. Among Yang's English translations of Chinese literature, one of the most notable was "*Li Sao*" 離騷 (Encountering Sorrow), attributed to the famous poet Qu Yuan 屈原

(340?–278 BC).[31] The poem epitomized the theme of integrity of a loyal retainer to his monarch in the face of slander. Qu Yuan, who completed suicide by drowning himself in protest, came to symbolize Confucian resistance to an oppressive state.[32] Yang's translation of this poem became the basis of his most significant exchange with Mao Zedong. In 1953 or early 1954, Yang was invited as part of a group of twenty other intellectuals (scientists, writers, and artists) to meet Chairman Mao. Standing in the reception line, Zhou Enlai introduced Yang as the translator of "Li Sao" into English. Mao, who was a poet himself and very familiar with "Li Sao," shook his hand and asked if he really thought that "Li Sao" could be translated.[33] Yang replied instinctively that all works of literature could be translated. Yang had translated "Li Sao" into mock-heroic couplets, and the British Sinologist David Hawkes (1923–2009) later joked that Yang's translation "bears as much resemblance to the original as a chocolate Easter egg to an omelette."[34]

The 1950s were the most prolific years for the Yangs' translation work. In addition to *Li Sao and Other Poems of Chu Yuan*, the Yangs translated a four-volume set of Lu Xun's writings.[35] They also translated the famous eighteenth-century Qing dynasty novel *The Scholars* by Wu Jingzi.[36] One of their most successful joint translations was *The Selected Stories of Lu Hsün*, first published in 1960. In 1956, the English-language magazine *Chinese Literature* was transferred to the Foreign Languages Press, and the Yangs became closely affiliated with it.[37] Later, after the Cultural Revolution receded, Yang became the chief editor of *Chinese Literature*. The state of euphoria that Yang felt in the early years of Communist rule in China did not last long. By 1955, a series of mass campaigns began to root out "hidden counter-revolutionaries."[38] Because of his pre-Liberation connections with foreign embassies and foreign friends, Yang's status began to change. From 1955 until his release from jail in 1972, he remained under a cloud of suspicion. In June 1957, Chairman Mao accused several people of being bourgeois "rightists" who sought to overthrow Communist Party leadership. Although Yang escaped being branded a "rightist," some of his best friends, including the historian Xiang Da and the director of the Foreign Languages Press Liu Zunqi, were labeled "rightists." Yang became disillusioned and his admiration for Mao dimmed. And yet his wit and wry humor never left him.

Yang claimed that the "madness" of the Cultural Revolution began ten years before the traditional starting date of 1966. He traced this attack against intellectuals to an intensifying series of oppressive movements, including the witch-hunt to uncover hidden counter-revolutionaries beginning in 1955, the Anti-Rightist Movement of 1957, and the Great Leap Forward Movement of 1958 to 1960. During this time, the political atmosphere of China became more and more radical while the social status of Chinese intellectuals sank lower and lower.[39] After a disruption of several years, Yang returned to translating histories with Sima Qian's famous dynastic history *Shiji* (Records of the Historian) (compiled 104–87 BC). The Foreign Languages Press allowed Yang to translate selections from the work, which he finished in 1961 or 1962.[40] However, the printing of the book was delayed until much later.[41] In 1964, he learned that a ban had been placed on publishing any work translated by him. In 1965, Yang was told to suspend his translation work on *Hongloumeng* (Dream of the Red Mansions) and not to translate any other works.

In July 1966, Mao issued his call from Tiananmen to purge the government and Party of counter-revolutionary elements. Inflamed by his words in "Red August," the Red Guards dragged tens of thousands of accused people into the street, beating and humiliating them. Thousands died, and the Beijing crematorium overflowed with corpses. When revolutionaries came demanding that Yang be handed over for a struggle meeting, the Foreign Languages Press refused to let him go. Consequently, he escaped the fate of his old friend, the writer Lao She, who was beaten during a struggle meeting and later found drowned in a lake. During Red August, struggle meetings raged and loudspeakers were driven through the streets night and day, blaring denunciations of people. The atmosphere was frightening and Yang, who during the Sino-Japanese War and civil war had been impervious to such distractions, became nervous and fearful. His paranoia grew and he suffered from auditory hallucinations, imagining that people were talking about him.[42] He was afraid to leave the Foreign Languages Building. During weekdays, he would go to his office and sit at the desk, but there was no translation work to do. He was assigned to clean the lavatories in the building and later sent to work in the kitchen.

At the beginning of 1968, Jiang Qing, Chairman Mao's wife, who was known for her political ambitions as part of the Gang of Four, made a speech warning about foreign spies which set off a campaign to find these "spies." On May Day of 1968, Yang and Gladys were arrested and imprisoned. Yang later joked about going off to jail in his slippers.[43] Their son and two daughters were sent to remote regions to do manual labor in a Cultural Revolution program of reeducation. Finally in the spring of 1972, the Yangs were released. Their apartment had been sealed off for four years and only a few rats had occupied it.[44] After their release from jail, they finished their translation of *Dream of the Red Mansions* (*Hongloumeng*). After Mao's death in 1976, peace was gradually restored. In 1978 or 1979, some security ministry officials came to the Foreign Languages Bureau to make a formal apology for the abusive treatment during the Cultural Revolution and blamed it all on the Gang of Four who had attempted an unsuccessful coup after Mao's death.

With the change in the political atmosphere, the Yangs were able to travel extensively in foreign countries from 1979 to 1986.

In the late spring of 1989, students began assembling at Tiananmen Square in Beijing, calling for political reform. In particular, they demanded more freedom of speech and press and the elimination of corruption and nepotism within the Party elites. Yang, who was by this point in his life an intellectual figure of some prominence, was sought out by foreign television networks. He gave several interviews in which he supported the students and criticized the government for its overly harsh response to their demands.[45] After the massacre on June 3 and 4, the intensity of his anger grew, and he denounced the Chinese government in a BBC interview, calling them fascists and worse than the northern warlords of twentieth-century China. The Yangs also gave a joint television interview condemning the government's brutality.

Personal tragedy had come in 1979 when their brilliant son, unable to reconcile his Eurasian sides, collapsed into insanity and completed suicide in Britain.[46] Gladys never got over his death. The pain of a difficult lifetime finally caught up with her, and she turned to alcohol for release. The effects began to cause her health to fail after 1990. At the suggestion of their youngest daughter, in 1994 the Yangs moved into one of the foreign experts' apartments in the Friendship Hotel in downtown Beijing, which was more convenient to the medical facilities Gladys needed. Yang cared for her until her death on November 18, 1999, at the age of eighty. Afterwards, Yang moved in with the family of his youngest daughter, Yang Zhi, and her husband David in their courtyard house north of the Forbidden City.[47] He missed Gladys. In his farewell poem to her he wrote: "I thought that you and I would fly away together but you have gone before."[48] Yang died on November 23, 2009, at the age of ninety-three.

NOTES

1. Yang Xianyi, *White Tiger: An Autobiography of Yang Xianyi* (Hong Kong: Chinese University Press, 2002), 1–4.

2. Yang, *White Tiger*, 8.

3. D. E. Mungello, "Necrology of Dr. John Dragon Young (楊意龍博士) (1949–1996)," *Sino-Western Cultural Relations Journal* XIX (1997): 1–5.

4. Yang, *White Tiger*, 13.

5. Yang, *White Tiger*, 2–9.

6. Yang, *White Tiger*, 11–15.

7. Yang, *White Tiger*, 19–20.

8. Yang, *White Tiger*, 24–35.

9. Yang, *White Tiger*, 27–28.

10. Yang, *White Tiger*, 37–42.

11. Yang, *White Tiger*, 58–59.

12. Yang, *White Tiger*, 73–81; Bill Jenner, "Obituary: Gladys Yang," *The Independent*, December 1, 1999; William H. Honan, "Gladys Yang is Dead at 80: Translated Chinese Classics," *New York Times*, November 24, 1999.

13. See E. R. Hughes, *The Great Learning & the Mean-in-Action* (New York: E. P. Dutton, 1943).

14. Yang, *White Tiger*, 80–81.

15. Yang, *White Tiger*, 93–99.

16. Yang, *White Tiger*, 75–76.

17. D. E. Mungello, *Western Queers in China* (Lanham, MD: Rowman & Littlefield Publishers, 2012), 67.

18. Yang, *White Tiger*, 101–07.

19. Yang, *White Tiger*, 109–15.

20. Yang, *White Tiger*, 131.

21. John Blofeld, *City of Lingering Splendour: A Frank Account of Old Peking's Exotic Pleasures* (London: Hutchinson, 1961).

22. Yang, *White Tiger*, 145–46.

23. Yang, *White Tiger*, 154–55.

24. Yang, *White Tiger*, 153.

25. Yang, *White Tiger*, 157–58.

26. Yang, *White Tiger*, 160–61.

27. John Gittings, "Yang Xianyi Obituary," *The Guardian*, November 23, 2009.

28. Jenner, "Obituary: Gladys Yang."

29. Yang, *White Tiger*, 185.

30. Jenner, "Obituary: Gladys Yang."

31. The China missionary and professor at Fu Ren University, Fr. Franz Xavier Biallas, SVD, had written his doctoral dissertation on Qu Yuan at the University of Leipzig in the 1920s. Entitled "K'üh Yüan's 'Fahrt in die Ferne,'" the work was published in *Asia Major* in 1927. Qu Yuan was the reputed author of the major poems in the collection *Chuci* (Songs of Chu) compiled and annotated by Wang Yi in the second century AD. "Fahrt in die Ferne" *Yuanyou* (Distant Journey) was one of the seventeen texts of the *Chuci*. See Michael Loewe, *Early Chinese Texts: A Bibliographical Guide* (Berkeley, CA: Society for the Study of Early China, 1993), 48–49.

32. Charles Hartman, "Ch'ü Yüan," in *Indiana Companion to Traditional Chinese Literature*, edited by William H. Nienhauser, Jr. (Bloomington, Indiana: Indiana University Press, 1986), 352.

33. Yang, *White Tiger*, 189–90.

34. Obituary of Yang Xianyi, *Telegraph*, December 10, 2009.

35. Lu Xun, Yang Hsien-I, and Gladys Yang, *Selected Works of Lu Xun, Volume One* (Beijing: Foreign Languages Press, 1956); *Volume Two* (1957); *Volume Three* (1959); and *Volume Four* (1960).

36. Wu Jingzi, Yang Xianyi, and Gladys Yang, *The Scholars* (Rulin waishi) (Beijing: Foreign Languages Press, 1957).

37. Yang, *White Tiger*, 195–96.

38. Yang, *White Tiger*, 199–207.

39. Yang, *White Tiger*, 209.

40. Yang, *White Tiger*, 221–22.

41. Ssu-ma Ch'ien and Yang Hsien-I, *Selections from Records of the Historian* (Beijing: Foreign Languages Press, 1979).

42. Yang, *White Tiger*, 229–33.

43. Yang, *White Tiger*, 235–37.

44. Yang, *White Tiger*, 255.

45. Yang, *White Tiger*, 283–91.

46. Jenner, "Obituary: Gladys Yang."

47. John Gittings, "Yang Xianyi Obituary," *The Guardian*, November 23, 2009.

48. Delia Davin, "Yang Xianyi: Translator Who Fell Foul of Authority during the Cultural Revolution," *The Independent*, November 29, 2009.

Conclusion

I.

Since the sixteenth century, East Asia had become an interracial melting pot focused initially in Macau, but later in Shanghai. The term Eurasian (*Ouya ren* 歐亞人) developed in the age of imperialism and reflected the highly conscious sense of race that was part of that period. The term is not well researched perhaps because it reflects a certain sensitivity to racial relations in these cultures. The term appears to have first emerged in the early nineteenth century as a reference to Indo-Britons and "half-castes." It was later extended to include British, Portuguese, Hindus, and Malays of mixed blood. Although the negative connotations of the term Eurasian belonged to the highly racialized consciousness of the nineteenth and early twentieth centuries, the objective meaning of racial blending embodied in the term was pre-Christian in origin and dated from the time of early contacts between people in eastern Europe, western Asia, and northern Africa.

The Eurasians of modern times in India, Ceylon, and East Asia were descendants of European adventurers of the sixteenth to eighteenth centuries. Catholic Portuguese explorers settled in Goa, India, and intermarried with native women. Relatively few native Portuguese settled in Portugal's extended empire. In 1590 there were probably no more than fourteen thousand European-born Portuguese in the important trading center of India. Far more numerous were Luso-Asians who played a mediating role between the Portuguese and native populations of Asia. By the beginning of the seventeenth century, Macau had become the leading trading center of East Asia with an estimated population of six to seven thousand, the majority of whom were Luso-Asians. After the golden age of triangular trade linking Portugal, India, and Macau ended in the 1650s, Macau survived as a Chinese and Macanese mixed race city.[1]

By the late eighteenth century, intermarriage between the Portuguese and Portuguese Eurasians with the Chinese had become commonplace.[2] A native

149

population of Macanese emerged created by the intermarriage of European Portuguese, Portuguese Asians, and Chinese—the *casados*. In 1896, there were 3,898 residents in Macau of Portuguese descent: 615 natives of Portugal, 177 born in other Portuguese possessions, and 3,106 of Macau birth.[3]

In Shanghai, the name Eurasian was not initially carried as a mark of pride. The Shanghai census returns for 1890 claimed that in the entire foreign population in the International Settlement of Shanghai, there were only forty-one Eurasian adults and 101 Eurasian children, which is suspiciously low. By the early twentieth century, the Eurasians in Shanghai were associated with the Portuguese who along with the Japanese occupied the poorest section, Hongkew (Hongkou 虹口), which lay on the eastern bank of Soochow (Suzhou) Creek across the Garden Bridge (*Waibaiduqiao* 外白度橋) from the Bund.[4] The Shanghai census of 1915 for the International Settlement (apart from residents of the French Concession) listed 1,323 Portuguese out of a total foreign population of 18,519.

The growing sensitivity of the identity of Eurasians was reflected in the apologetic tone of an article that appeared in 1917 in *The Encyclopaedia Sinica*.[5] This article, written by a Christian minister named Arnold Foster, reflected the growing sense of social injustice that Eurasians were feeling. The outlier state of Eurasians in Shanghai was indicated by the founding in 1914 of the Thomas Hanbury School in Shanghai primarily as a boarding and day school for Eurasian children. However, most Eurasians in Shanghai were not destitute. Complaints were published in the *North China Herald* in 1916 and 1917 by British Eurasians who had not received their fair rewards for service in the British Army as volunteers. Proposals to exclude Eurasians from public schools were considered but rejected on several occasions. Eurasian schoolchildren performed at comparable levels to European and American children.

The Shanghai historian Betty Peh-T'i Wei describes the Eurasians in Shanghai during the nineteenth and early twentieth centuries by dividing them into two groups, based on their paternity.[6] Those with foreign surnames (foreign fathers and Chinese mothers) were far more numerous than those with Chinese surnames (Chinese fathers and foreign mothers). Eurasians in Shanghai tended to be isolated from Chinese society and lacked the respect and status that their counterparts enjoyed in Hong Kong. Nevertheless, those with foreign fathers had foreign nationality and were able to enter spheres forbidden to the Chinese. They were bilingual and were generally regarded as being intelligent and good-looking.

Some Eurasians, such as Eric Cumine of both Shanghai and Hong Kong, achieved prominence. Cumine's grandfather was one of two brothers who came from Scotland and established households with two Chinese women (Tang and Wu) from Hainan. Cumine said his family felt comfortable in both societies—whether the men were going to the horseraces and mixing with the wealthy taipans or whether the women were playing mahjong with Chinese women. Apart from those who headed their own firms, most of the Eurasians worked in Shanghai's civil service (the municipal government of the Imperial Maritime Customs). The most well-known Eurasian family in Shanghai were the McBains. George McBain came from Scotland and became wealthy importing petroleum products from Indonesia, housing his business at the prestigious address of No. 1 on the Bund. He married a Eurasian woman of Chinese and Austrian descent and procreated children and grandchildren, one of whom became a member of the prestigious Shanghai Municipal Council.

II.

Love affairs take many forms which are driven by a range of motives from the very practical to the utterly romantic. When the Dowager Empress Cixi pulled Edmund Backhouse to his feet and kissed him on his mouth several times in front of an important court official (if Backhouse's account is to be believed), she was expressing romantic affection and assuring him that he would not be poisoned like her other European lovers.[7] Backhouse included the description of that kiss to show that his relationship to Cixi was more than sexual and involved a love affair—*fengliu yunshi* 風流韻事 or *affaire de coeur*—albeit one of questionable intensity. It is hard to fathom why Cixi would have had a romantic interest in Backhouse. Unlike her other two supposed European lovers—the well-built twenty-three-year-old Wallon and the lustful Raab—Backhouse was an effete English gentleman-scholar. And yet he possessed a knowledge of Chinese and scholarly abilities that were traditionally admired by the Chinese. Moreover, Backhouse was in his youthful thirties in 1904 to 1908, the period when he claimed to have had sexual relations with Cixi. Is it possible that their romantic coupling was prompted by sexual curiosity on Cixi's part? Or was their attraction just a projection of Backhouse's overactive literary imagination?

The dismal decline of Manchu male virility in the imperial family had created not only a practical problem but also a political crisis. These circumstances, combined with the bizarre rumors of sexual relations between the young, virile René Leys and the Chinese Dowager Empress Longyu in Victor Segalen's novel, lend hypothetical support to the notion that Cixi was interested in European men because of their sexual virility and fecundity. On the other hand, we must question whether these literary sexual couplings at the peak of European imperialism existed in reality or only in the miscegenous and overcharged imaginations of Europeans of that time. (This mentality is reflected in the fact that the very word miscegenation appears to have come into circulation in Europe and the United States in the late nineteenth century.) Did these purported sexual couplings between European men and Manchu imperial women spring perhaps more from European imaginations than from their libidos?

Lao She's account of the abortive love affairs of the two Ma's may have been literary fiction, but the British racial bias against Chinese in England in the 1920s was very real and appears to have been a driving force in Lao She's creation of this novel. He dealt with this humiliating racism and triumphed intellectually over British prejudice by writing a parody that mocked the lower middle classes of England for their ignorance.

With Han Suyin's romantic relationships, we move more clearly into a non-fictional interracial world, but one made problematic by her Eurasian consciousness. These relationships included her first husband (the Nationalist General Tang Baohuan), her second husband (the British Special Branch Assistant Superintendent Leonard Comber), her Australian lover (the journalist Ian Morrison), and her third husband (the Indian colonel Vincent Ratnaswamy). The nature of her relationships to each of these four men was romantic in different ways. Han Suyin made clear that a suspicion of interracial relationships and interracial progeny in Eurasians was a very active subcurrent in revolutionary China.

By contrast, the racially sensitive American culture that Pearl Buck absorbed from her family probably caused her interracial love affair with a Chinese to take a more sublimated form. Her romance with the charismatic Chinese poet Xu Zhimo appears to have been more than a flirtation but stopped short of being a full-blown love affair. Yet because they met at a time of Buck's emotional vulnerability when her first marriage was disintegrating and the hopelessness of her daughter's mental illness was becoming crushingly apparent, the relationship served as an important form of romantic reassurance in her life. Unable to procreate seven children like her mother, Pearl Buck sublimated her powerful maternal feelings and adopted seven children, using her influence as a prominent author to create an adoption agency to find homes for abandoned biracial Amerasian children with American families.

Two of the love affairs discussed in this book blended traditions of Chinese marriage and concubinage with foreign partners. The love affair of Emily Hahn and the author-publisher Shao Xunmei was unique among these relationships in that it involved a Chinese marriage in which Hahn was on amicable terms with Shao's first Chinese wife Zoa as well as his nine children who referred to Hahn with affection as "Foreign Mother." The long-term romantic affair of Lu Gwei-djen with Joseph Needham sprang from different causes. It was rooted not only in their intellectual collaboration, but also in practical needs. Lu Gwei-djen was a refugee from Nanjing at a time when China was being brutally invaded by the Japanese, and she needed shelter. Needham was in a position of power to help her, and his sexual passion needed gratification. Their relationship was distinguished by its Chinese concubinage nature and stood starkly at odds with the early twentieth-century Western trend toward divorce which Xu Zhimo famously aped in becoming the "first man to divorce" in China. The love affair of Needham and Lu Gwei-djen was characterized not only by Needham's continuing loyalty to his marriage, but also their collaborative contribution to scholarship in the form of the monumental *Science and Civilisation in China*.

Robert Winter's same-sex attractions were driven by innate feelings and frustrations that caused him to escape to the freer atmosphere of China. Later Chinese revolutionary homophobia emerged to suppress and obscure most of the landmarks of his same-sex relationships with Chinese men, leaving a hidden landscape of secret relationships. The remaining evidence of these relationships is scant. We have only one surviving fragment in the form of Winter's oil painting of a "Fisherman at Tsingtao (Qingdao)" who is depicted as holding a seahorse (a homosexual symbol). Little is known about the romantic tie between this Chinese fisherman and Robert Winter, although the universal affections of a love affair might be projected from this painting. Like many same-sex romantic relationships, it is buried in the sands of history. Given that Winter was part of an interracial gay subculture in Beijing in the 1930s, it is likely that he was very familiar with homosexual life in China prior to the sexually puritanical years of the Communist regime and it is likely that Winter had several (even numerous) Chinese male lovers.

The last romantic relationship treated in the book presents the interracial relationship of Yang Xianyi and Gladys Yang. It was a relationship that took the most romantically conventional form of a long fifty-seven-year happy marriage with three biracial children. However, it included a series of misfortunes, including government interrogations in the 1950s, mutual government incarcerations in 1968 to 1972, the tragic suicide of their son in 1979, and Gladys' turn to alcohol in her sorrow over this loss.[8] Their son's anxiety was a price paid by many Eurasians.

The interracial love affairs discussed in this book were generated by human passion and affection, but they also came at a cost, particularly to their Eurasian and Amerasian offspring. It is a striking fact that only two of the interracial love affairs discussed in this book produced offspring. The marriage of Zhou Wei and Marguerite Denis produced four children (one boy and three girls) who survived beyond infancy, including Han Suyin who remained biologically childless. Yang Xianyi and Gladys Yang gave birth to three children (two girls and one boy). Han Suyin struggled her entire life with the fact that she was a Eurasian who wanted to be accepted as Chinese. The son of Yang Xianyi and Gladys Yang also appears to have struggled with being Eurasian. His struggles intensified during the Cultural Revolution when he and his two sisters were sent to remote regions of China to work in farms and factories.[9] In an attempt to protect their son from the excesses of the Cultural Revolution, the Yangs sent him to London. He never recovered, but he descended into mental illness and completed suicide in 1979 by burning down the house in which he lived.[10] In contrast to this scarcity of progeny, there were numerous biracial offspring produced by the indiscriminate sexual coupling of American servicemen with Korean women in the 1950s and Vietnamese women in the 1960s and 1970s. The fathers of many of these children were Black. These children were largely rejected in both their Asian and American homelands. Pearl Buck's love for these children made her a leader in finding adoptive parents for them in America. Her last years made her vulnerable to her male flatterers and flawed her legacy, but her contribution to helping these spurned biracial children survives as an enduring monument to interracial love.

NOTES

1. Philippe Pons, *Macao*, translated by Sarah Adams (London: Reaktion Books, Ltd, 2002), 72; Donald F. Lach and Edwin J. Van Kley, *Asia in the Making of Europe. Volume III: A Century of Advance. Book One: Trade, Missions, Literature* (Chicago: University of Chicago Press, 1993), 8, 169.

2. Jonathan Porter, *Macau, The Imaginary City: Culture and Society, 1557 to the Present* (Boulder, CO: Westview Press, 1996), 77.

3. Arnold Foster, "Eurasians," in *Encyclopaedia Sinica*, edited by Samuel Couling (Shanghai: Kelly and Walsh, Ltd, 1917), 169.

4. Harriet Sergeant, *Shanghai Collision Point of Cultures 1918/1939* (New York: Crown Publishers, 1990), 179.

5. Foster, "Eurasians," 169–70.

6. Wei, *Shanghai Crucible of Modern China*, 107–09.

7. Edmund Trelawny Backhouse, *Décadence Mandchoue: The China Memoirs of Sir Edmund Trelawny Backhouse*, edited by Derek Sandhaus (Hong Kong: Earnshaw Books, 2011), 237.

8. Bill Jenner, "Obituary: Gladys Yang," *The Independent*, December 1, 1999.

9. John Gittings, "Yang Xianyi Obituary," *The Guardian*, November 23, 2009; Delia Davin, "Yang Xianyi: Translator Who Fell Foul of Authority during the Cultural Revolution," *The Independent*, February 19, 2009.

10. Willian H. Honan, "Gladys Yang is Dead at 80," *New York Times*, February 19, 2013.

Bibliography

Arlington, L. C., and William Lewisohn. *In Search of Old Peking*. Peking: Henri Vetch, 1935.

Auden, W. H., and Christopher Isherwood. *Journey to a War*. 1939; New York: Paragon House, 1967.

Backhouse, Edmund Trelawny. *The Dead Past*. Peking 1943. Third edition. Edited by Reinhard Hoeppli and Peter Jordaan. Coppell, TX: Alchemie Books, 2021.

———. *Décadence Mandchoue: The China Memoirs of Sir Edmund Trelawny Backhouse*. Edited by Derek Sandhaus. Hong Kong: Earnshaw Books, 2011.

Backhouse, E., and J. O. P. Bland. *Annals & Memoirs of the Court of Peking (from the 16th to the 20th Century)*. Boston: Houghton Mifflin Company, 1914.

Bays, Daniel H. "The Growth of Independent Christianity," in Daniel H. Bays, ed., *Christianity in China from the Eighteenth Century to the Present*. Stanford, CA: Stanford University Press, 1996.

Bernard, Emily. *Carl von Vechten & the Harlem Renaissance*. New Haven, CT: Yale University Press, 2012.

Bland, J. O. P., and Edmund Backhouse. *China under the Empress Dowager: The History of the Life and Times of Tzu Hsi*. 1910; Hong Kong: Earnshaw Books, 2009.

Blofeld, John. *City of Lingering Splendour: A Frank Account of Old Peking's Exotic Pleasures*. London: Hutchinson, 1961.

Boorman, Howard L., ed. *Biographical Dictionary of Republican China*. Five volumes. New York: Columbia University Press, 1967–1971.

Buck, Pearl S., trans. *All Men Are Brothers* [Shui Hu Chuan]. With an introduction by Lin Yutang and illustrations by Miguel Covarrubias. New York: The Heritage Press, 1933.

Buck, Pearl S. *The Exile*. New York: John Day, 1936.

———. *Fighting Angel*. New York: John Day Company, 1936; reprinted 1957.

———. *The Good Earth*. New York: Simon & Shuster, original copyright 1931, renewed 1958.

———. *My Several Worlds*. New York: John Day Company, 1954.

Burton, Charles. "Loved China. Maybe Too Much. Also Loved Women." *Globe and Mail*, May 31, 2008.

Ch'en, Jerome. "The Last Emperor of China." *Bulletin of the School of Oriental and African Studies* 28 (1965): 336–55.

Chang, Pang-Mei Natasha. *Bound Feet and Western Dress*. New York: Anchor Books, 1997.

Clark, Anthony E. *China Gothic: The Bishop of Beijing and His Cathedral*. Seattle: University of Washington Press, 2019.

Classic of Mountains and Seas. Translation with introduction and noted by Anne Birrell. London: Penguin, 1999.

Clifford, Nicholas R. *Spoilt Children of Empire: Westerners in Shanghai and the Chinese Revolution of the 1920s*. Hanover, NH: University Press of New England, 1991.

Conn, Peter. *Pearl S. Buck: A Cultural Biography*. Cambridge, England: Cambridge University Press, 1996.

Couling, Samuel. *The Encyclopedia Sinica*. Shanghai: Kelly & Walsh, 1917.

Crow, Carl. *Foreign Devils in the Flowery Kingdom*. 1940; republished Hong Kong: Earnshaw Books, 2007.

Cuthbertson, Ken. *Nobody Said Not to Go: The Life, Lovers, and Adventures of Emily Hahn*. Boston: Faber and Faber, 1998.

Davin, Delia. "Yang Xianyi: Translator Who Fell Foul of Authority during the Cultural Revolution." *The Independent*, November 29, 2009.

Demel, Walter. "Wie die Chinesen gelb wurden: Ein Beitrag zur Frühgeschichte der Rassentheorien." *Historische Zeitschrift* 255 (1992): 625–66.

Dickinson, G. Lowes. *Letters from John Chinaman*. London: Brimley Johnson, 1901.

Dikötter, Frank. *Mao's Great Famine*. London: Bloomsbury Publishing Plc., 2010.

Duyvendak, J. J. L. "Ching-Shan's Diary a Mystification." *T'oung-Pao* 33, book 3/4 (1937): 268–94.

Eberhard, Wolfram. *A Dictionary of Chinese Symbols*. Translated by G. L. Campbell. London: Routledge, 1986.

Fairbank, John K. *East Asia: Tradition and Transformation*. Boston: Houghton Mifflin Co, 1973.

Fairbank, Wilma. *Liang and Lin: Partners in Exploring China's Architectural Past*. Philadelphia: University of Pennsylvania Press, 1994.

Finkelstein, David, and Beverly Hooper. "57 Years Inside China: An American Odyssey." *Asia* 2 (January-February 1980): 10–11, 46.

Forsythe, Michael. "Pierre Ryckmans (1935–2014)." Obituary, *New York Times*, August 15, 2014.

Gittings, John. "Yang Xianyi Obituary," *The Guardian*, November 23, 2009.

Gunther, John. *Inside Asia*. New York: Harper & Brothers, 1939.

Hahn, Emily. *China to Me: A Partial Autobiography*. Garden City, NY: Country Life Press, 1944.

———. *The Soong Sisters*. 1941; New York: Open Road Integrated Media, 2014.

Han Suyin. *Birdless Summer*. Great Britain: Jonathan Cape Ltd., 1968; republished Frogmore, St. Albans, Herts: Panther Books Ltd, 1972.

———. *The Crippled Tree*. 1965; reprinted at Frogmore, St. Albans, Herts, Panther Books, 1972.

————. *My House Has Two Doors* 吾宅双门. Great Britain: Triad/Granada, 1982.

Harris, Theodore F., in consultation with Pearl S. Buck. *Pearl S. Buck: A Biography.* New York: John Day Company, 1969.

Hollinger, David A. *Protestants Abroad: How Missionaries Tried to Change the World But Changed America.* Princeton, NJ: Princeton University Press, 2017.

Honan, William H. "Gladys Yang is Dead at 80: Translated Chinese Classics." *New York Times,* November 24, 1999.

Hsia, C. T. *A History of Modern Chinese Fiction 1917–1957.* New Haven: Yale University Press, 1961.

Hsu, Kai-yu, ed. and tr. *Twentieth Century Chinese Poetry: An Anthology.* Garden City, NY: Anchor Books, 1964.

Hughes, E. R. *The Great Learning & the Mean-in-Action.* New York: E. P. Dutton, 1943.

Hummel, Arthur W., ed. *Eminent Chinese of the Ch'ing Period (1644–1912).* Washington, DC: Government Printing Office, 1943.

Hussein, Aamer. "On Not Teaching Han Suyin and Other 'Third-World' Matters." YouTube interview, June 14, 2021.

Hyatt, Irwin T., Jr. *Our Ordered Lives Confess: Three Nineteenth-century American Missionaries in East Shantung.* Cambridge, MA: Harvard University Press, 1976.

Indiana Companion to Traditional Chinese Literature, edited by William H. Nienhauser, Jr. Bloomington, IN: Indiana University Press, 1986.

Isaacs, Harold R. *Images of Asia: American Views of China and India* (originally published in 1958 under the title *Scratches on Our Minds*). New York: Harper and Row, 1972.

Jacobsen, Stefan Gaarsmand Jacobsen. "Chinese Influences or Images? Fluctuating Histories of How Enlightenment Europe Read China." *Journal of World History* 24 (2013): 623–60.

Jenner, Bill. "Obituary: Gladys Yang." *The Independent,* December 1, 1999.

Israel, John. *Lianda, A Chinese University in War and Revolution.* Stanford: Stanford University Press, 1999.

Johnson, David K. *The Lavender Scare: The Cold War Persecution of Gays and Lesbians in the Federal Government.* Chicago: The University of Chicago, 2004.

Johnson, Ian. "Religion in China: Zurück ins Zentrum von Politik und Gesellschaft." *China Heute* 37 (2018): 110–17.

Kam, Louis Kam. "Constructing Chinese Masculinity for the Modern World: With Particular Reference to Lao She's *The Two Mas.*" *The China Quarterly* 164 (December 2000): 1062–78.

Kates, George N. *Chinese Household Furniture.* London: Harper & Brothers, 1948.

Kinnear, Angus I. *The Story of Watchman Nee: Against the Tide.* First published 1973. Wheaton, IL: Tyndale House Publishers, 1978.

Lach, Donald F., and Edwin J. Van Kley. *Asia in the Making of Europe. Volume III: A Century of Advance. Book One: Trade, Missions, Literature.* Chicago: University of Chicago Press, 1993.

Ladany, Lazlo. *The Catholic Church in China.* New York: Freedom House, 1987.

Lao She. *Mr. Ma & Son a Sojourn in London* 二馬。 Bilingual Chinese-English edition. Translated by Julie Jimmerson. Beijing: Foreign Language Press, 2001.

Lao She [Shu Qingchun]. *Rickshaw [Luotuo xiangzi]*. Translated by Jean M. James. Honolulu: University of Hawaii Press, 1979.

Laurence, Patricia. *Lily Briscoe's Chinese Eyes: Bloomsbury, Modernism, and China.* Columbia, SC: University of South Carolina Press, 2003.

Lee, Erika. *At America's Gates: Chinese Immigration during the Exclusion Era, 1882–1943.* Chapel Hill: University of North Carolina Press, 2002.

Lee, Joseph Tse-Hei. "Watchman Nee and the Little Flock Movement in Maoist China." *Church History* 74, 1 (March 2005): 68–96.

Lee, Leo Ou-fan. *The Romantic Generation of Modern Chinese Writers.* Cambridge, MA: Harvard University Press, 1973.

Leong, Karen. J. *The China Mystique: Pearl S. Buck, Anna May Wong, Maylong Soong, and the Transformation of American Orientalism.* Berkeley: University of California Press, 2005.

Leung, Gaylord Kai Loh. "Hsü Chih-mo and Bertrand Russell." *Renditions* 14 (autumn 1980): 27–38.

Leys, Simon [Pierre Ryckman]. *The Burning Forest: Essays on Chinese Culture and Politics.* New York: Henry Holt and Co, 1986.

Li Hung-chang and China's Early Modernization, edited by Samuel C. Chu and Kwang-Ching Lu. Armonk, NY: M. E. Sharpe, 1994.

Lian, Xi. *Redeemed by Fire: The Rise of Popular Christianity in Modern China.* New Haven: Yale University Press, 2010.

———. *The Conversion of Missionaries: Liberalism in American Protestant Missions in China, 1907–1932.* University Park, PA: Pennsylvania State University Press, 1997.

Lim Boon Keng (Wen Ching). *The Chinese Crisis from Within.* London: Grant Richards, 1901.

Lo, Hui-min. "The Ching-shan Diary: A Clue to Its Forgery." *East Asian History*, 1 (June 1991): 98–124.

Loewe, Michael. *Early Chinese Texts: A Bibliographical Guide.* Berkeley, CA: Society for the Study of Early China, 1993.

Lownie, Andrew. *Stalin's Englishman: Guy Burgess, the Cold War, and the Cambridge Spy Ring.* New York: St. Martin's Press, 2015.

Lu Xun. "On Seeing Shaw and Those Who Saw Shaw," in *Selected Works.* Third edition. Translated by Yang Xianyi and Gladys Yang. Beijing: Foreign Language Press, 1980. Volume 3.

———. *Selected Works of Lu Xun.* Translated by Yang Hsien-I and Gladys Yang. Volume one (Beijing: Foreign Languages Press, 1956), volume two (1957), volume three (1959), and volume four (1960).

MacKinnon, Janice, and Stephan R. MacKinnon. *Agnes Smedley: The Life and Times of an American Radical.* Berkeley: University of California Press, 1988.

Malatesta, Edward J., and Gao Zhiyu, eds. *Zhalan: Departed, Yet Present, the Oldest Christian Cemetery in Beijing.* Macau: Instituto Cultural de Macau and Ricci Institute, University of San Francisco, 1995.

Mariani, Paul P. *Church Militant: Bishop Kung and Catholic Resistance in Communist Shanghai.* Cambridge, MA: Harvard University Press, 2011.

May, Grace Y. "Watchman Nee and the Breaking of Bread: The Missiological Forces That Contributed to an Indigenous Chinese Ecclesiology." Doctor of Theology, Boston University, 2000.

Mitchell, Leslie. *Maurice Bowra: A Life.* Oxford: Oxford University Press, 2009.

Morrison, G. E. *An Australian in China.* London: Horace Cox, 1895.

Mungello, D. E. *The Catholic Invasion of China: Remaking Chinese Christianity.* Lanham, MD: Rowman & Littlefield, 2015.

———*Curious Land: Jesuit Accommodation and the Origins of Sinology.* Stuttgart: Franz Steiner Verlag, 1985.

———. *Drowning Girls in China: Female Infanticide since 1650.* Lanham, MD: Rowman & Littlefield, 2008.

———. *The Great Encounter of China and the West.* Fourth revised edition. Lanham, MD: Rowman & Littlefield, 2013.

———. *Leibniz and Confucianism: The Search for Accord.* Honolulu: University of Hawaii Press, 1977.

———"Necrology of Dr. John Dragon Young (楊意龍博士) (1949–1996)." *Sino-Western Cultural Relations Journal* XIX (1997): 1–5.

———. *The Spirit and the Flesh in Shandong, 1650–1785.* Lanham, MD: Rowman & Littlefield, 2001.

———. *This Suffering Is My Joy: The Underground Church in Eighteenth-Century China.* Lanham, MD: Rowman & Littlefield, 2021.

———. *Western Queers in China: Flight to the Land of Oz.* Lanham, MD: Rowman & Littlefield, 2012.

Nee, Watchman. *What Shall This Man Do?* Digest of spoken ministry compiled by Angus I. Kinnear, ed. Wheaton, Illinois: Tyndale House Publishers, 1978.

Needham, Joseph, and Wang Ling, *Science and Civilisation in China. Volume 1 Introductory Orientations.* Cambridge, England: Cambridge University Press, 1954; *Volume 2 History of Scientific Thought.* Cambridge, England: Cambridge University Press, 1956.

Nienhauser, William H., Jr., ed. *The Indiana Companion to Traditional Chinese Literature.* Bloomington, IN: Indiana University Press, 1986.

Nugent, Richard Bruce. *Gay Rebel of the Harlem Renaissance.* Edited by Thomas H. Wirth. Durham, NC: Duke University Press, 2002.

Pan Ling. *In Search of Old Shanghai.* Hong Kong: Joint Publishing Co., 1982.

Pons, Philippe. *Macao.* Translated by Sarah Adams. London: Reaktion Books, Ltd., 2002.

Porter, Jonathan. *Macau, The Imaginary City: Culture and Society, 1557 to the Present.* Boulder, CO: Westview Press, 1996.

Pu, Songling. *Strange Tales from a Chinese Studio.* Translated and edited by John Minford. London: Penguin Books, 2006.

Roberts, John Stuart. *Siegfried Sassoon (1886–1967).* London: Richard Cohen Books, 1999.

Ross, Heidi A. "'Cradle of Female Talent': The McTyeire Home and School for Girls, 1892–1937," in Daniel H. Bays, ed. *Christianity in China: From the Eighteenth Century to the Present*, 209–27. Stanford: Stanford University Press, 1996.

Segalen, Victor. *René Leys*. Édition présentée et annotée par Marie Dollé et Christian Doumet. Paris: Librairie Génerale Française, 1999.

———. *René Leys*. Translated by J. A. Underwood. New York: NYRB Classics, 2003.

Sergeant, Harriet. *Shanghai Collision Point of Cultures 1918/1939*. New York: Crown Publishers, 1990.

Shen Fu, *Six Records of a Floating Life* (*Fu sheng liu ji*). Translated by Leonard Pratt and Chiang Su-hui. London: Penguin, 1983.

Shen Xuebin. "Die 'Union Version' der Bibel und die Sinisierung des Christentums." *China heute* XL (2021): 106–10.

Spence, Jonathan D. *Emperor of China: Self-portrait of K'ang-his*. New York: Vintage, 1975.

———. *The Gate of Heavenly Peace: The Chinese and Their Revolution, 1895–1980*. New York: Viking Press, 1981.

———. "The Question of Pearl Buck." *The New York Review of Books*, October 14, 2010.

Spurling, Hilary. *Burying the Bones: Pearl Buck in China*. London: Profile Books, Ltd., 2010.

Stern, Bert. *Winter in China: An American Life*. Xlibris LLC, 2014. This book has been translated into Chinese as *Wende xiansheng: qin li Zhongguo liu shi nian de chuan qi jiao shou* 溫德先生：親歷中國六十年的傳奇教授 (Mr. Winter: the long poetic drama of his sixty-year personal experience as a professor in China) by Bote Site'en zhu 伯特。斯特恩著 (Bert Stern 1930–), Ma Xiaowu 馬小悟 (translator) and Yu Wanhui 余婉卉 (translator). Hong Kong: Xianggang Zhonghe Chuban Youxian Gongsi 中和出版有限公司, 2016.

Stirling, Nora. *Pearl Buck: A Woman in Conflict*. Piscataway, NJ: New Century Publishers, 1983.

Sullivan, Michael. "A Small Token of Friendship." *Oriental Art* 35, 2 (summer 1989): 76–85.

Sydenstricker, A., and Zu Baohui (transl.). *Si fuyinshu* 四福音書 (The Books of the Four Gospels). Shanghai: Presbyterian Mission Press, 1913.

Terrill, Ross. *The White-Boned Demon: Biography of Madame Mao Zedong*. New York: William Morrow, 1984.

Trevor-Roper, Hugh. *Hermit of Peking: The Hidden Life of Sir Edmund Backhouse*. Harmondsworth, Middlesex, England: Penguin Books, 1976.

Van Gulik, R. H. *Sexual Life in Ancient China*. Leiden: Brill, 1961.

Waller, Nancy Thomson. *My Nanking Home 1918–1937*. Cherry Valley, NY: Willow Hill Publications, 2010.

Wei, Betty Peh-T'i. *Shanghai Crucible of Modern China*. Oxford: Oxford University Press, 1987.

Wenzel-Teuber, Katharina. "Statistik zu Religionen und Kirchen in der Volksrepublik China und in Singapur. Ein Update für das Jahr 2021." *China heute* 2022/1: 26–40.

White, Edward. *The Tastemaker: Carl van Vechten and the Birth of Modern America.* New York: Farrar, Straus and Giroux, 2014.

Wilbur, C. Martin. *The Nationalist Revolution in China, 1923–1928.* Cambridge, UK: Cambridge University Press, 1983.

Wilkinson, Endymion. *Chinese History. A Manual.* Cambridge, MA: Harvard University Asia Center, 1998.

Williams, C. A. S. *Chinese Symbolism and Art Motifs.* Third revised edition. Rutland, VT: Charles E. Tuttle Company, 1993.

Winchester, Simon. *The Man Who Loved China.* New York: HarperCollins, 2008.

Witchard, Anne. *Lao She in London.* Hong Kong: Hong Kong University Press, 2012.

Wu Jingzi. *The Scholars (Rulin waishi* 儒林外史). Translated by Yang Xianyi and Gladys Yang. Beijing: Foreign Languages Press, 1957.

Zetzsche, Jost Oliver. *The Bible in China: The History of the Union Version or The Culmination of Protestant Missionary Bible Translation in China.* Nettetal, Germany: Steyler Verlag, 1999.

Index

163

Xianfeng emperor, 1
Xiang Da, 139, 144
Xu Jigai, 67
Xu Zhimo, xviii, 40, 63–77, 103, 104,
    130–131, 153
Xu, Peter, 68–69
Xuanzong (emperor), 7

Yang Guifei, 6
Yang Xianyi, xix, 20, 137–146; accused
    counter-revolutionary, 143; B. Litt.,
    139; imprisonment, 145; romantic
    relationship, 153; son, 145, 153–154
Yang, Amy, 142
Yang, Gladys Taylor, xix, 20, 123, 137,
    139, 140–146, 153; British passport
    of, 142; imprisonment, 145; romantic
    relationship, 153; son, 153–154
Yang, Zhi, 146
Yangtszepoo, xiii, 103
Yanjing University, 16, 26, 32, 77, 118
Yaukey, Grace Sydenstricker, 75, 77, 81
Yaukeys, 74
Year of the Tiger, 137
Yellow Peril, 17
yellow, xx

yin-yang dialectic, 28–29, 30, 32
YouTube, 31
Young, John Dragon, 138
Yu, Dora, 55
Yuan Shikai, 138
Yuanmingyuan, 5

Zao Simay. *See* Shao Xunmei
Zhalan, 3
Zhang Jiasen (Carson Chang), 63, 67
Zhang Youyi, 63–70
Zhao Deming, 123
Zhenjiang (Chinkiang), 38, 39, 48
Zhou Enlai, 30, 31, 32, 34, 85,
    112, 123, 132
Zhou Guanghu (Rosalie Matilda
    Kuanghu Chou), 23, 26
Zhou Wei, xviii, 20, 23, 28, 39, 153
Zhou Zuoren, 139
Zhou, Marianne, 26, 32
Zhou, Tiza, 26, 32
Zhu Baohui, 45
Zi-ka-wei, xiii
Zoa, wife of Shao Xunmei, 103,
    107, 112, 152

About the Author

For the past half-century **D. E. Mungello** has been a leading scholar in Sino-Western history. From 1979 to 2016 he founded and edited a journal dedicated to the post–Mao Zedong era revival of contacts between Chinese and foreign historians. His books include *Leibniz and Confucianism*; *Curious Land*; *The Great Encounter of China and the West, 1500–1800*; *The Spirit and the Flesh in Shandong, 1650–1785*; *Drowning Girls in China: Female Infanticide since 1650*; *Western Queers in China: Flight to the Land of Oz*; *The Catholic Invasion of China*; and *This Suffering Is My Joy: The Underground Church in Eighteenth-Century China*. He is professor of history emeritus at Baylor University.

Made in the USA
Middletown, DE
18 July 2023

35424930R00109